Welcome to the Premiere edition of Ice Fishing Ontario. This book has been designed as the most complete angling guide to some of the best ice fishing locations in the province. The invaluable information on such things as access, facilities, stocking and fish species will allow you to choose that ideal lake or water body for your winter fishing adventure. The amazing feature of this guidebook is that it provides you with the first ever-detailed information on where in Ontario to ice fish. This information is invaluable to increase your success and is especially important to anglers looking to explore this great province during the winter months.

Ontario has long been a popular ice fishing destination and is riddled with both small and large lakes offering boundless fishing opportunities. Visitors to the region will find hundreds of beautiful lakes and water bodies to explore, including some proven popular spots such as Lake Nipissing and Lake Simcoe. Ice fishing has quickly become a popular winter sport and is only getting more popular. One of the current problems with ice fishing in Ontario is that wanna be ice anglers really do not know where to go other than the main lakes that everyone knows of. The idea of this guidebook is to help unravel the inaccessibility and mystique of ice fishing so that anglers can better explore the province.

In this boo[illegible] including depth charts, access maps and detailed information on hundreds of the best lakes and water bodies for ice fishing found in Ontario. To ensure you have a successful trip, we have also provided information on access, facilities, stocking and fishing hints. The lakes in the region vary from large water bodies such as Owen Sound, to small out of the way interior access lakes. We have also included information on most of the more popular ice fishing destination lakes such as Lake Simcoe.

Ontario offers a well developed system of roads, providing easy access to many of Ontario's fine ice fishing lakes. There is also hundreds of harder to reach lakes in the province that are only accessible by snowmobile. For more detailed access information to all the lakes in this book, we recommend consulting the Backroad Mapbook Series of guidebooks. Backroad Mapbooks provide very detailed maps along with information on everything from trail systems to other fishing opportunities. It is the perfect compliment to the Ice Fishing Ontario guidebook.

No other source combines such detailed information on the best ice fishing lakes in Ontario. Whether you are visiting the region for the first time or simply looking for a new lake to fish, we are certain you will find Ice Fishing Ontario an invaluable guide.

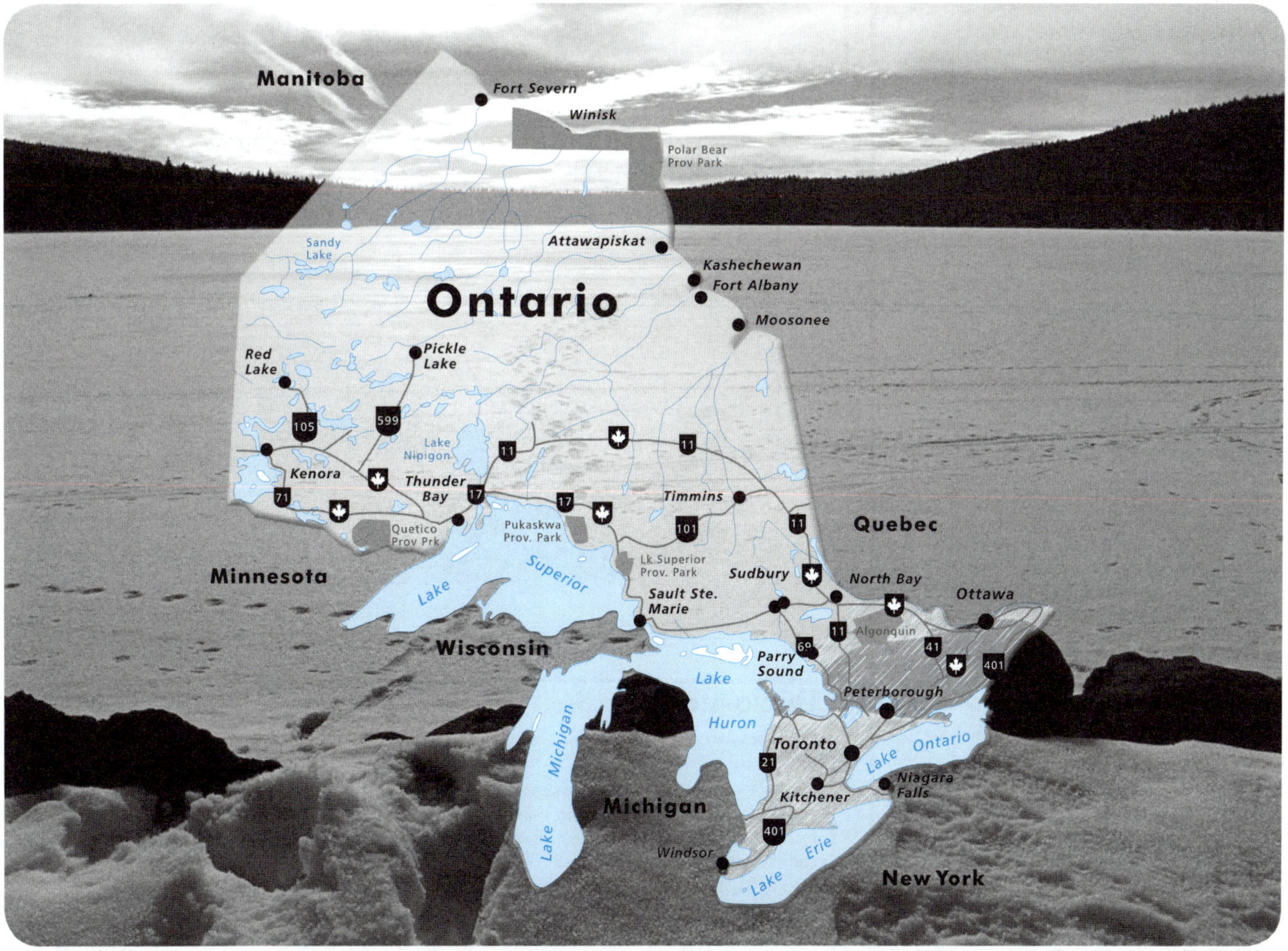

FISHING ONTARIO

DIRECTORS
Russell Mussio
Wesley Mussio
Penny Stainton-Mussio

COVER DESIGN & LAYOUT
Farnaz Faghihi

CREATIVE CONTENT
Russell Mussio
Wesley Mussio

PRODUCTION
Andrew Allen
Shawn Caswell
Shaan Desai
Tara Dreyer
Farnaz Faghihi
Brett Firth
Chris Taylor
Grace Teo
Dale Tober

SALES /MARKETING
Jason Marleau
Kerry Welch

WRITER
Jason Marleau

National Library of Canada Cataloguing in Publication Data

ISBN: 1-894556-40-2

Published by:

5811 Beresford St
Burnaby, BC, V5J 1K1
P. (604) 438-3474 F. (604) 438-3470
E-mail: info@backroadmapbooks.com
www.backroadmapbooks.com

Acknowledgement

This book could not have been compiled without the relentless effort of Jason Marleau. He headed the research and writing effort and did a fabulous job of digging up countless fishing opportunities and describing them in a creative, yet appealing way. His efforts have been aided by the hard work and dedication of the Mussio Ventures Ltd. staff, Andrew Allen, Shawn Caswell, Shaan Desai, Tara Dreyer, Farnaz Faghihi, Brett Firth, Chris Taylor, Grace Teo and Dale Tober. Without this teamwork, this comprehensive mapbook would never have been completed as thoroughly as it was.

In addition, we would like to thank all those individuals, retailers and tourism personnel for their knowledge and assistance in the production of this fishing guidebook. A special thanks goes to Kerry Welch and his help on the sales end.

Most of all we would like to thank Heather K. and River J. Marleau as well as Allison, Devon, Nancy, Madison and Penny Mussio for their continued support of the Fishing Ontario Series. As our family grows, it is becoming more and more challenging to break away from it all to explore our beautiful country.

Help Us Help You

A comprehensive resource such as ***ICE FISHING ONTARIO*** could not be put together without a great deal of help and support. Despite our best efforts to ensure that everything is accurate, errors do occur. If you see any errors or omissions, please continue to let us know.

Please contact us at:
Mussio Ventures Ltd.
5811 Beresford St, Burnaby, B.C. V5J 1K1
Email: updates@backroadmapbooks.com
P: 604-438-3474 toll free 1-877-520-5670 F: 604-438-3470

All updates will be posted on our web site:
www.backroadmapbooks.com

Disclaimer

The lake charts contained in this book are not intended for navigational purposes. Uncharted rocks and shoals may exist.

Mussio Ventures Ltd. does not warrant that the information contained in this guide is correct. Therefore, please be careful when using this or any source to plan and carry out your outdoor recreation activity. Also note that travelling on logging roads and trails is inherently dangerous, and you may encounter poor road conditions, unexpected traffic, poor visibility, and low or no road/trail maintenance. Please use extreme caution when travelling logging roads and trails.

Please refer to the Ontario Recreational Fishing Regulations for closures and restrictions. It is your responsibility to know when and where closures and restrictions apply.

Table of Contents

Ice Fishing In Ontario .... Page 4-8

- Regional Breakdown .... Page 4
- Stocking in Ontario .... Page 5
- Special Restrictions .... Page 5
- Catch & Release .... Page 5
- Fish Species .... Page 5-7
- Fishing Techniques .... Page 7
- Equipment .... Page 7-8

Safety .... Page 9

Southwestern Ontario .... Page 11-16
- Covering .... 26 Lakes

Cottage Country Ontario .... Page 17-56
- Covering .... 140 Lakes

Eastern Ontario .... Page 57-75
- Covering .... 98 Lakes

Algoquin Region Ontario .... Page 76-86
- Covering .... 67 Lakes

Near North Ontario .... Page 87-94
- Covering .... 120 Lakes

Index .... Page 95

Backroad Mapbooks

www.backroadmapbooks.com

Important Phone Numbers

Ministry of Natural Resources

General Inquiry .... (800) 667-1940
.... (800) 667-1840 (French)
.... e-mail: mnr.nric@mnr.gov.on.ca
Outdoors Card (Licenses, Customer Service) .... (800) 387-7011

Southwestern Ontario

Aurora, Greater Toronto Area .... (905) 713-7400
Aylmer .... (519) 773-9241
Chatham .... (519) 354-7340
Clinton .... (519) 482-3428
Guelph .... (519) 826-4955
Owen Sound .... (519) 376-3860
Vineland .... (905) 562-4147

Cottage Country

Bracebridge .... (705) 645-8747
Minden .... (705) 286-1521
Midhurst .... (705) 725-7500
Peterborough .... (705) 755-2001

Eastern Ontario

Bancroft .... (613) 332-3940
Kemptville .... (613) 258-8204
Kingston .... (613) 531-5700
Tweed .... (613) 478-2330

Algonquin Region

Algonquin .... (613) 637-2780
Pembroke .... (613) 732-3661

Near North

North Bay .... (705) 475-5550
Sudbury .... (705) 564-7823

Parks

Reservations .... (888) ONT-PARK
.... www.ontarioparks.com

Crime Stoppers (Poaching) .... (800) 222-TIPS (8477)

Invading Species Hotline .... (800) 563-7711

Sportfish Contaminant Monitoring Programme .... (800) 820-2716

Updates .... www.backroadmapbooks.com

Tourism, Resorts & Lodges

Ontario Tourism .... (800) ONT-ARIO
Resorts Ontario .... (705) 325-9115

Ice Fishing in Ontario

Ice fishing can be done by simply auguring a hole through the ice of a lake, or it can be done in style, inside the heat and comfort of an ice fishing hut. Over the past decade or so, ice fishing has been evolving quite rapidly. There are many new toys and people have been experimenting with technique. The popularity of the sport has also grown rapidly. While ice fishing in most of Ontario has always been a way of life, the recent growth of the sport has resulted in some overcrowding on lakes. Hopefully a book like this will help alleviate that problem.

Regional Breakdown

Ice fishing opportunities in Ontario vary depending on the region and lake. Each region has its own unique set of lakes and its own set of opportunities. Regardless of the region, there are plenty of fantastic lakes that are available to ice fish.

In the body of this book you will find the ice fishing information separated into five different regions. These regions correlate with the popular **Backroad Mapbook** Series; in fact, the map key at the beginning of each region is borrowed from that series. On each map key you see the area covered in each region along with a fish icon denoting where the various ice fishing lakes are found. Below is a general breakdown of each region and the fishing opportunities available:

Southwestern Ontario

Southwestern Ontario essentially covers from the Golden Horseshoe southwest to Windsor and from Long Point all the way to the tip of the Bruce Peninsula. Some of the more popular ice fishing destinations include Lake Erie, the many bays around Owen Sound as well as some of the smaller lakes scattered through the Bruce Peninsula.

Cottage Country

Cottage Country is one of the more popular outdoor destinations in the province. This region covers the many lakes from just north of Toronto all the way to Parry Sound. The western limit would be around the town of Collingwood, while the eastern most limit would be just past the city of Peterborough. This area includes Muskoka, the Kawarthas and the areas around Haliburton. For more information on these popular sub-regions, look for our other **Fishing Ontario** titles.

Eastern Ontario

Eastern Ontario continues to be an underutilized region, especially due to its close proximity to centres such as Ottawa, Kingston and Belleville. The region basically stretches from just east of Peterborough all the way to the Quebec border. From the popular Bay of Quinte all the way to Bancroft and the Madawaska Highlands, this region has countless lakes for ice anglers to explore. More information on the popular summer destination lakes in this region is found in the Eastern Ontario version of our **Fishing Ontario** series.

Algonquin Region

The Algonquin region may be deceiving due to the fact that ice fishing is banned in Algonquin Park itself. However, the region is about three times the size of the park and includes areas such as Pembroke, Mattawa and Sundridge. Essentially, all the vast areas around the park offer plenty of ice fishing opportunities and are a great place to explore in the winter months.

Near North

The Near North is best known for lakes such as Lake Nipissing and Lake Nosbonsing. The region stretches north from Parry Sound all the way to just past North Bay and Sudbury. Ice fishing in this region is not just a pastime; it is a way of life. Anglers can literally spend a lifetime exploring this vast and beautiful region.

Stocking in Ontario

Many lakes that offer ice fishing opportunities in Ontario are stocked in order to provide better fishing opportunities to anglers. Most stocking in the region is done on a put and take type basis and usually on a one to two year cycle depending on the fishing pressure on the lake. Splake, the brook trout/lake trout hybrid, is also stocked in a number of lakes in the region. Splake provide decent angling opportunities in lakes that are suitable for trout species. Splake not only help reduce pressure on fragile natural lake trout and brook trout lakes in the region but they also grow very quickly to good sizes. This makes them an attractive stocking and angling option.

Walleye are also one of the few species that are stocked in Ontario. Most walleye plantings are done in Eastern Ontario or around the Georgian Bay area near Manitoulin Island. However, there have been plantings in a few other areas, such as the Marten River area in Near North. Walleye stocking continues to be a debated topic in the province since the results in most circumstances are quite poor. There is scientific data pointing to the fact that unlike trout species, young walleye tend to feed ferociously on each other greatly reducing the chances of large numbers of young walleye to grow to adulthood.

Special Restrictions

A few of the restrictions anglers should be aware of during ice fishing on some Ontario lakes are slot size limits, line limits and bait restrictions. A slot size limit is the restriction of what size of fish must be released and what size you can keep from a lake. For example, on Bennett Lake, in order to keep walleye they must be greater than 41 cm (16 inches) in length. The idea is to release fish that are at a healthy maturity and the prime breeding stock of the lake. This gives the fish a better opportunity to reproduce.

On most Ontario lakes two lines may be used through the ice, although on a few of the more popular lakes, only one line is permitted. This regulation is obviously in effect to reduce the chance for anglers to harvest fragile stocks.

Bait restrictions are also quite common on lakes that are inhabited by trout species. Trout lakes are quite fragile ecosystems and the introduction of baitfish can literally decimate the ecosystem's ability to support trout, especially brook trout. Hundreds of times over the past decades trout lakes have been ruined by the introduction of foreign species such as bass from anglers using baitfish for ice fishing. Anglers have carelessly dumped buckets of live baitfish into lakes. Since the baitfish are very aggressive feeders they often out compete the trout for food.

All of these regulations are having positive effects on fishing quality in the region and are in place strictly for the benefit of future angling.

Catch and Release

Expanded awareness of anglers has increased the practice of voluntary catch and release, which is vital for a healthy sport fishery in Ontario. Anglers must realize that the fishery is not 'unlimited' and that the days of filling the freezer after a fishing trip are long gone. Ice fishing, in particular, is a very efficient but potentially devastating method of angling. As a result, more and more of the popular lakes are being closed to ice fishing. We can all help to keep more lakes open in the winter by practicing catch and release.

Catch and release can be effective in helping maintain a fishery, although extra attention and care must be taken to ensure sportfish survive the trauma of being pulled through the ice. In extreme cold conditions (approximately below -15 degrees Celsius), once fish come through the ice their eyes can freeze very rapidly rendering a live release ineffective. As well, be sure to pay attention to the depth you are catching sportfish. If you are bringing fish up from extreme depths such as 10+ m (33+ ft), they often cannot regulate their pressure properly and are impossible to revive if returned to the water. Larger fish, however, can often regulate properly, especially if they have put up a fight when coming in.

Fish Species

There are over 25 fish species that are angled for sport in the Province of Ontario and most species are regulated to some degree. The most popular species in Ontario are listed below:

1. Atlantic Salmon

Atlantic Salmon were native to Lake Ontario and became extinct by 1900 mainly due to over fishing by European settlers. There have been many attempts to introduce Atlantics into the Great Lakes and a few North Bay area lakes, although success has been limited. North Bay area Atlantics are locally known as Ouininache. Although the species is rare, the salmon are caught periodically in Trout Lake and Nosbonsing Lake while fishing for other sportfish species. The Ontario record is 11 kg (24 lbs).

2. Bass (Smallmouth and Largemouth)

In the body of this book, many readers may notice that there is only brief mention of bass in most of the lakes. Smallmouth and largemouth bass are present in the majority of Ontario's ice fishing lakes, although bass become quite lethargic in the winter and are basically impossible to catch through the ice. Unlike cool water species such as trout and pike, which can be quite feisty at times, bass simply are warm water species and the cold temperatures basically renders them into hibernation.

3. Brook Trout

Brook trout are native to Ontario and inhabit cool streams and smaller lakes throughout the region. Brook trout are also known as speckled trout due to the red spots with blue halos on their sides. Brookies are often a fickle and difficult fish to catch and some of the most ardent anglers can be skunked during a day's outing for brook trout. Stream brook trout are generally small and rarely reach sizes in excess of 30cm (12 in), while lake brook trout can be found to 1 kg (2.2 lbs) and sometimes larger.

One of the most effective ice fishing methods of angling for brookies is by jigging. Small spoons tipped with worms can be productive, and is the recommended set up when fishing for brook trout through the ice. The Ontario record brook trout was caught on a fly in the Nipigon River and weighed a whopping 6.58 kg (14.5 lbs).

4. Lake Trout

This trout species is one of the most sought after fish species in the province. Unfortunately the prized fish is suffering and populations are either in steady decline or have become extinct in many parts of Ontario. The dramatic declines in lake trout stocks in these lakes are due mainly to over harvesting by anglers.

Lake trout grow very slowly and mature at an older age (6-8 years of age) than most other species; therefore, the use of catch and release fishing can go a long way in helping maintain populations. Lakers can grow to sizes exceeding 6 kg (13 lbs) and can be found near the surface at times in winter. Spoons, jigs, or anything that imitates the lake trout's main food source, the minnow, are good choices when ice fishing for lakers. The Ontario record lake trout is 28.6 kg (63.12 lbs).

5. Muskellunge

Muskellunge are the largest freshwater sportfish species in Ontario and can reach over 16 kg (35 lbs) in size. Often referred to as "musky" this warm water predator feeds mainly on other fish and on frogs, mice, muskrat, and the occasional waterfowl. The best method for finding these large fish in the winter is by using minnows as bait. However, ice fishing can be very slow for these warm water predators.

A true musky angler releases their catch to grow larger and to fight another day. The Ontario record muskellunge was caught in 1989 in Blackstone Harbour of The Massasauga Provincial Park off Georgian Bay and weighed 29.5 kg (65 lbs). This great fish would not have made it to a record size if not for catch and release angling.

6. Northern Pike

Pike are the cousin of the muskellunge and inhabits weedy, murky waters throughout Ontario. Pike are very aggressive and readily strike anything imitating a good meal. Northern pike can be found over 8 kg (17.6 lbs) in size and colourful spoons or jigs can be very productive winter baits.

Pike are most active during the darker times of day; hence, early morning and evening are the most productive periods to fish. Ontario's record northern pike is a 19.11 kg (42.13 lb) lunker.

7. Pacific Salmon

These were introduced into the Great Lakes and include pink, Chinook and Coho salmon. Pink salmon were accidentally introduced into the Current River, a tributary of Lake Superior, in 1956 and have since spread throughout the Great Lakes and established spawning runs on many streams of the Great Lakes basin. The Ontario record pink salmon is 5.9 kg (13.1 lbs).

Chinook and Coho salmon have been the focus of numerous Great Lakes stocking introductions since 1873 and Chinook salmon continue to be stocked in large numbers. The famous Wilmot Hatchery was one of the pioneers of Chinook introductions and the species is a prized catch. Even though many Great Lakes streams have healthy spawning runs of both Chinook and Coho salmon, the reproduction success has been dismal with the future of Chinook and Coho being solely dependent on stocking programs.

Jigging spoons or using that imitation minnows can take all three pacific salmon species. The bays of Lake Huron are the only area where ice fishing for these salmon is productive. Chinook are the most prevalent of the three species, while pinks and Coho are a little harder to find through the ice. The Ontario record Coho salmon is 12.1 kg (26.64 lbs) and Chinook salmon is 20.6 kg (45.38 lbs).

8. Panfish

Panfish have quickly become a very popular fish species while ice fishing. In some parts of the province, anglers ice fish solely for these aggressive and easy to catch fish. Some of the more popular panfish found in the province include pumpkinseed and bluegill.

9. Rainbow Trout

Native to the Pacific Northwest, rainbow trout have been introduced into a number of inland lakes in Ontario and provide for exciting ice fishing opportunities. Inland lake sizes of rainbow trout usually average 35-45 cm (14-18 in) and are found generally in smaller lakes. Similar to most trout species, small silver or gold spoons can be productive. The Ontario record rainbow trout is 13.2 kg (29.12 lbs).

10. Splake

Splake are a sterile cross between lake trout and brook trout and were developed specifically to stock lakes uninhabited by other trout species or lakes where trout were either extinct or near extinction. The fast growing hybrid not only helps reduce fishing pressure on native trout lakes but also enhances angling opportunities.

Splake grow very rapidly similar to brook trout and to sizes similar to lake trout. Often, anglers don't know that they have caught a splake and mistake the hatchery fish for natural lake trout. Splake are most active in winter and in spring just after ice off. Similar to lake trout, they will strike shiny spoons.

11. Walleye

Also known as pickerel, walleye are perhaps the most prized sportfish in Ontario due in part to its acclaim as a great tasting fish. The walleye's diet is made up of mainly baitfish, although they do take leeches and other grub like creatures. However, jigs are the lure of choice for walleye either through the ice or during open water season.

Walleye travel in loose schools and once you find them, you should be able to catch more than one. Jigging in set locations is a productive method through the ice. Try to find an anomaly in the bottom structure where baitfish may congregate. Another trick is to try during the darker times of day, such as early morning and evening, when walleye are more active. The Ontario record walleye is 10.1 kgs (22.25 lbs).

12. Whitefish

Whitefish are found in many lakes in Ontario and can provide some great angling opportunities from the Great Lakes to the Hudson Bay. The species is not one of the prized sportfish, although it is increasingly becoming more popular.

Whitefish feed mainly on insects similar to trout, although are much more aggressive than trout and less spooky. In winter, whitefish will readily strike spoons or other shinny lures. They average 2-3 kg (4-7 lbs) in size and the Ontario record is a stunning 6.53 kg (14.38 lbs).

13. Yellow Perch

Yellow Perch do not grow very big and only average 20-30 cm (8-12 in) in size. What they lack in size, they make up for in eating quality. In this regard, they are often compared to walleye.

The feisty fish is active throughout the year, especially during ice fishing season. Perch are aggressive feeders and are best caught by still fishing with minnows or even worms. They are found in many warm water lakes throughout the province and the Ontario record is 1 kg (2.25 lbs).

Please Note: There are angling regulations in effect on all water bodies in Ontario in order to preserve the future of the resource. Some of the more specific regulations may include bait bans, special limits, slot size restrictions and closures. Penalty for breaking these regulations can include heavy fines, seizure of equipment and/or imprisonment. Always check the annual Ontario Recreational Fishing Regulations Summary before fishing!

Season

Southern Ontario's ice fishing season begins later than in the cooler areas of northern Ontario. In general, winter sets in around mid-November and ice is often formed on lakes by mid to late December. By early January many of the lakes are safe enough to ice fish.

Ice off in Southern Ontario usually occurs around mid April. But the ice conditions vary greatly and several lakes start to become unsafe to fish as early as the beginning of March. Be sure to check locally for ice conditions before heading out.

Fishing Techniques

Years ago, ice fishing techniques were quite basic, usually a line on a pole, hook and minnow. Today, things have changed. Below, we have outlined some of the current ice fishing options used today. For more information on these methods and proper equipment, visit your local retailer or pick up one of the many ice fishing guides on the market.

Jigging

Jigging has become one of the more frequently used ice fishing methods used anywhere. Jigging is, basically, moving the lure up and down periodically. The idea behind jigging is quite simple; the action of the lure will attract more fish to bite. Jigging may also add light reflection to the lure or even create added sound in the water. These other factors may contribute to the added success found through jigging.

Tip Ups

A tip up is a contraption that an angler can bait and set over a hole. The contraption is set with a spring so that when a fish comes by and hits the bait, the rod will recoil, hopefully helping set the hook. These contraptions are normally equipped with a bell or flag to help alert the angler to the strike. You can purchase a tip up set at any reputable fishing retailer.

Bouncing Rod

There are many different set ups that anglers have created over the years for ice fishing. The bouncing rod is a rod that is attached to the wall of a hut positioned over a hole. The base of the rod is equipped with something like a door stopper type spring, hence when a strike arrives, the rod will bounce.

Rod Mount

Perhaps the most popular angling method is to simply hook a bell to the tip of a ice fishing rod and mount the tip over the hole. There are mounts that you can buy, but a simple stick with a 'Y' will usually do fine. When a strike happens, the rod will bend and the bell will sound.

Equipment

Below is some basic information on some of the equipment used in finding fish through the ice.

Huts

Ice fishing huts have multiple purposes for the angler. One purpose is the most obvious, anglers can fish through the ice in some warmth and a little comfort. Recently, huts have become a great place for anglers to socialize and simply enjoy a part of winter. While most huts are quite small, suitable for two or three people, a major change has occurred in the past decade. Huts have advanced to the point that anglers can now even sleep and cook out on the lake. Some hardcore anglers are known to enjoy several days out on the ice without even coming to shore.

Portable Huts

In the past some anglers have attempted to make their own portable shelters or even collapsible huts. As a result, enterprising entrepreneurs have created numerous collapsible hut options. These can be found at any reputable fishing retailer and are designed to be easily towed by a snowmobile making them highly portable from lake to lake.

Snowmobiles

The snowmobile has become synonymous with ice fishing. Snowmobiles are the main mode of transport on all lakes in the province and are very handy in accessing interior ice fishing lakes. Along with the access ability of snowmobiles, they are indeed fun to ride.

Augers

There are two ways to get through the ice of a lake. For decades anglers have been physically grinding their augers through the ice by hand. Today, the hand augerer is a dying breed. The advent of the power auger, which grinds through the ice in seconds with little physical exertion, has made ice fishing a lot more enjoyable. There are a couple of drawbacks with the power augers. They are very noisy and often scare the fish away. They also make drilling holes almost too easy and some lakes are literally riddled with holes making for sometimes unsafe walking conditions.

Rods

Although some anglers still use the old manual hand coil rod, ice fishing rods have come a long way. Many anglers now use an specific ice fishing rod with a spincasting reel. These rods are simply a much smaller and more sensitive version of open water rods.

Lures

At any of your local tackle shops, you will find a seemingly endless array of tackle. Here is a quick rundown of ice fishing lures and what they are mainly used for:

Spoons

Spoons come in a mix of sizes and colours. Spoons are more commonly used when fishing for northern pike and trout; however, they can be productive for other species as well. For pike, the larger presentations with brighter colours, like red or yellow, are the spoons of choice. For trout, smaller silver or gold spoons with shades of blue, or green can be productive. A popular brand name for trout spoons is the Little Cleo.

Jigs

Jigs are made up of a weighted head and plastic body. Both the head and body come in a wide range of colours, shapes and sizes. As with any lure, the key to finding the right shape, size or colour is done mainly through trial and error. Jigs work well for bass and are a favourite lure of walleye anglers. Trout anglers have recently began to use jigs, especially for lake trout. While a lake trout will rarely hit a jig in the spring or summer, they seem to be drawn to it in the winter months.

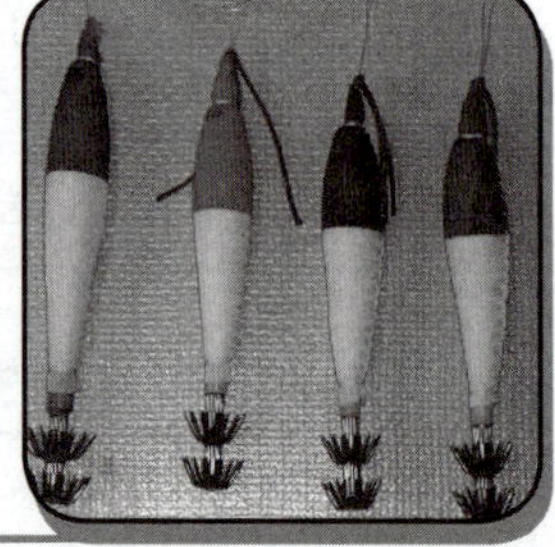

Others

Many anglers are beginning to push the limits of ice fishing to include different lures. One of the increasingly more popular lures is to jig crankbaits or any minnow imitation lure through the ice. This makes sense, if they will bite a live minnow in winter, why not an imitation.

Bait

Baitfish are still one of the primary lures of choice for ice anglers in Ontario. Minnows and on occasion worms are quite effective on most water bodies. Many have an opinion on how to hook a minnow for ice fishing. One of the more effective methods is the simple hook it through the top of the snout. This way the baitfish can still swim and it is upright, providing an enticing meal for a walleye or pike. If you do use baitfish, please adhere to all restrictions and bans. Literally hundreds of Ontario lakes have been decimated due to the improper use of baitfish.

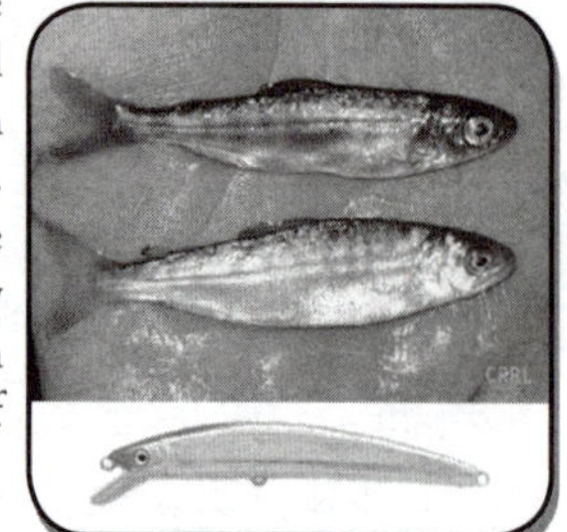

How To Read The Depth Charts

Knowing how to read the depth charts provided in this or the other **Fishing Ontario** books will definitely improve your fishing success. Depth charts are the best way to find clues to where fish are hanging out. When reading depth charts there are some general rules that can help your angling success.

When analyzing a depth chart, look for hidden islands, drop-offs and shoals. A hidden island is a relatively flat, shallow area that is slightly submerged, while being surrounded by deeper water. A drop-off is a rapid decline in the depth on the chart. A shoal is a slowly declining area of the lake, which then drops off into the depths. In larger lakes, shoals can also be characterized as shallow irregularities in the bottom of the lake, essentially, a bump in the bottom. In some lakes there may be only one or two of these significant shoal sites. As a result, these are often the sites of some of the best angling on the lake. This is because shoals are often the site of aquatic vegetation, which is home to the baitfish that larger sportfish feed on.

When looking for a species like the brook trout, depth information can be very handy. As an example, during winter, brook trout often forage for food in the shallower areas of the lake. On some lakes, there may only be one specific area of the lake where lake trout will find the required depth needed to find food. With a depth chart in hand, these spots can be easily located.

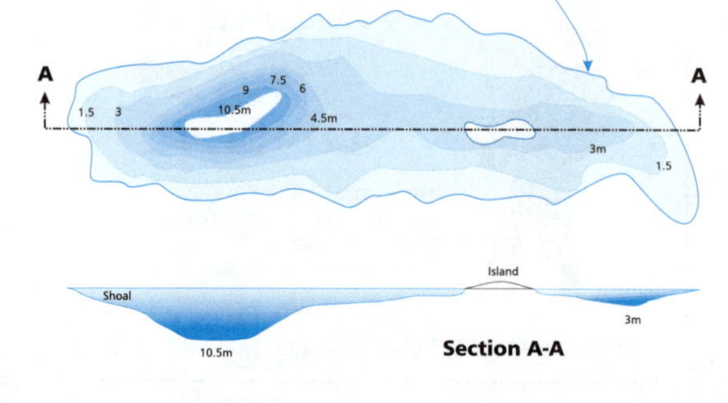

Safety

Ice Thickness

The number one thing to remember about ice safety is that no ice is ever 100% safe. Even if ice is extremely thick, it can be broken up by sudden changes in weather conditions. As an example, in the mid 1990's there was a very strong windstorm in Southern Ontario in mid February resulting in the widespread break up of very thick ice on Lake Simcoe. Ice in some areas was reported at over 18 inches thick, a safe thickness for vehicle travel, yet it still broke up. Several anglers had to be lifted to safety by helicopters and a few anglers even lost their vehicles.

So when heading out on any lake, be sure to be aware of the current conditions. Most local bait shops or even local police stations should be able to provide that information. If you are even in doubt, do not risk it. As a general guideline, we have included the following chart for ice safety. Although the chart indicates that at a certain thickness vehicles can be driven on ice, it is wise to know that there is no insurance company in Canada that will honour your policy if an accident of any type occurs on a frozen lake with your vehicle.

Clothing

When venturing out on a lake in the dead of winter it is very important to be properly clothed in order to be comfortable and safe. Footwear is perhaps one of the most important items that should not be overlooked. Your boots should be well insulated and you should be wearing at least thermal type socks or even a couple pairs of heavy wool socks. Of course, comfort varies from person to person. After standing on a sheet of ice for a few hours, the cold can penetrate some of the best footwear. Many first time ice anglers have to cut their visit short due to frozen feet.

Many ice anglers are opting to wear a full thermal survival suit. This is a very good idea, as the suit not only keeps you warm, it acts as a floatation device in the event of ice breakage. While these suits can be expensive, they have saved hundreds of lives. As an alternative to a thermal suit, water resistant snow pants and jacket are good choices. Regardless of what you choose to wear, be sure to dress in layers. You can always take a layer off and you will surely regret not having enough layers once you are out on the ice in the bitter cold.

Mitts are also very important, as your hands and fingers are often one of the first areas that become cold. While some people prefer gloves to mitts, a glove with double the insulation of a mitt often cannot do a proper job insulating your fingers. Mitts are designed for cold and a good water resistant mitt will definitely make your outing more enjoyable.

Finally, headwear should not be overlooked. The majority of all heat loss when exposed to the cold is through your head. A fine wool toque is often all that is needed. However, in extreme conditions, a balaclava is recommended. The added protection can save your face from becoming numb and potentially frostbitten.

Hypothermia

Hypothermia is a condition that can set in almost immediately when immersed in freezing water or over a slow period after constant exposure to wet, windy and cold conditions. The first defense to hypothermia is to be safe so that you do not go through the ice. If you are exposed to extreme conditions for a long period, the best defense is to be properly dressed. Clothing should begin with a water resistant layer with several layers after that ending with long underwear.

Symptoms of hypothermia can include shivering, white coloured skin and in more extreme situations the skin will turn blue. The affected person will also potentially have slurred speech, stiff muscles and be confused about basic things. If medical help is available nearby, ensure the victim gets there as soon as possible.

If medical help is not readily available, there are a few things you can do to greatly improve the victim's condition. Be sure to seek shelter right away, remove all wet clothing and replace with dry clothing. Keep the victim active in order to help generate internal heat and get the victim in front of a heat source such as a fire. Skin to skin body contact helps to greatly improve the body temperature of the victim. Hot drinks and food high in carbohydrates will also help. Be sure not to take this condition lightly as it can lead to heart failure and death if left untreated.

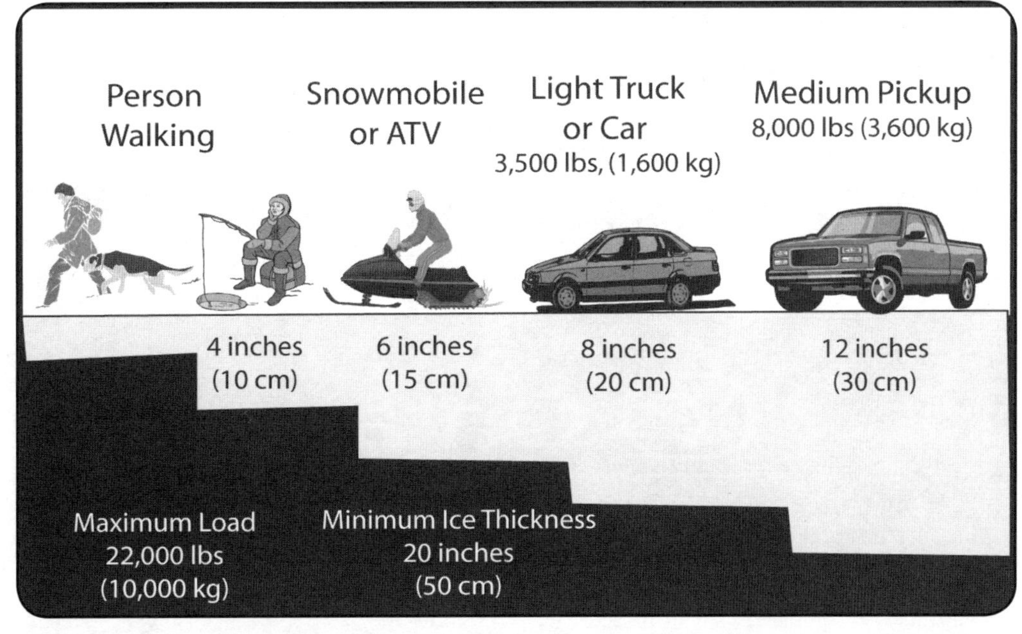

Southwestern Ontario Mapkey

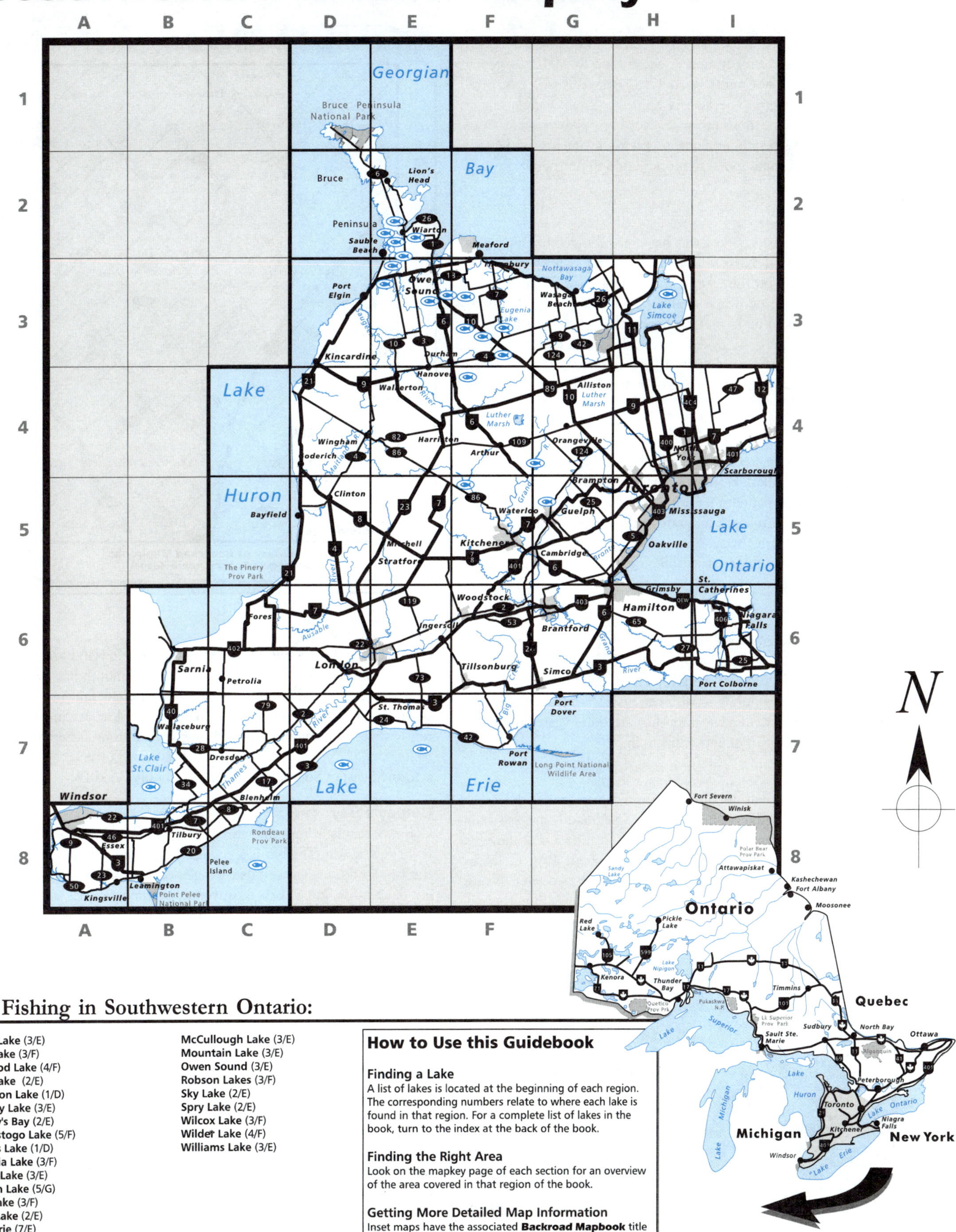

Ice Fishing in Southwestern Ontario:

Arran Lake (3/E)
Bells Lake (3/F)
Belwood Lake (4/F)
Boat Lake (2/E)
Cameron Lake (1/D)
Chesley Lake (3/E)
Colpoy's Bay (2/E)
Contestogo Lake (5/F)
Cyprus Lake (1/D)
Eugenia Lake (3/F)
Gould Lake (3/E)
Guelph Lake (5/G)
Irish Lake (3/F)
Isaak Lake (2/E)
Lake Erie (7/E)
Lake Simcoe (3/H)
Lake St. Clair (8/B)
McCullough Lake (3/E)
Mountain Lake (3/E)
Owen Sound (3/E)
Robson Lakes (3/F)
Sky Lake (2/E)
Spry Lake (2/E)
Wilcox Lake (3/F)
Wilder Lake (4/F)
Williams Lake (3/E)

How to Use this Guidebook

Finding a Lake
A list of lakes is located at the beginning of each region. The corresponding numbers relate to where each lake is found in that region. For a complete list of lakes in the book, turn to the index at the back of the book.

Finding the Right Area
Look on the mapkey page of each section for an overview of the area covered in that region of the book.

Getting More Detailed Map Information
Inset maps have the associated **Backroad Mapbook** title and the page that it is found on.

Arran Lake

This long lake is located east of Port Elgin and can be accessed at the Arran Lake Conservation Area off Side Road 10. To reach Side Road 10, follow County Road 17 (Gustavus Road) east from downtown Port Elgin. The lake is home to a fair population of smallmouth bass and northern pike. Northern pike provide all of the action during the winter months with fish averaging 1.5 kg (3.5 lbs). Try jigging a small spoon to attract cruising northerns through the ice.

Belwood Lake

The damming of the Grand River has created a good fishing destination in Belwood Lake. Some big pike and panfish make up most of the action on the lake in winter. Pike over 75 cm (30 in) are caught on occasion, while smaller pike in the 3+ kg (6.5+ lb) range can be picked up as evening approaches. Access to Belwood Lake is from the Belwood Lake Conservation Area found just outside of the town of Fergus. Inquire locally or consult the Backroad Mapbook for Southwestern Ontario for detailed directions to the lake.

Bells Lake

Bells Lake has been stocked periodically with both rainbow trout and brook trout. The lake is a fine winter fishing destination but like all trout lakes, patience is certainly needed. Try jigging a small silver or gold spoon to hook into one of these trout, which average 30 cm (12 in) in size. Access to the lake is via the 70 Side Road west of the village of Markdale. There are special season regulations on Bells Lake.

Boat Lake

This popular fishing destination is accessible via the Boat Lake Road southwest of Wiarton or by County Road 13, which travels along the northern shore of the lake. The weedy lake offers northern pike and walleye during ice fishing season. Fishing seems to be hit and miss for pike, as some days they are quite aggressive while other days they are almost impossible to find.

Cameron Lake

Cameron Lake lies within Bruce Peninsula National Park and is home to walleye and smallmouth bass. Smallmouth are basically dormant in the winter months, although fishing for walleye is known to be generally fair. Walleye average about 1 kg (2 lb) in size with the odd 2+ kg (4.5+ lb) fish caught on occasion. White coloured jigs can be effective. If the walleye are not biting, there is usually plenty of panfish action on this lake. Be sure to check the regulations for special season restrictions before heading out.

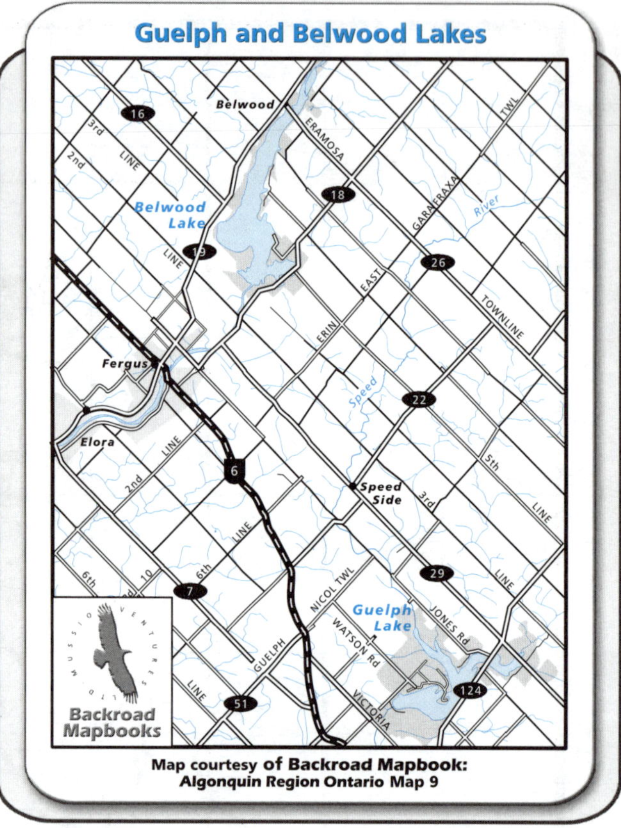

Map courtesy of Backroad Mapbook: Algonquin Region Ontario Map 9

Chesley Lake

Chesley Lake is a very weedy lake that lies in a lowland area of the Bruce Peninsula. The lake is inhabited by smallmouth bass, walleye and northern pike. Fishing for walleye is generally fair for average sized pickerel, while success for pike can be slow at times. Currently there is a sanctuary period on the lake from December 15th to January 31st in order to reduce catches through the ice. The lake is located east of Southampton just off County Road 14.

Colpoy's Bay

Colpoy's Bay is a long shaped bay that can be accessed from the town of Wiarton. The bay is a popular ice fishing destination, when the ice conditions are suitable. Anglers can expect to find a variety of sportfish in the bay, most notably rainbow trout, lake trout, whitefish and the odd Chinook salmon. Jigging spoons is a popular method in finding these sportfish, although many swear by minnows. Some good-sized trout and salmon can be caught in this bay in the winter months.

Contestogo Lake

The damming of the Contestogo River northwest of Kitchener/Waterloo created this popular recreational lake. Anglers visiting the lake can look forward to the opportunity to catch some big northern pike. Pike can reach over 75 cm (30 in) in size and average 3 kg (6 lbs). If the pike are not hitting there are usually plenty of panfish nipping at the lines.

Cyprus Lake

Found within Bruce Peninsula National Park, Cyprus Lake is home to a large campground. As a result, the lake receives significantly

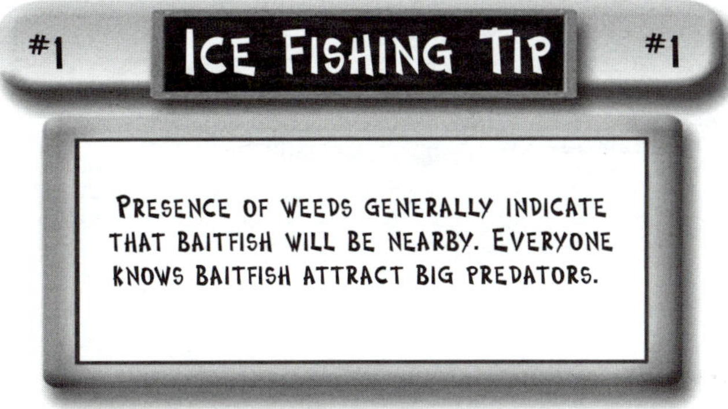

more angling pressure than nearby Cameron Lake, especially during the summer. Walleye are the main attraction for anglers visiting this lake in the winter months. The fishing is usually slow but jigging chartreuse or white coloured jigs can be effective. Be sure to check the regulations for any special restrictions before heading out.

Eugenia Lake
Brown trout, brook trout and rainbow trout have all been stocked in Eugenia Lake at one time. Today, rainbow trout are the only species that are being stocked, however, there are still occasional reports of brook trout being caught. Rainbow seem to provide most of the action during ice fishing season. Check for special season regulations before heading out.

Gould Lake
Gould Lake is a weedy, marsh like lake that is located southeast of Sauble Beach. There are several cabins and camps along the shore of the lake. Bass are the main species found in the lake during the summer months, but there are populations of walleye and pike available for ice fishers. While walleye and northern pike tend to be smaller than average, there are some good-sized fish found on occasion. Access is best via the tent and trailer park located off County Road 14.

Guelph Lake
Perhaps one of the most overlooked fishing spots in the region is Guelph Lake. The lake is home to a healthy population of bass and also sports decent northern pike and panfish populations for winter fishing. Since the lake is a reservoir, there are plenty of old stumps and other underwater debris creating ideal habitat. Pike fishing in the lake is generally fair for pike that average around 45 cm (16 in) in size. When the pike are not biting in the winter, there are usually plenty of panfish to keep you occupied. The lake is accessible from the Guelph Lake Conservation Area found north of the city of Guelph.

Irish Lake
Rainbow trout are stocked in Irish Lake every few years and provide for fair to good fishing throughout the season. Rainbow average around 22 cm (9 in) in size and can be caught jigging small jigs or spoons. Access to this lake is found off the Artemesia-Glenelg Townline south of the town of Markdale. There are special season regulations on this lake. Inquire locally or consult the Backroad Mapbook for Southwestern Ontario for directions.

Isaak Lake
Isaak Lake lies to the north of Boat Lake and can be reached by Isaak Lake Road off the west side of Highway 6. At the end of the road you will find a picnic area with a rough access area. The weedy lake is a popular summer destination for its smallmouth and largemouth bass, however northern pike and walleye are the main ice fishing attraction. Fishing seems to be hit and miss for pike.

Lake Erie
Once considered a polluted waterbody, Lake Erie has certainly been cleaned up over the past several decades. Today, it is one of the cleaner Great Lakes, and as a result, the sportfishing industry is thriving. The main sportfish anglers are after in the lake are walleye, but lake trout and coho salmon are quite popular as well. Other species include perch and northern pike.

This big lake can be overwhelming to new anglers, but it is a simple as finding a sheltered bay to get into some of the ice fishing action. A few of the more popular areas for ice fishing are Pigeon Bay, Rondeau Bay near Leamington or Long Point Bay near Port Rowan. Walleye are the most prized catch in the winter, but perch are a close second and provide the bulk of the winter action. Anglers are also occasionally surprised by a big northern pike when fishing for perch or walleye. Ice fishers will find lake trout are concentrated near the eastern portion of the lake.

Lake Simcoe
See Pages 14-15

Lake St. Clair
With the cities of Detroit, London and Windsor so close, it is amazing how resilient Lake St. Clair remains. The big lake remains a good destination for a day out on the ice. The main sportfish pursued by anglers is walleye. With some luck and patience, good size walleye can be found regularly in the lake. Perch are also a big draw to the lake, especially in the winter. (Continued on page 16)

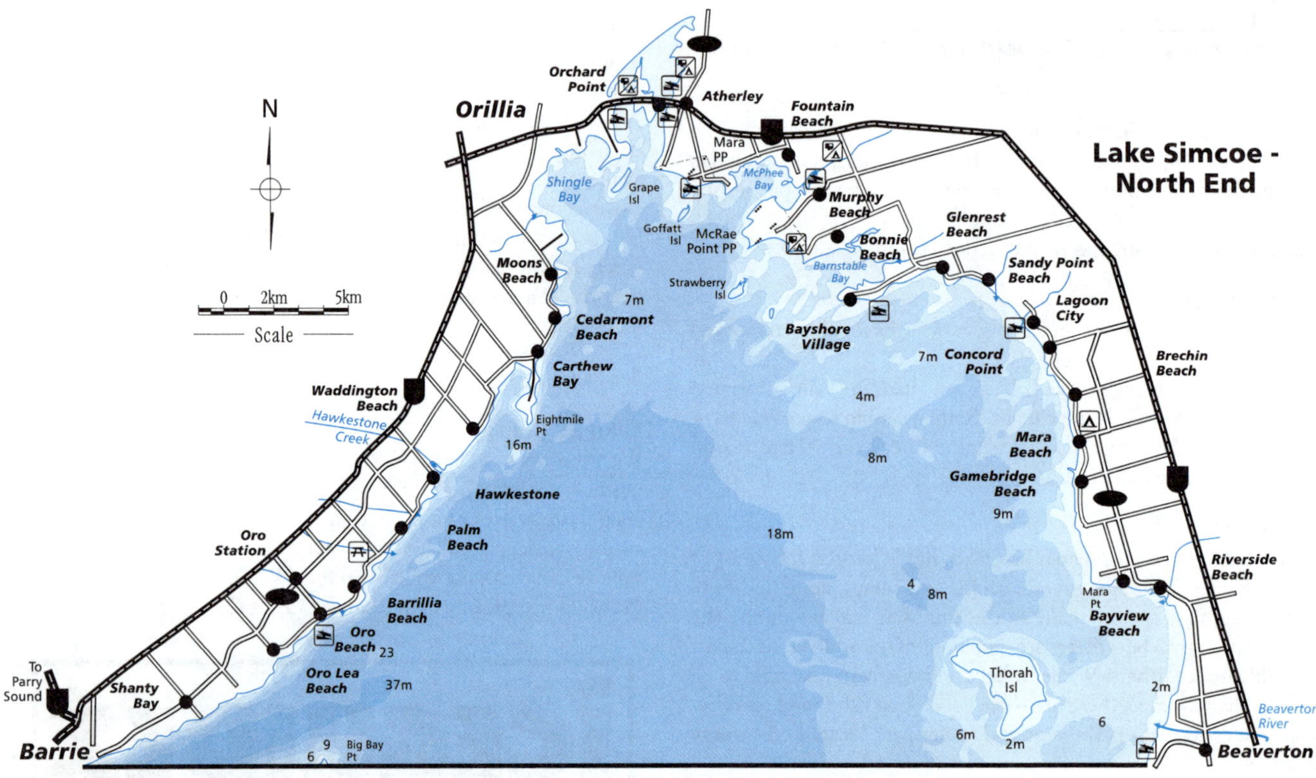

Access

Lake Simcoe is one of Ontario's largest inland lakes and is a thriving outdoor recreational playground. Although you can access this big lake from numerous areas, the main access area for the northern portion is from the Orillia area. The scenic lakeside community has thrived over the years due in part from the popularity of Lake Simcoe. There are a few boat launch areas and marinas in town that can be found off the south side of Highway 12. Highway 12 can be easily reached by travelling north along Highway 11 from the Barrie area.

The most popular area to access the southern portion of the lake is from the city of Barrie. Barrie lies along the beautiful shores of Kempenfelt Bay and has grown substantially in size over the past decade. It rightfully promotes itself as an outdoor lifestyle community.

There are several other access points to the lake shown on the lake depth chart. Many of these boat launch areas are used by people to get out on the lake, either by snowmobile or in a vehicle. Before travelling over the ice with a vehicle, it is essential to find out if the ice is safe. Please inquire locally.

Fishing

Lake Simcoe is the largest lake in the Trent-Severn Waterway system. The lake has long been a popular destination for the Metro Toronto region and continues to grow as an outdoor centre. The big lake is stocked annually with over 100,000 yearling lake trout, which provide for decent fishing throughout the season, especially during the winter. Northern Pike and walleye round out the main sport fish species found in Lake Simcoe in the winter. Some big northerns can be found in this lake, while walleye success is sporadic and depends on the area you are fishing.

The main method of fishing on this lake in the winter months is by bait fishing. A minnow hooked to a tip up or rod with a bell is the method of choice. However, some anglers swear by jigging, especially for the bigger predatory sportfish. In particular, white jigs have been known to attract lake trout. Sometimes a change like this is all it takes to attract the attention of one of those big cruising fish in Lake Simcoe.

Lake Definition

Mean Depth: 8.7 m (28.8 ft)
Max Depth: 41.4 m (136 ft)
Way Point: 44° 25' 00" Lat - N
79° 20' 00" Long - W

Facilities

The town of Orillia is a growing lakeside community that is home to hotels, motels, and retail stores that provide all the essentials to make your fishing adventure a success. If you prefer, there are several other smaller lakeside communities around the shore that offer basic amenities and access to the lake. Barrie is the focal point of the southern portion of Lake Simcoe since it offers all the amenities of a larger city, but still retains that small town feel. Accommodations and retailer outlets are readily found in the city providing the perfect base for your outdoor adventure.

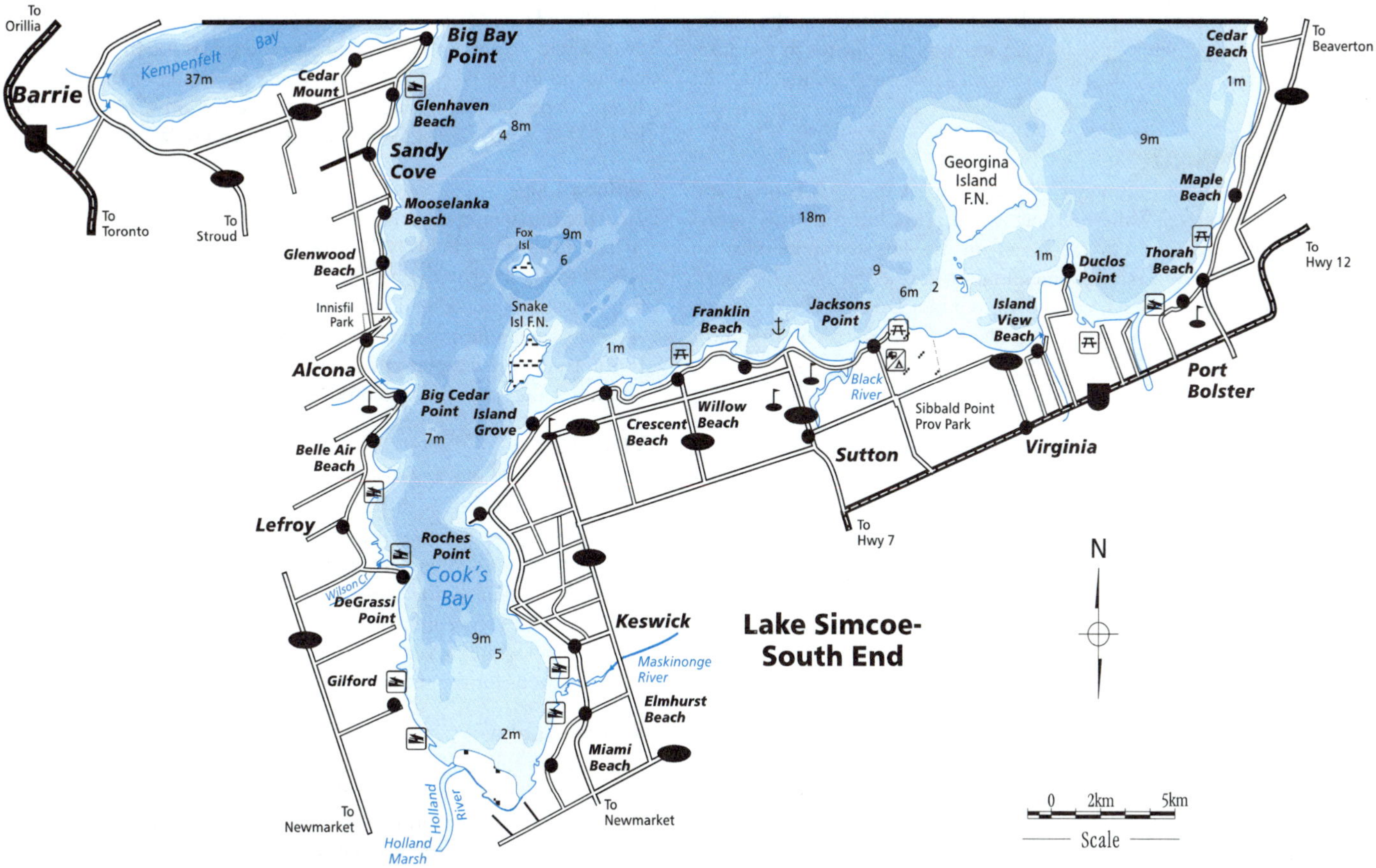

Lake Simcoe-South End

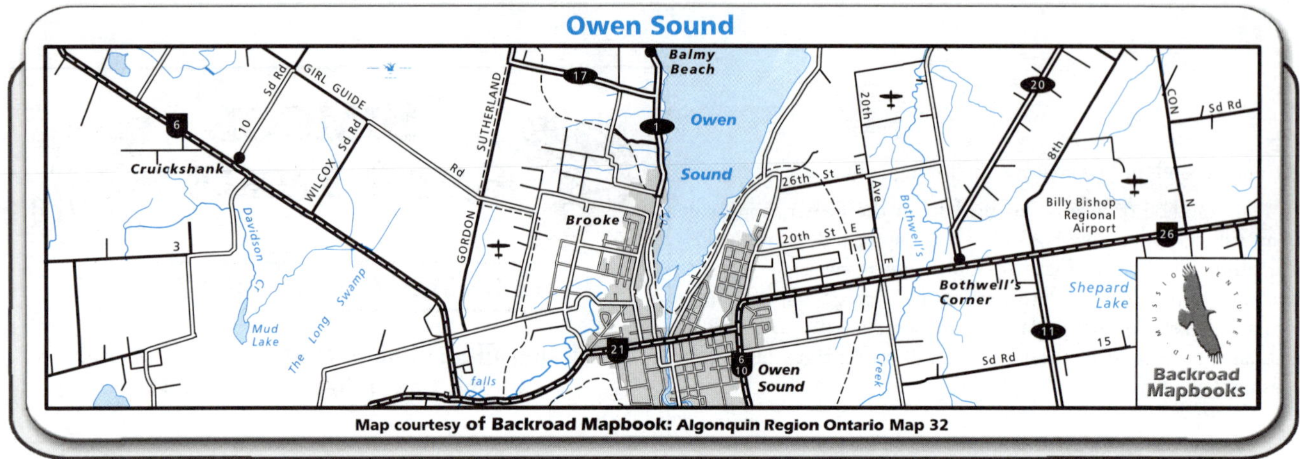

Map courtesy of Backroad Mapbook: Algonquin Region Ontario Map 32

Lake St. Clair is also known to hold northern pike and big muskellunge. Musky can take your ice fishing gear for a wild ride, while northerns are usually smaller and a bit more manageable. However, pike do reach 10 kg (22 lbs) in size on occasion. Be sure to check the regulations thoroughly before fishing in Lake St. Clair, a number of special regulations apply.

McCullough Lake

McCullough Lake is inhabited by natural populations of northern pike and smallmouth bass. However, it is the stocked brook trout/lake trout hybrid, splake, that provides most of the good fishing in the winter. Try jigging small silver spoons through the ice for both splake and northern pike. Splake are usually caught in the 30 cm (12 in) range, while pike can get much bigger. To reach the lake, take McCullough Lake Road west off Highway 6, south of Owen Sound.

Mountain Lake

Anglers visiting Mountain Lake can expect to catch panfish and the odd walleye. Walleye fishing is often slow but the prized sportfish can reach up to 60 cm (24 in) in size. Jigging can be effective at times or try a minnow presentation for added success. Found north of Owen Sound, access to Mountain Lake is off Concession 17 Road or from the tent and trailer park located along the north shore of the lake.

Owen Sound

Owen Sound, the water body, is accessible many ways, but most notably from the town of Owen Sound. The bay offers populations of popular game fish such as lake trout, rainbow trout, chinook salmon and whitefish, with some panfish available as well. Rainbow trout and lake trout are the two main species sought after through the ice. Success for these sportfish is slow to fair, with the best action usually coming during overcast periods. Ensure caution when travelling on the sound by snowmobile and be sure to check locally for ice conditions before heading out.

Robson Lakes

The Robson Lakes are a collection of small lakes found southeast of Owen Sound. The lakes are stocked with splake and are also inhabited with generally small northern pike. Both pike and splake will hit under the ice and are active late day feeders. Access to the lakes is found by taking Highway 10 south of Chatsworth to Side Road 20. Side Road 20 passes just north of the Robson Lakes.

Sky Lake

Anglers visiting Sky Lake in the summer months are often there in search of its active bass fishery. However, in winter the fishery turns to walleye and northern pike. Walleye and pike are generally average in size, although the odd large pike can surprise anglers. The weedy nature of Sky Lake provides ideal habitat but can affect the quality of the ice on the lake. Please be careful. Access to Sky Lake is found by travelling north of Wiarton via Highway 6 to Red Bay Road. Red Bay Road passes by the southern end of the lake.

Spry Lake

Due to the close proximity and easy access to Spry Lake from Wiarton, the lake receives significant angling pressure throughout the year. While smallmouth bass and largemouth bass are the main species found in the lake, northern pike and panfish offer the only ice fishing opportunities during the cool winter months. Look for the lake on the north side of County Road 13, west of Wiarton.

Wilcox Lake

Another fine winter destination in the Markdale area, Wilcox Lake is found south of Highway 10, not far from County Road 4. The lake is stocked regularly with brook trout, which provide for good fishing at times in winter. Ice anglers should try jigging a small silver spoon or even a flashy gold spoon for brookies. The odd rainbow or brown trout is also reportedly caught every season. Check the regulations for the special season on this lake.

Wilder Lake

Found east of Highway 6 north of Mount Forest, Wilder Lake has been heavily stocked with brook trout and as a result fishing success can be good at times. Ice anglers can have a lot of fun at this lake, as brookies can be very aggressive at times during the winter. In the evening or during overcast periods brookies will often move closer to shore in search of food. Jigging a small silver spoon or even a small white jig is often effective. Be sure to consult the fishing regulations for the special season available on Wilder Lake.

Williams Lake

The Williams Lake Conservation Area lies along the southeastern shore of Williams Lake and provides access to the lake. The conservation area lies just off Highway 10 south of the village of Chatsworth. The lake is stocked regularly with brook trout, which can provide good fishing through the ice in the winter. There are also reports of rainbows and brown trout caught on occasion. Special season regulations apply. Check your regulations before heading out.

Cottage Country Ontario Mapkey

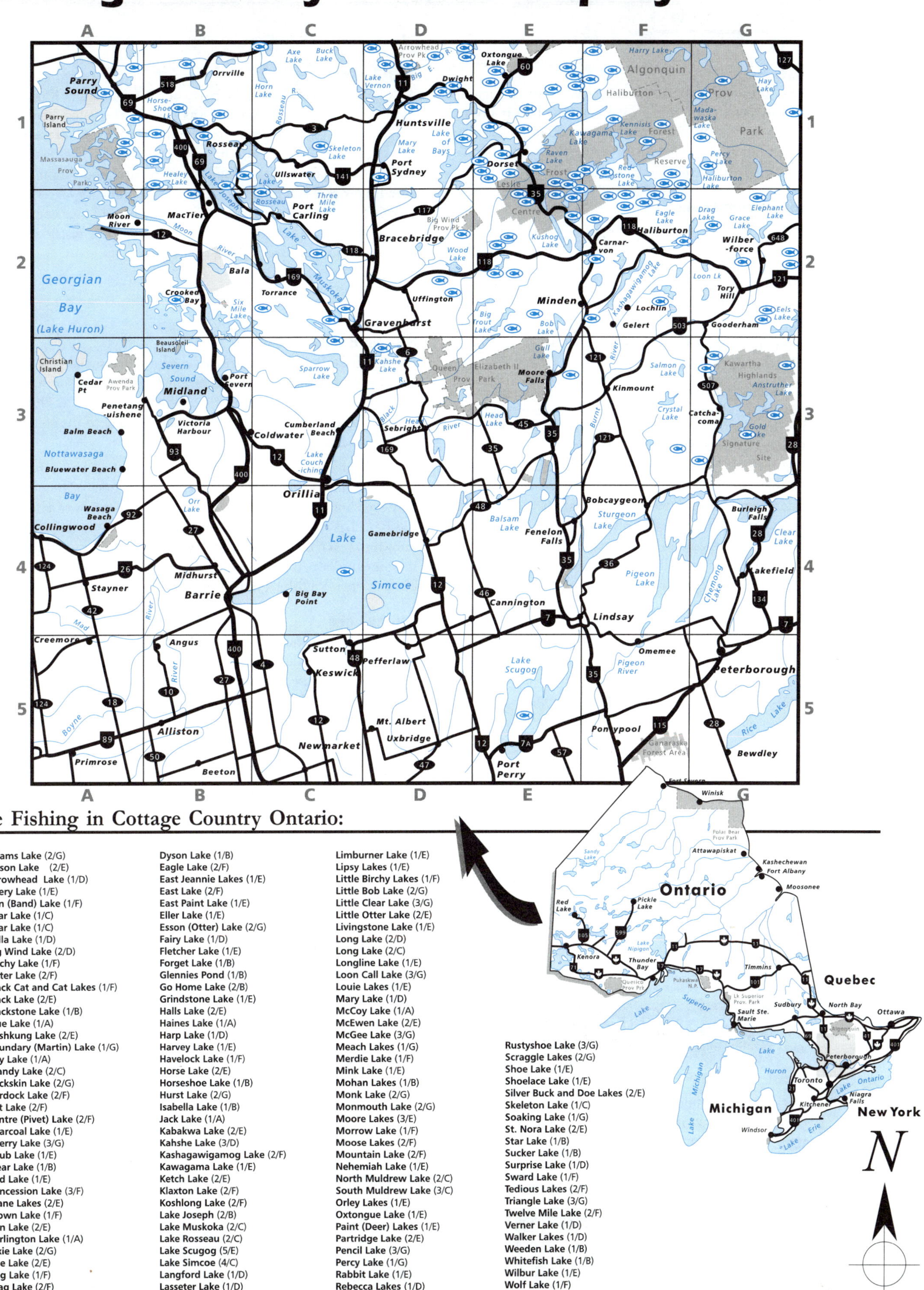

Ice Fishing in Cottage Country Ontario:

Adams Lake (2/G)
Anson Lake (2/E)
Arrowhead Lake (1/D)
Avery Lake (1/E)
Ban (Band) Lake (1/F)
Bear Lake (1/C)
Bear Lake (1/C)
Bella Lake (1/D)
Big Wind Lake (2/D)
Birchy Lake (1/F)
Bitter Lake (2/F)
Black Cat and Cat Lakes (1/F)
Black Lake (2/E)
Blackstone Lake (1/B)
Blue Lake (1/A)
Boshkung Lake (2/E)
Boundary (Martin) Lake (1/G)
Boy Lake (1/A)
Brandy Lake (2/C)
Buckskin Lake (2/G)
Burdock Lake (2/F)
Cat Lake (2/F)
Centre (Pivet) Lake (2/F)
Charcoal Lake (1/E)
Cherry Lake (3/G)
Chub Lake (1/E)
Clear Lake (1/B)
Cod Lake (1/E)
Concession Lake (3/F)
Crane Lakes (2/E)
Crown Lake (1/F)
Dan Lake (2/E)
Darlington Lake (1/A)
Dixie Lake (2/G)
Doe Lake (2/E)
Dog Lake (1/F)
Drag Lake (2/F)
Duck Lake (1/F)
Dutton Lake (1/F)
Dyson Lake (1/B)
Eagle Lake (2/F)
East Jeannie Lakes (1/E)
East Lake (2/F)
East Paint Lake (1/E)
Eller Lake (1/E)
Esson (Otter) Lake (2/G)
Fairy Lake (1/D)
Fletcher Lake (1/E)
Forget Lake (1/B)
Glennies Pond (1/B)
Go Home Lake (2/B)
Grindstone Lake (1/E)
Halls Lake (2/E)
Haines Lake (1/A)
Harp Lake (1/D)
Harvey Lake (1/E)
Havelock Lake (1/F)
Horse Lake (2/E)
Horseshoe Lake (1/B)
Hurst Lake (2/G)
Isabella Lake (1/B)
Jack Lake (1/A)
Kabakwa Lake (2/E)
Kahshe Lake (3/D)
Kashagawigamog Lake (2/F)
Kawagama Lake (1/E)
Ketch Lake (2/E)
Klaxton Lake (2/F)
Koshlong Lake (2/F)
Lake Joseph (2/B)
Lake Muskoka (2/C)
Lake Rosseau (2/C)
Lake Scugog (5/E)
Lake Simcoe (4/C)
Langford Lake (1/D)
Lasseter Lake (1/D)
Lee Lakes (1/D)
Liebeck Lake (1/B)
Limburner Lake (1/E)
Lipsy Lakes (1/E)
Little Birchy Lakes (1/F)
Little Bob Lake (2/G)
Little Clear Lake (3/G)
Little Otter Lake (2/E)
Livingstone Lake (1/E)
Long Lake (2/D)
Long Lake (2/C)
Longline Lake (1/E)
Loon Call Lake (3/G)
Louie Lakes (1/E)
Mary Lake (1/D)
McCoy Lake (1/A)
McEwen Lake (2/E)
McGee Lake (3/G)
Meach Lakes (1/G)
Merdie Lake (1/F)
Mink Lake (1/E)
Mohan Lakes (1/B)
Monk Lake (2/G)
Monmouth Lake (2/G)
Moore Lakes (3/E)
Morrow Lake (1/F)
Moose Lakes (2/F)
Mountain Lake (2/F)
Nehemiah Lake (1/E)
North Muldrew Lake (2/C)
South Muldrew Lake (3/C)
Orley Lakes (1/E)
Oxtongue Lake (1/E)
Paint (Deer) Lakes (1/E)
Partridge Lake (2/E)
Pencil Lake (3/G)
Percy Lake (1/G)
Rabbit Lake (1/E)
Rebecca Lakes (1/D)
Ronald Lake (1/E)
Ross Lake (1/F)
Rustyshoe Lake (3/G)
Scraggle Lakes (2/G)
Shoe Lake (1/E)
Shoelace Lake (1/E)
Silver Buck and Doe Lakes (2/E)
Skeleton Lake (1/C)
Soaking Lake (1/G)
St. Nora Lake (2/E)
Star Lake (1/B)
Sucker Lake (1/B)
Surprise Lake (1/D)
Sward Lake (1/F)
Tedious Lakes (2/F)
Triangle Lake (3/G)
Twelve Mile Lake (2/F)
Verner Lake (1/D)
Walker Lakes (1/D)
Weeden Lake (1/B)
Whitefish Lake (1/B)
Wilbur Lake (1/E)
Wolf Lake (1/F)
Wood Lake (2/D)
Wren Lakes (1/E)

Adams Lake
Adams Lake is a secluded lake that can be found east of Tory Hill on foot from the rough road off Highway 121. The lake is stocked periodically with brook trout and offers fair to good fishing at times through the ice and in the spring for trout that can exceed 35 cm (14 in). Live fish may not be used as bait in this lake.

Anson (Montgomery) Lake
Anson Lake is a secluded lake that lies east of the Poker Lakes and south of the Leslie M. Frost Centre. Near the north end of Kushog Lake, take the Austin Lake Road south off Highway 35. The road continuously gets rougher and requires either an ATV or snowmobile to negotiate. This old road system eventually leads to the northern shore of Anson Lake. This beautiful lake is stocked every few years with the lake trout/brook trout hybrid, splake. Splake action usually picks up in the winter.

In addition to splake, there are rumours that bass have made their way into Anson Lake. These reports have not been confirmed.

Arrowhead and Little Arrowhead Lakes
Located in Arrowhead Provincial Park, Arrowhead Lake is a heavily used lake that offers slow fishing for small brook trout. During summer anglers can also find smallmouth bass. Little Arrowhead Lake is a little more difficult to access and usually offers better fishing. The smaller lake is home to both brook trout and lake trout. Access into the lakes is through the park, which can be found north of Huntsville off Highway 11.

Avery Lake
This small Leslie M. Frost Centre lake is found on the north side of Sherborne Road. The lake stocked with splake every few years that can provide good fishing through the ice for average sized fish. Try small spoons through the ice and streamer patterns in the spring.

Ban (Band) Lake
Ban Lake is a small, secluded lake found in the Haliburton Forest that offers good fishing for small brook trout. The lake is stocked about every two years and is mainly fished in the winter through the ice. Inquire at the Haliburton Forest Reserve gatehouse for directions to the lake.

Bear Lake
Bear Lake is located east of Orrville just off the south side of Highway 518. The medium sized lake provides fair fishing for northern pike to 3.5 kg (8 lbs) and even slower fishing for walleye. Ice fishing for perch is popular.

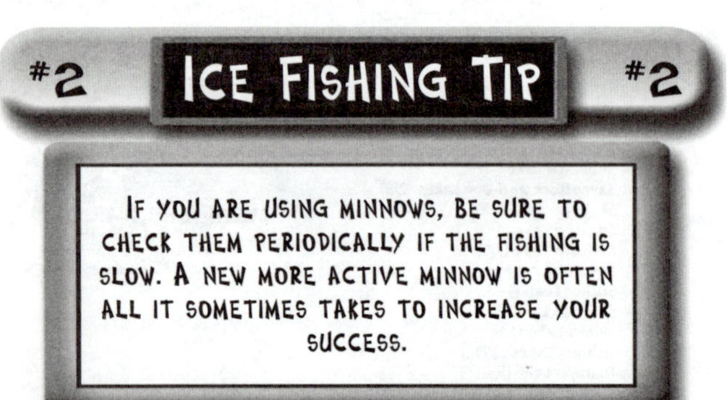

Bear Lake
This Bear Lake is found to the north of the much larger Kawagama Lake. It can be accessed by snowmobile via the gated Bear Lake Road or through Livingston Lake. Both options begin off the south side of County Road 12 northeast of Dorset. Bear Lake was once stocked with lake trout to supplement natural populations, however, it now relies on natural regeneration. Fishing for lakers is slow to fair through the ice. There is also a small, very elusive population of brook trout in the lake. Watch for slot size restrictions on lake trout and special ice fishing regulations.

Bella Lake
See Page 19

Big Wind Lake
Bigwind Lake is part of a rustic backcountry provincial park that is found east of Bracebridge. To access the lake from the south, follow Highway 118 east from it's junction with Highway 11 to Bird Lake Road. This lake snakes north, eventually leading to the south end of Bigwind Lake.

Bigwind Lake was once thought to be inhabited by both brook trout and lake trout. Although there are rumours of brook trout and even rainbow trout, lake trout are the sportfish of choice in the lake. Lakers are stocked every few years into the lake and are known to reach 65 cm (26 in) in size. Spoons, jigs, or anything that imitates the lake trout's main food source, the minnow, are good choices when ice fishing in Bigwind Lake.

Birchy Lake
Birchy Lake is a small, secluded lake found just south of Kennisis Lake near the Haliburton Forest Reserve. From County Road 7 near the gatehouse, a snowmobile accessible road branches west and leads close to the shore of the small lake. Birchy Lake offers generally slow fishing for small brook trout. Ice fishing produces better action.

Bitter Lake
Bitter Lake is located off County Road 7 (Kennisis Lake Road) north of Haliburton. Look for the snow covered road leading east at the north end of Tedious Lake. Bitter Lake is stocked almost annually with lake trout and fishing can be good at times in winter or in spring just after ice off. Try working a small white jig through the ice for the best opportunity to catch these sometimes lethargic trout.

Black Cat and Cat Lakes
The Cat Lakes lie just to the west of Kennisis Lake in the Leslie M. Frost Centre. These lakes are accessible by snowmobile only and are stocked every few years with brook trout. Fishing for brookies is fair and can be good at times in the winter months.

Black Lake
Black Lake can be accessed by snowmobile along a series of portage trails leading west from Wren Lake of the Leslie M. Frost Centre. Black Lake is stocked every few years with splake that can provide good fishing in the winter.

Blackstone Lake
See Page 22

Access

Bella Lake is found northeast of Huntsville, not far from Algonquin Park. From Huntsville, travel east on Highway 60 to County Road 8, then proceed along County Road 8 eastward. Just after you pass J. Albert Bauer Provincial Park, you will come to the community of Brooks Mill. This is where the access road to Bella Lake branches north. The road doubles as the main access road to Rebecca Lake.

Visitors can also find the lake by following County Road 8 a bit further east to Billie Bear Road. This road leads to a boat launch on the northeast side of the lake.

Fishing

The most sought after sportfish in Bella Lake is lake trout. Since this lake is one of the area's few natural reproducing lake trout lakes, it is essential to practice catch and release to help maintain the fishery. Contrary to public opinion, lake trout are indeed a fragile species and have a much lower reproduction rate than most of Ontario's sportfish. Although these fish grow big, they also very slow. A trout from Bella Lake weighing merely 2 kg (4.5 lb) can be over 10 years of age.

Ice fishing is one of the better times to fish for lake trout in Bella Lake. Lakers are often found in shallower water and will take well presented, shiny spoons. During summer, most of the angling action is for smallmouth bass. Watch for special restrictions on Bella Lake such as lake trout slot size limits.

Facilities

In addition to the boat launch on the northeast side of the lake, there are many cottages along the shores of Bella Lake. Periodically a few of these are available for rent. Inquire locally for more information on the possibility of renting a cottage in the area.

Lake Definition

Surface Area: 324 ha (800 ac)
Mean Depth: 14.6 m (48 ft)
Max Depth: 36 m (118 ft)
Way Point: 46° 26' 00" Lat - N
79° 02' 00" Lon - W

400m 0 400m 800m 1200m 1600m
Scale

To Big East River
private
To Hwy 8
N
2m 3 6 12m 24 18 24m 30 24 36m
1m 2 3m 6 12m
18 12 6 3 2m
To Hwy 8 & Benson Lake
To Hwy 8 & Brooks Mill
To Hwy 8
Bravender Creek

Blue Lake
Blue Lake is a small Cottage Country lake found off Blue Lake Road south of Parry Sound. The lake is stocked semi-annually with splake and fishing for splake can be good through the ice or in spring just after ice off. There are also rumours of a small population of lake trout remaining in the lake. These catches are rare and may only be confused anglers mistakenly identifying a splake as a lake trout.

Boshkung Lake
See Page 21

Boundary (Martin) Lake
Also known as Martin Lake, this lake is found just west of the Algonquin Park southern panhandle northeast of Haliburton Lake. During winter a snowmobile is needed to follow the series of roads leading from either Percy Road or the private East Lake Road, which both begin at the northeast end of Haliburton Lake. Boundary Lake is stocked every few years with brook trout. Anglers can expect fair to good fishing through the ice or for brook trout that average 25-35 cm (10-14 in) in size.

Boy Lake
The Long Lake East and Pinewood Roads leading east from Highway 124 north of Parry Sound can access this lake. Although home to a few cottages on its northern shore, there is not much activity in the area in winter. Splake are stocked every few years and average 35 cm (14 in). Ice fishing can be fairly productive for this hybrid fish. During summer anglers will also find average sized smallmouth bass.

Brandy Lake
See Page 23

Buckskin Lake
Buckskin Lake can be found via the unplowed Rock Lake Road south off Highway 118, just east of the Highway 503 junction. Buckskin Lake is stocked yearly with lake trout, which provide for good success during the ice fishing season or in spring after ice off. There is the occasional report that rainbow and splake have been caught, although these reports are becoming less frequent since these species are no longer stocked

Burdock Lake
To reach Burdock Lake, follow Highway 118 west from Haliburton to the Kennisis Lake Road (County Road 7). The Kennisis Lake Road travels north, eventually passing by the western end of Burdock Lake. This small lake is heavily stocked with brook trout and fishing for brookies can be good at times, especially in the winter. Ice fishing is most productive along shoreline areas since brook trout usually cruise closer to the surface where oxygen levels are at their best. Try jigging a small spoon or light coloured jigs in 3-5 m (10-16 ft) of water. Live fish are not permitted for use as bait in this lake.

Cat Lake
Cat Lake is a remote access lake that is stocked semi-annually with brook trout. The fishing can be quite good through the ice by slow jigging. Access to the lake is via snowmobile from the much larger Kennisis Lake. Kennisis Lake can be reached by the Kennisis Lake Road (County Road 7) off Highway 118 northwest of Haliburton.

Centre (Pivet) Lake
Centre Lake lies off the Kennisis Lake Road (County Road 7) northwest of the town of Haliburton. The small lake has been stocked with splake every few years and fishing can be good during ice fishing season and in spring. A population of whitefish is also available in the lake.

Charcoal Lake
Charcoal Lake is a hidden lake located off the east side of Highway 35 just north of the village of Dorset. The lake is stocked every few years with brook trout and fishing for brookies in the 20-30 cm (8-12 in) range is fair through the ice.

Cherry Lake
Cherry Lake lies in the heart of the remote Kawartha Highlands Provincial Park north of Peterborough. The lake can only be accessed by snowmobile and there is a main trail that can be picked up from the Missassugua Gold Lake Road. Cherry Lake is stocked with lake trout and most of the action happens during ice fishing season.

Chub Lake
Chub Lake is an easily accessible lake that can be reached by snowmobile not far off Paint Lake Road. Paint Lake Road branches off County Road 117 southwest of Dorset. While the main species fished for in this lake is smallmouth bass in the summer, there remains a small population of brook trout for people visiting the lake in winter. Fishing success can be slow for these brookies.

Boshkung Lake

Fishing

The deep lake has an average depth of 23 m (76 ft) and a maximum depth of 71 m (233 ft). This bodes well for the natural population of lake trout, which remain a popular target during the winter ice fishing season. Anglers jig though the ice for lake trout with small spoons and other various lures. A few of the more productive ice fishing locations are located off any of the points found along the lake. In order to maintain the natural lake trout fishery, slot size and special ice fishing regulations have been established.

Access

Boshkung Lake is located just outside of the village of Carnarvon. Highway 35 travels along the eastern shore of the lake and offers a few places to access the lake by foot in the winter. The close proximity of the lake to Highway 35 makes it a popular year round destination.

Facilities

Visitors interested in staying overnight will find the **Clansman Motel and Cottages** is open during the winter. In addition to accommodations, they also provide ice fishing packages. Alternatively, basic supplies such as groceries and fishing gear are available in Carnarvon.

Lake Definition

Elevation:	303 m (1,010 ft)
Surface Area:	71 ha (178 ac)
Mean Depth:	22.8 m (76 ft)
Max Depth:	70 m (229 ft)
Perimeter:	18 km (11 mi)
Way Point:	45° 04' 00" Lat - N 78° 44' 00" Lon - W

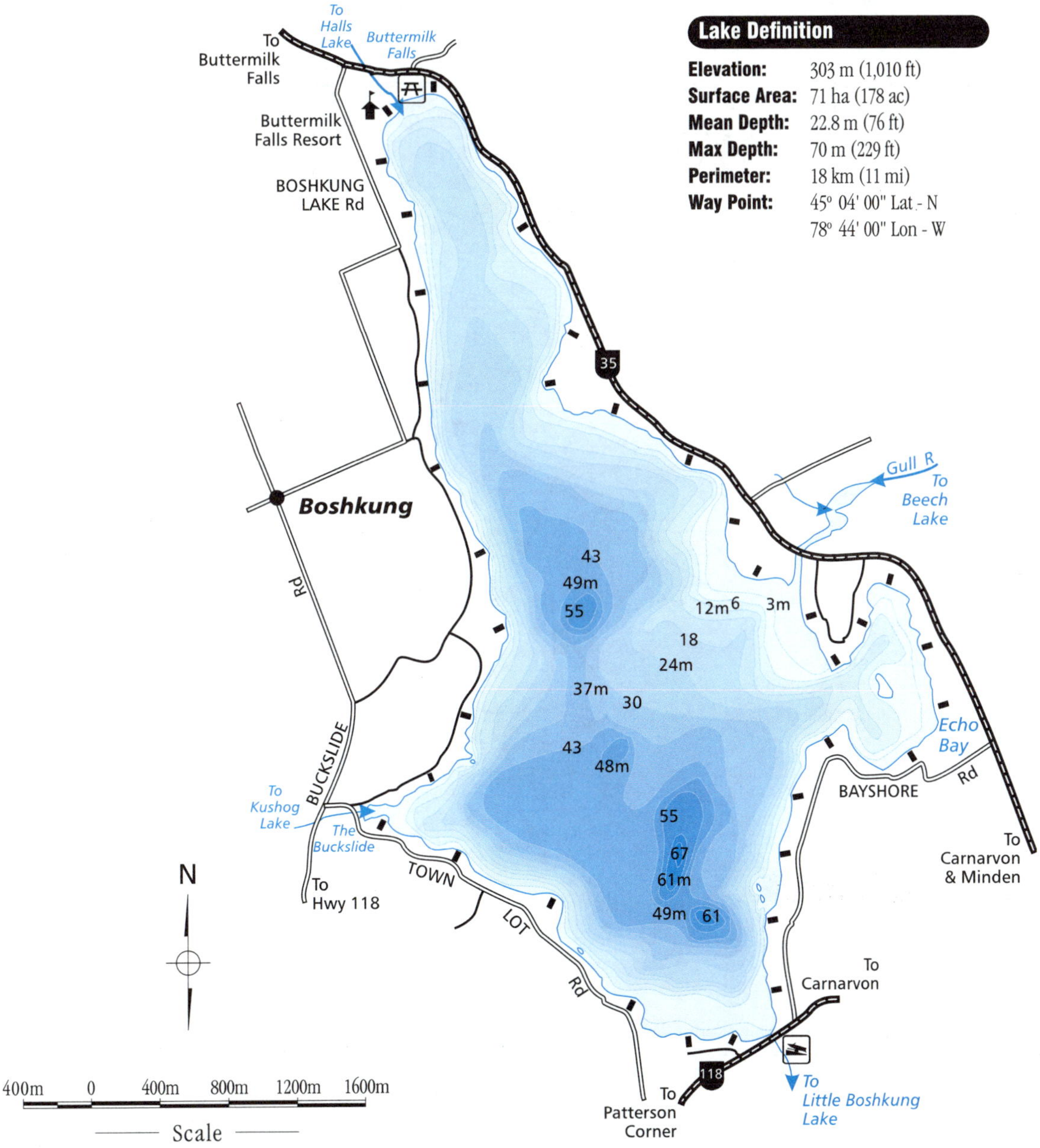

Scale: 400m 0 400m 800m 1200m 1600m

Depth Chart Not Intended for Navigational Use

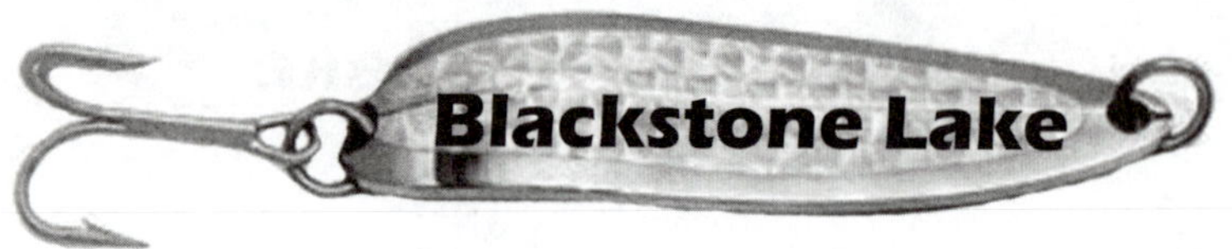

Access

Blackstone Lake can be found by taking the Black Road south from Highway 69 at exit 214 just south of the Parry Sound visitor centre. This road leads to Crane Lake Road, which leads west. Anglers can access Blackstone Lake from a few different places along this road. Alternatively, Jacklins Road branches east from Black Road and leads to a boat/snowmobile launch.

Fishing

Blackstone Lake offers fishing for a wide variety of sportfish. The most abundant of which are largemouth and smallmouth bass. Since these fish are inactive in the winter, ice fishing is mainly for walleye and stocked lake trout. There are also northern pike and the odd muskellunge that will surprise the unsuspecting angler with their size and power. Walleye fishing is usually fair for average sized walleye. Even though lake trout are stocked in Blackstone Lake every few years, fishing is often slow for this elusive species.

Be sure to check the regulations before heading out on Blackstone Lake. There are special sanctuary restrictions in place as well as special limits to help the ailing walleye population. Ice fishing is also limited to one line per angler.

Facilities

There are a number of cottages on Blackstone Lake that periodically come up for rent on a weekly or weekend basis. Enquire locally for more details on these opportunities.

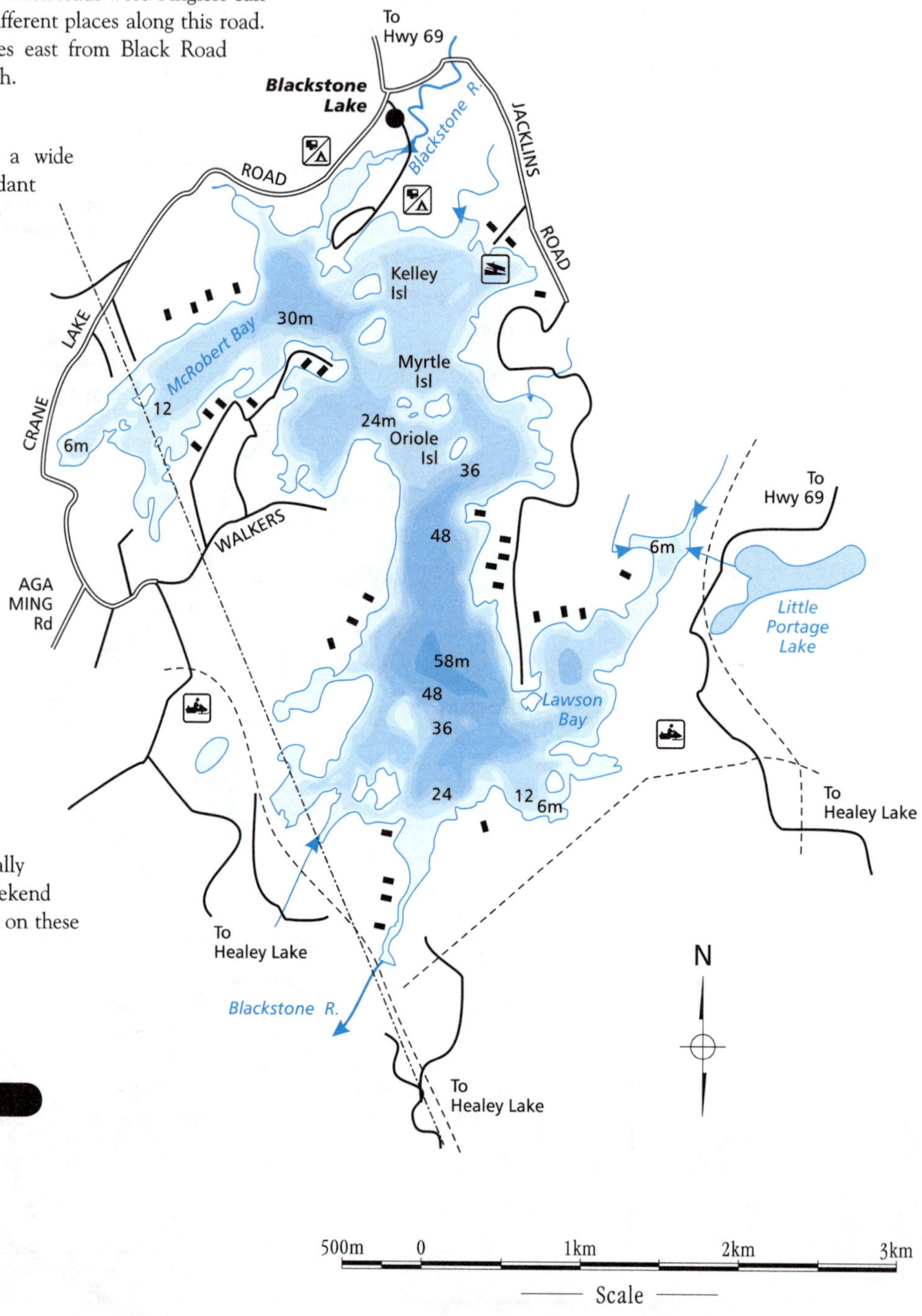

To Hwy 69
Blackstone Lake
Blackstone R.
JACKLINS ROAD
ROAD
CRANE LAKE
Kelley Isl
30m
McRobert Bay
Myrtle Isl
12
6m
24m
Oriole Isl
36
WALKERS
48
AGA MING Rd
To Hwy 69
6m
Little Portage Lake
58m
48
Lawson Bay
36
24
12
6m
To Healey Lake
To Healey Lake
Blackstone R.
To Healey Lake
N

Lake Definition

Elevation:	200 m (655 ft)
Surface Area:	515.5 ha (1,274 ac)
Mean Depth:	30.5 m (100 ft)
Max Depth:	54.8 m (180 ft)
Perimeter:	34.75 km (21.6 mi)
Way Point:	45° 14' 00" Lat - N 79° 53' 00" Lon - W

500m 0 1km 2km 3km

Scale

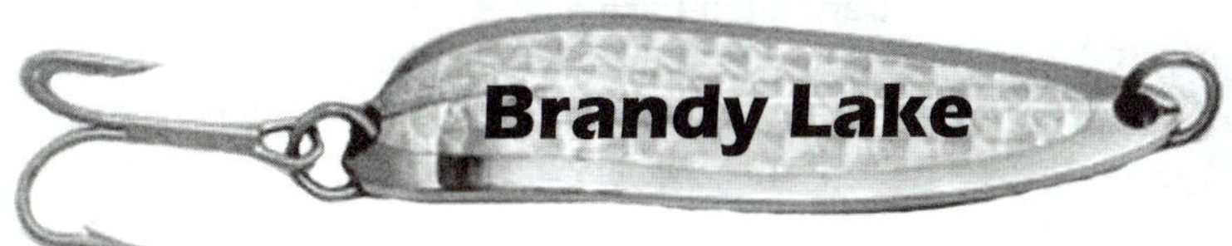

Access

Brandy Lake is located just east of Port Carling off County Road 118. Just east of the County Road 25 junction, look for the main cottage road leading north. This road leads to an informal access point. Alternatively, the much quieter County Road 25 passes by the north side of the lake. Please be sure not to trespass when accessing the lake.

Fishing

Walleye and northern pike inhabit the lake, but fishing is generally slow for both species. These fish see a lot of pressure throughout the year and as a result, their numbers are low. Try fishing closer to dusk to increase your chances of finding these roaming fish. During summer most anglers will find that bass provide the best action on the lake.

Facilities

Other than periodic cottage rentals, there are no facilities offered at Brandy Lake. Nearby Port Carling is a busy summer destination that is certainly much quieter in the winter. Visitors to the area should still be able to find accommodations and basic supplies.

Other Options

Leonard Lake can be found east of Brandy Lake off County Road 118. The lake is visible from the highway, while Leonard Lake Road, which can be picked up off the highway, travels along the west side of the lake. The lake offers fishing for stocked rainbow trout and a very small population of walleye.

Lake Definition

Elevation:	243.8 m (800 ft)
Surface Area:	104.8 ha (259 ac)
Mean Depth:	3 m (9.8 ft)
Perimeter:	9.81 km (6.1 mi)
Way Point:	45°07' 00" Lat - N 79°31' 00" Long - W

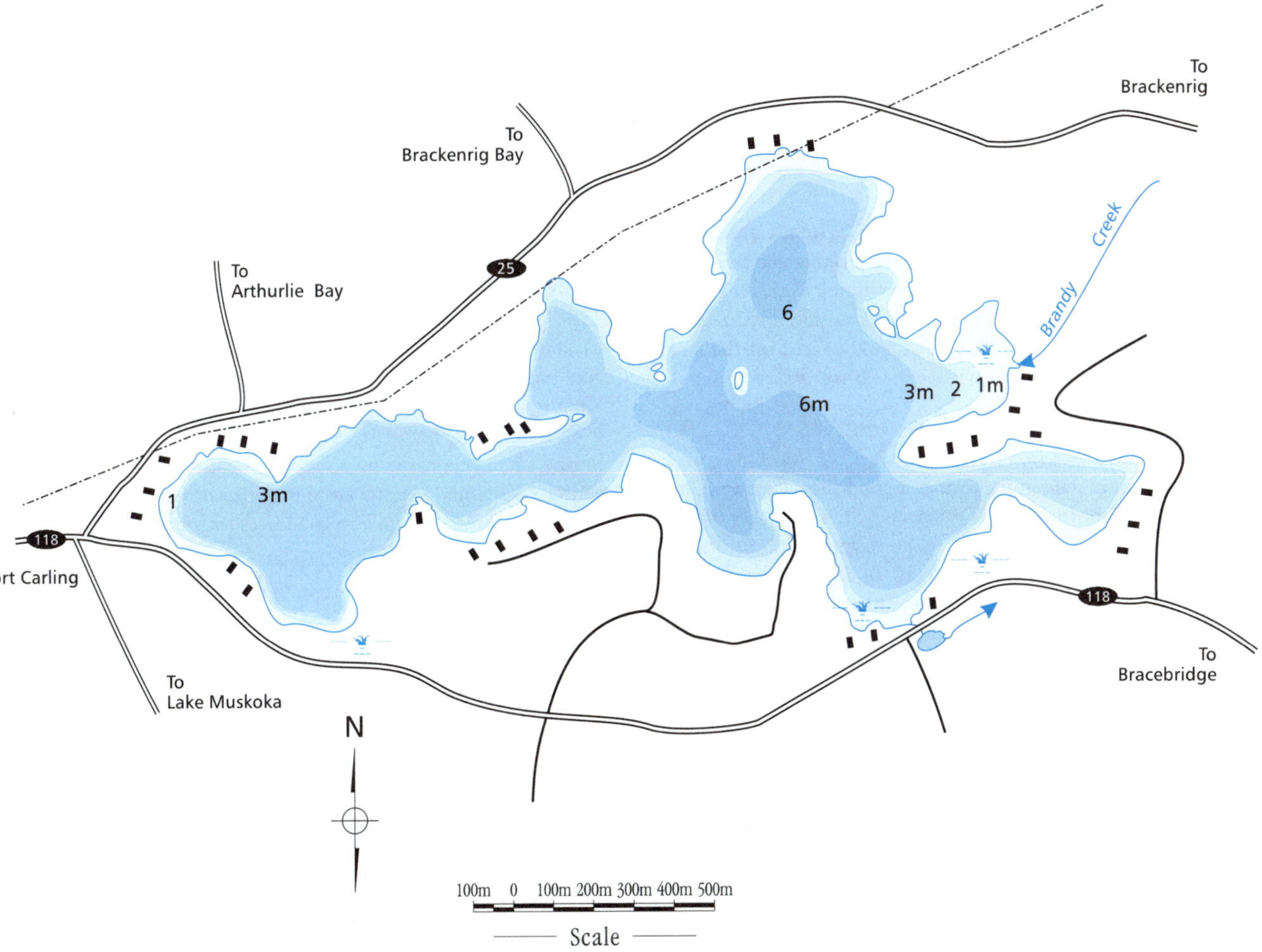

To Brackenrig
To Brackenrig Bay
To Arthurlie Bay
25
Brandy Creek
6
0
6m
3m 2 1m
1
3m
118
To Port Carling
To Lake Muskoka
118
To Bracebridge
N
100m 0 100m 200m 300m 400m 500m
Scale

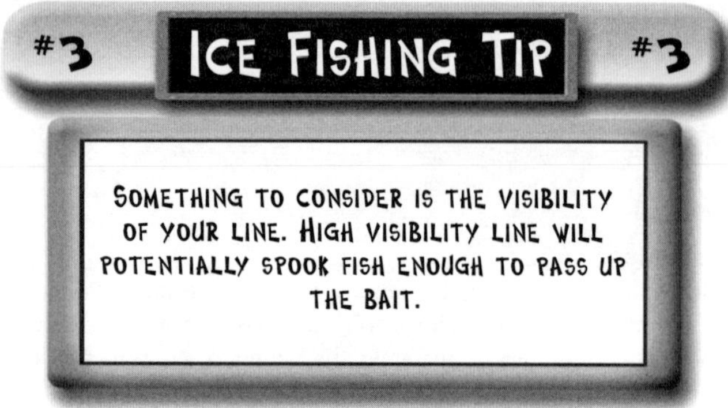

Clear Lake

Clear Lake receives heavy fishing pressure throughout the year, which creates a rather challenging fishery. Fishing for natural lake trout is often slow in this lake in the winter. A fair population of whitefish is also available. There are slot size restrictions in place for lake trout as well as special ice fishing regulations.

Cod Lake

Cod Lake can be accessed via snowmobile along a rough roadway that branches north off Highway 35 north of Dorset. The lake is stocked every few years with brook trout and anglers can expect fishing for brookies to 30 cm (12 in) to be good at times through the ice.

Concession Lake

Concession Lake is stocked regularly with lake trout. There is no real road access to the lake, although snowmobiles can be used for access in the winter. The trail can be picked up along the southern end of Crystal Lake near Kinmount. Ice fishing for lakers can be good for trout that average 0.5-1 kg (1-2 lbs) in size and can reach up to 2 kg (4.5 lbs).

Crane Lakes

The Crane Lakes are part of the Poker Lake System Canoe Route and are stocked every few years with splake. Fishing can be good at times for splake in the 30 cm (12 in) range during ice fishing season or in the spring just after ice off. Small spoons jigged through the ice can be quite productive. There is a parking area off the south side of Highway 118 west of the village of Carnarvon.

Crown Lake

Found a few kilometres from Algonquin Park, Crown Lake can be accessed via snowmobile in the winter. To find the access trail, take County Road 12 northeast of Dorset and drive past Livingstone Lake to the trailhead. The lake offers fair fishing opportunities for brook trout that average 25-35 cm (10-14 in). The lake is best fished through the ice or in spring just after ice off. The use of a Backroad Mapbook for Cottage Country will greatly increase your chances of finding this lake.

Dan Lake

Dan Lake is stocked with splake about every two years, which offer good fishing at times for nice sized splake. Fishing is most productive through the ice or in spring just after ice off. Small spoons or jigs can be productive during ice fishing season. Dan Lake lies in the Leslie M. Frost Centre to the west of Highway 35. The lake can be found via snowmobile north from the unplowed Sawmill Access Road.

Darlington Lake

Found just north of Parry Sound, Darlington Lake offers fair fishing in the winter months for stocked lake trout. Jigging a small white jig through the ice can be productive for lakers that average 30 cm (12in) in size.

Dixie Lake

This small, secluded lake is stocked every few years with brook trout and fishing for brookies to 30 cm (12 in) can be good during ice fishing season or in spring after ice off. A main snowmobile trail passes the west side of the lake and can be picked up off Highway 648 near Harcourt.

Doe Lake

Doe Lake is a secluded lake found east of South Anson Lake that has good fishing for stocked brook trout. Ice fishing is popular on the lake and can be quite productive at times. There are no established snowmobile trails passing near the lake, therefore a GPS unit and a good map, such as the Backroad Mapbook for Cottage Country is almost essential to find the lake.

Dog Lake

Located just south of the Haliburton Forest Reserve, this lake can be accessed via snowmobile east of Redstone Lake. Dog Lake is stocked every few years with brook trout that provide good fishing through the ice or in spring just after ice off. Brook trout average 25-35 cm (10-14 in) in size, although can be found bigger later in the year.

Drag Lake

This large lake lies just east of Haliburton and can be accessed from its southern or northwestern shore. To find the southern access, follow Highway 121 east to Long Lake Road and head north. Long Lake Road quickly passes Jones Drive, which travels west to a boat launch along the southern shore of the lake. The northwestern access can be reached by taking Harburn Road (County Road 19) north from Haliburton to Indian Point Road. Head east on Indian Point Road and watch for boat launch signs.

Drag Lake is one of the more popular lakes in the Haliburton area and is a busy cottage destination lake during the summer months. This clear lake is extremely deep with its average depth at 18 m (59 ft) and a maximum depth of a whopping 56 m (180 ft). The crisp cool nature of the lake is prime habitat for lake trout and there is a natural population of lakers in the lake. Fishing success for lake trout is definitely better in the winter months and just after ice off. Jigging small spoons along shoal areas can be effective for finding winter lake trout. Due to an abundance of baitfish in Drag Lake, its resident trout can grow to good sizes with trout in the 65 cm (26 in) range caught on occasion.

In order to protect the long-term viability of this natural lake trout population, slot size and winter ice fishing regulations have been established. Be sure to check your provincial regulations for details and please practice catch and release.

Duck Lake

Access to Duck Lake is via a private road or trail from near Redstone Lake. Owners of private property in the area have permitted access to the lake in the past and since the lake is stocked with government-funded fish, there should remain public access in the future. Please do not trespass without permission from landowners.

Duck Lake is stocked regularly with brook trout and fishing can (continues on page 27)

Fairy Lake

Access

The town of Huntsville lies along the western shore of Fairy Lake and is known by many as the gateway town to Algonquin Park's main corridor. Huntsville is situated near the junction of Highway 11 and Highway 60 north of Bracebridge. There are a few access points to Fairy Lake with the main access point being found along the north shore of the lake just off Highway 60.

Fishing

Even though Fairy Lake is a very popular lake, the fishing continues to be fairly good. Lake trout are stocked every few years and provide for slow to fair fishing throughout the season. Although, Fairy Lake is over 61 m (200 ft) deep in areas, the lake trout are usually closer to the surface and easier to catch in the winter.

Facilities

Fairy Lake provides a public boat launch area on the north shore as well as a number of resorts and lodges around the lake and in the immediate area. The town of Huntsville has a full downtown business area providing all the major needs of any outdoor outing.

Lake Definition

Elevation:	284 m (931 ft)
Surface Area:	711.4 ha (1,758 ac)
Mean Depth:	33.2 m (108.8 ft)
Max Depth:	69.5 m (228 ft)
Perimeter:	28.5 km (17.7 ft)
Way Point:	45° 20' 00" Lat - N 79° 11' 00" Lon - W

Access

Horseshoe Lake is located south of the town of Parry Sound off the northeast side of Highway 69. When travelling north, the lake and access point is found off the east side of the highway just as you pass the junction with Highway 141.

Fishing

Due to Horseshoe Lake's proximity to Highway 69 and Parry Sound, the lake is heavily fished throughout the year. Even with the angling pressure, the lake continues to produce decent catches of a variety of sportfish including bass, lake trout and northern pike.

Ice fishers will find that the northern pike are the most aggressive and largest predator in the lake. They can be found in the shallow bays during spring and periodically during ice fishing season. However, most people visiting the lake in winter are in search of lake trout. The lake is home to a natural population of lakers that are starting to see the results of over fishing. Fishing success has dropped dramatically over the past few decades. If possible, please practice catch and release for these fragile trout.

Facilities

There are a number of facilities offered at Horseshoe Lake including a small marina and a few tent and trailer parks. However, these sites are closed in the winter. For supplies and accommodations, the city of Parry Sound is only about 20 km away and has plenty to offer the weekend tripper. Horseshoe Lake is also home to several private cottages and camps.

Lake Definition

Elevation:	229 m (750 ft)
Surface Area:	370 m (914 ac)
Perimeter:	10.5 m (34.4 ft)
Mean Depth:	20.4 m (67 ft)
Max Depth:	31.5 km (19.6 mi)
Way Point:	45° 18' 00" Lat - N 79° 51' 00" Lon - W

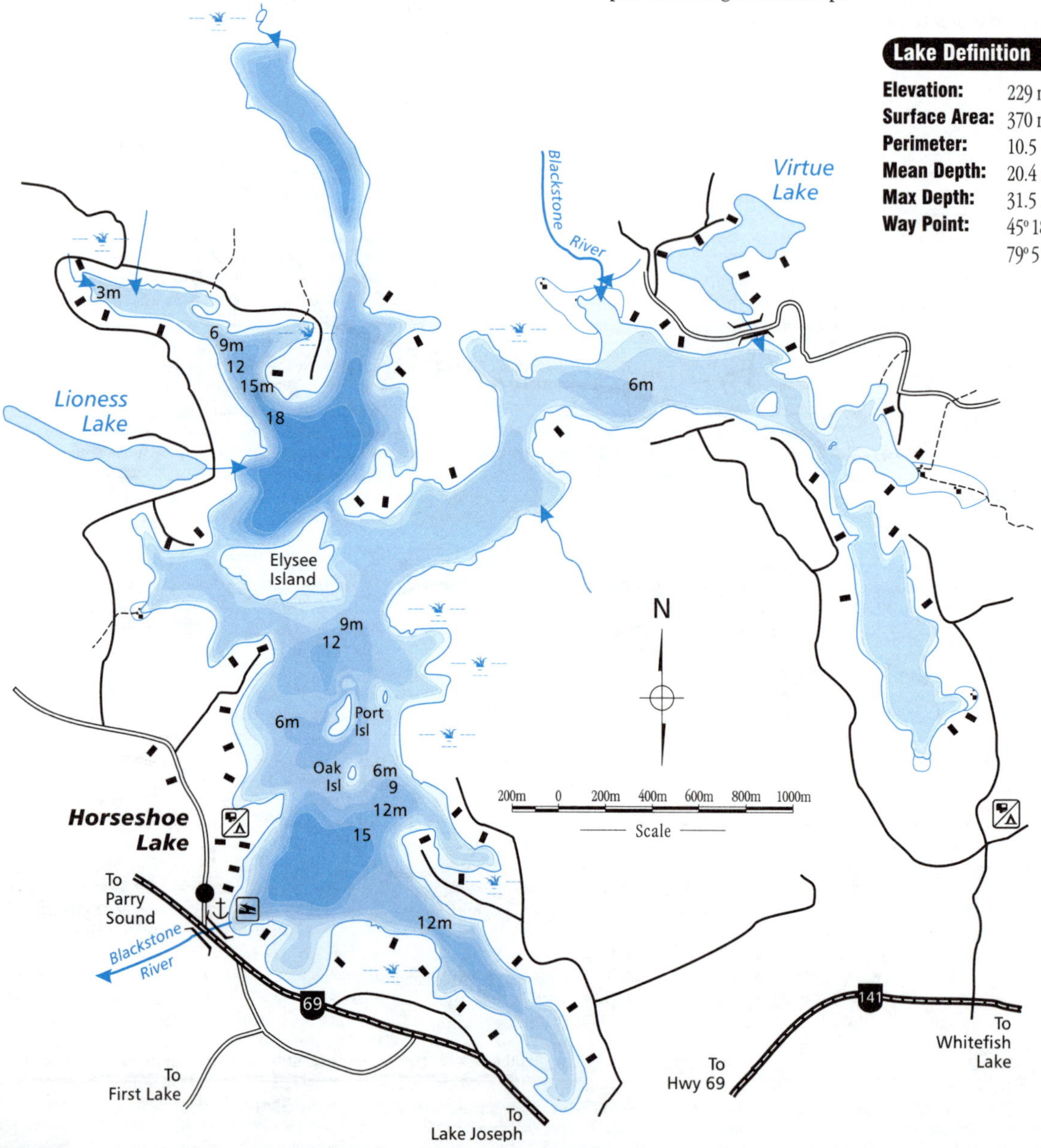

Depth Chart Not Intended for Navigational Use

be good, especially in the winter months and in the early spring. Through the ice, brookies can be caught in the 4-8 m (13-26 ft) range by jigging small spoons along shoals. It is thought that a natural population of lake trout once existed in Duck Lake, however, there have been no recent reports of catches.

Dutton Lake

Set in the heart of the Haliburton Forest Reserve, Dutton Lake is an interior reserve lake that lies minutes east of Little Kennisis Lake. The main route to the Haliburton Forest Reserve is to take Highway 118 to the Kennisis Lake Road (County Road 7). Follow the Kennisis Lake Road north to the Haliburton Forest Reserve gatehouse where further directions can be found.

Dutton Lake is stocked every few years with splake. Fishing success for splake is best in the winter, although spring and late fall are also fine times to try for these brook trout/lake trout hybrids. Splake in Dutton Lake average around 35-40 cm (14-16 in) in size, although are caught bigger on occasion. Jigging spoons or smaller sized white jigs can work well through the ice.

Dyson Lake

Dyson Lake is located south of Rosseau, just west of the much larger Lake Rosseau. To find the lake, take Highway 141 to Rosseau then follow Highway 632 south. There is a main access road about 1 km south of Morgan Bay of Lake Rosseau off the east side of the highway. Follow the access road east for about 3 km to Dyson Lake and the public access point on the north shore of the lake.

Fishing in Dyson Lake is mainly done in the summer months for its resident bass population. However, there remains a very small population of lake trout that can provide fair action in the winter. If you do target lake trout in Dyson Lake, please practice catch and release to help give the fragile species a chance at surviving in the lake. Heavy fishing pressure and lake pollution from cottages has created a large uphill battle for the ailing lake trout population in this lake.

Eagle Lake

Located off Eagle Lake Road (County Road 14) north of Haliburton, this lake has a number of cottages along its shoreline. There is a public access area on the southern shore of the lake. Anglers can expect fair fishing for lake trout that average 40 cm (16 in) in size and in the summer, fair to good fishing for smallmouth bass. Anglers will also find a fair population of whitefish. Watch for slot size restrictions on lake trout and special ice fishing regulations.

East Jeannie Lakes

These two small lakes are located off the gated, unplowed Bear Lake Road, which branches south off County Road 12 northeast of Dorset. The lakes and are stocked every few years with brook trout. Fishing for brookies in the 20-30 cm (8-12 in) range is fair and can be good in the spring or through the ice in winter.

East Lake

The East Lake Road is a private road that is rarely plowed in the winter. If you are unable to travel this road, then a snowmobile can be used to access Percy Lake Road and the series of logging roads heading north from Percy Lake to East Lake. Either road can be picked up off the Haliburton Lake Road at the northeast end of Haliburton Lake. East Lake contains a self-sustaining population of brook trout. Anglers can expect fair to good fishing through the ice or in spring for brook trout that average 25-35 cm (10-14 in) in size.

East Paint Lake

East Paint Lake is one of the quieter lakes in the Leslie M. Frost Centre due to its more remote access. Winter visitors can access the lake with a snowmobile via the old road that leads to the Red Pine Dam. Directions can be found at the Frost Centre main building or pick up a copy of the Backroad Mapbook for Cottage Country. The lake is stocked every few years with splake and offers good fishing through the ice. Splake average 30 cm (12 in) and can be found much bigger.

Eiler Lake

Eiler Lake is a small lake found just to the west of Highway 60 near Oxtongue Lake. Brook trout are stocked in Eiller Lake and provide for fair fishing on occasion. Try working a small spoon through the ice in winter. The lake can be accessed via a cross-country ski trail or snowmobile from the north end of Oxtongue Lake.

Esson (Otter) Lake

East of Haliburton, following Highway 121 can reach Esson Lake to County Road 4. County Road 4 continues east eventually passing by the southern end of the lake and an access area. A natural population of lake trout exists in Esson Lake; however, the long-term viability of the species is in question, as shoreline development, pollution and over fishing has put the naturally reproducing population in sharp decline. Over the past few years, a stocking program has been established to supplement existing stocks in order to provide additional sport fishing opportunities. Special slot size and ice fishing regulations have also been established to aid the ailing natural lake trout population. Please practice catch and release for these fragile sportfish.

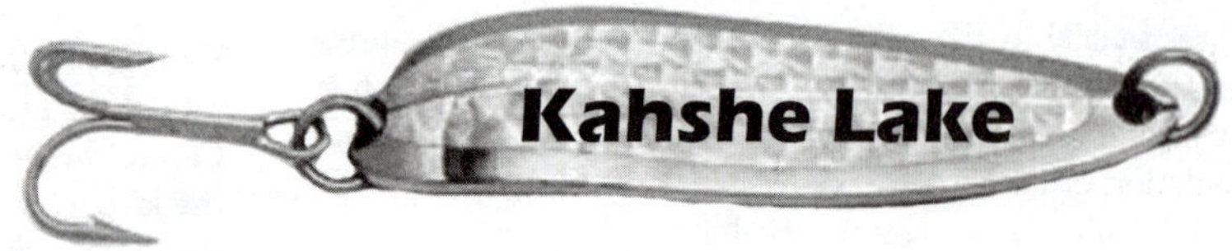

Access

Found north of Orillia just off Highway 11, there are two main access areas to Kahshe Lake. When travelling north, the first access can be found by taking South Kahshe Lake Road east off Highway 11. South Kahshe Lake Road leads directly to a public dock on the southern tip of the lake. The second access area is found via the North Kahshe Lake Road off Highway 11. There are two separate marinas and public docks on the northwest end of the big lake.

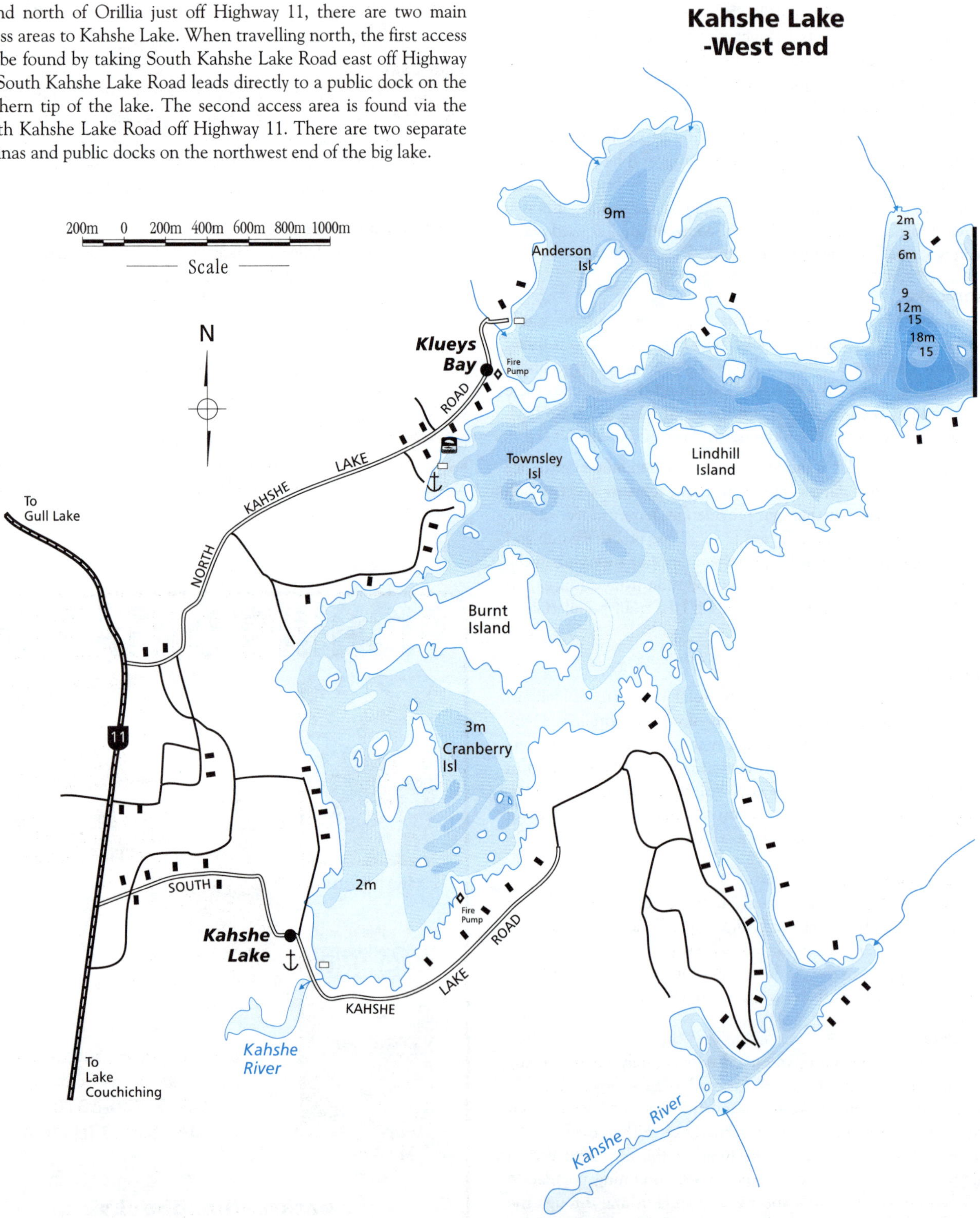

Kahshe Lake -West end

200m 0 200m 400m 600m 800m 1000m
Scale
N
Anderson Isl
9m
2m
3
6m
9
12m
15
18m
15
Klueys Bay
Fire Pump
NORTH KAHSHE LAKE ROAD
Townsley Isl
Lindhill Island
To Gull Lake
Burnt Island
11
3m
Cranberry Isl
2m
SOUTH KAHSHE LAKE ROAD
Fire Pump
Kahshe Lake
Kahshe River
To Lake Couchiching
Kahshe River

Fishing

Even though Kahshe Lake is a busy cottage destination lake, the lake continues to provide good fishing year to year. In winter, walleye are the most sought after sportfish. Ice fishing is often the most productive season for walleye. Jigging during darker periods, such as during overcast periods or at dusk, can improve your chances for success through the ice.

Muskellunge are the biggest predatory fish in the lake and can reach good sizes, although fishing success is often very slow in the winter. Die hard muskie anglers will find Kahshe Lake a challenging and rewarding lake to fish, although many other anglers often hook into these predators by chance. Be sure to check for new muskellunge regulations on all inhabited lakes. In particular, watch for fishing sanctuary areas around the Kahshe River.

Facilities

Kahshe Lake is a well-developed lake with many cottages, two marinas and three public docks. During winter it is best to inquire locally about accommodations in the area.

Lake Definition

Surface Area: 751 ha (1,856 ac)
Perimeter: 85.3 km (53 mi)
Mean Depth: 4.9 m (16 ft)
Max Depth: 21.3 m (70 ft)
Way Point: 44° 50' 00" Lat - N
79° 18' 00" Lon - W

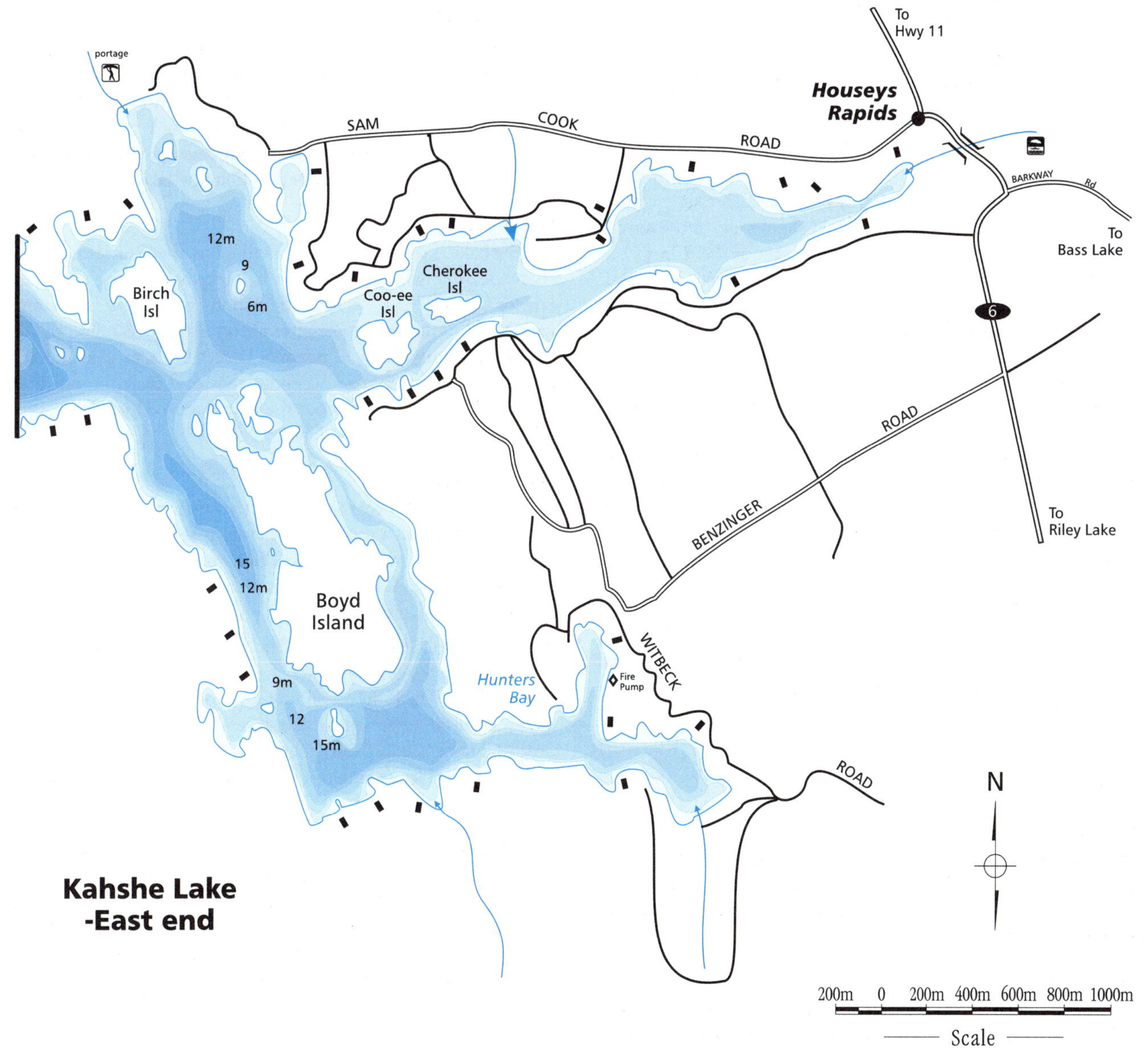

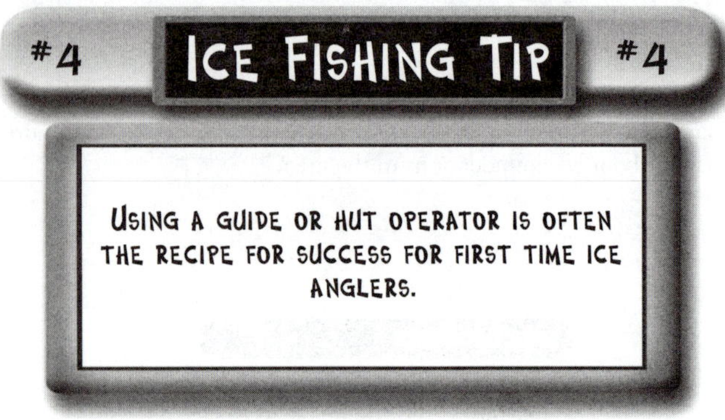

Fairy Lake

See Page 25

Fletcher Lake

Fletcher Lake is located northeast of Dorset on the north side of County Road 12. A public access point is found on Buck Bay near the western end of the lake.

Anglers visiting Fletcher Lake can expect to fish for lake trout. Lake trout are stocked periodically and provide for slow to fair fishing for average sized lakers. It is also rumoured that a population of brook trout once inhabited Fletcher Lake. Unfortunately, there have been no recent reports of brook trout catches.

Ice fishing is a popular pastime on this lake and lake trout success is usually at its best during this time. Jig off shoal areas and over any anomalies in the lake bottom such as over one of the 9 m (30 ft) humps found in the eastern end of the lake or in Buck Bay. While lake trout can be found in other areas of the lake, these two deeper ends of the lake seem to be the primary zones.

Forget Lake

To find Forget Lake, take the Black Road south from Highway 69 at exit 214 just south of the Parry Sound visitor centre. This road leads to Crane Lake Road, which skirts the south end of Forget Lake. The lake is stocked every few years with lake trout and provides good fishing for lakers through the ice. Lake trout success tails off significantly as summer approaches and smallmouth bass become the targeted species.

Glennies Pond

Glennies Pond is accessible via snowmobile off the Sherborne Lake Road in the Leslie M. Frost Centre property. The pond is stocked every few years with brook trout and fishing is good through the ice for brookies to 35 cm (14 in).

Go Home Lake

See Pages 34-35

Grindstone Lake

This Leslie M. Frost Centre lake can be found just off the west side of Highway 35 south of Dorset. The lake is stocked every few years with splake and provides good fishing for average sized splake through the ice and in the spring just after ice off.

Halls Lake

North of the village of Carnarvon, Halls Lake is easily accessible off Highway 35. A boat/snowmobile launch is available not far off Highway 35, while there is another access point also available not far off Highland Road along the east side of the lake.

Halls Lake is home to a fair population of lake trout. Fishing for lake trout is generally slow throughout the year, but the action does improve through the ice or in the spring just after ice off. Slot size and ice fishing restrictions are in place on Halls Lake. Please consult the Ontario Ministry of Natural Resources Fishing Regulations for details.

Haines Lake

This lake can be found off Highway 518 southeast of Parry Sound. Anglers can expect fair fishing for northern pike in the 1-2 kg (2-4.5 lb) range. Pike can be found much bigger, although they are usually small. Fishing for walleye is fair during late spring and can be productive through the ice. Please consult the fishing regulations before heading out.

Harp Lake

About 8 km east of Huntsville, you will find Harp Lake Road branching north from Highway 60. This road leads to the south end of the lake. Harp Lake is stocked every few years with lake trout, which provide for decent fishing through the ice or in the early spring just after ice off. The Little Cleo is always a favourite lure, although other silver flashing spoons will usually suffice. Harp Lake was once home to a natural population of brook trout; however, it is believed that over fishing and habitat degradation over the years has resulted in the trout's extinction from the lake.

Harvey Lake

Harvey Lake is a fairly remote lake that has a few cottages along its shoreline. The lake is stocked with splake and fishing is generally fair for average sized splake. The action is usually a bit better in winter and in the spring just after ice off. Anglers can find the lake by taking County Road 12 north of Dorset to Otter Lake. Look for the snowmobile trail/road access at the bend near the north end of Otter Lake. From this road, the first main road leading east will take you to the west side of Harvey Lake.

Havelock Lake

Havelock Lake lies in the northern boundary of the Haliburton Forest Reserve and a road access permit is required to travel to the lake. The main entrance to the Haliburton Forest Reserve can be reached near the end of the Kennisis Lake Road (County Road 7). Follow the road signs to the permit office.

If you plan on heading out on Havelock Lake in the winter, it is best to focus your efforts off shoal areas. Many anglers prefer to ice fish off the 1.5 m (5 ft) shoal found in the middle of the lake. Jigging a small jig or spoon in deeper water beside the shoal can be deadly. Before heading out, check the regulations as there are slot size and special ice fishing restrictions in place to maintain the lake trout population.

Horse Lake

Found via snowmobile in the Leslie M. Frost Centre property, Horse Lake offers fishing opportunities for stocked splake. Anglers can expect good fishing at times for nice sized splake. Fishing is most productive through the ice or in spring just after ice off. Small spoons or jigs can be productive during ice fishing season.

Horseshoe Lake

See Page 26

Kawagama Lake

Access

As one of the largest lakes in the region, there are a few ways to access Kawagama Lake. One of the main and more developed access points is located at Russell Landing. To reach the access, take Highway 35 north from Dorset to County Road 8. Take County Road 8 east and look for signs pointing to the Russell Landing access road. The road leads to an established boat launch, which doubles as a rustic snowmobile launch in the winter.

Other less formal access points are found off the north side of Kawagama Road. This road is the continuation of County Road 8 when the road enters the north end of the Leslie M. Frost Centre.

Fishing

As one of the largest lakes in the region, Kawagama Lake can be intimidating to anglers. The key to success for all of its resident sportfish is to locate structure. The depth chart provided below should help you locate some good areas to sample.

Many anglers visit Kawagama Lake for its natural population of lake trout. Fishing for these lakers can be fair at times with the bulk of catches coming in the winter during ice fishing season and in the early spring. In the past, natural brook trout and stocked rainbow were found in the lake. Although a few brook trout may have survived, it is believed that the rainbow are now gone.

Check the provincial fishing regulations before heading out onto Kawagama Lake, as there are slot size restrictions for lake trout and only one line is permitted when fishing through the ice.

Facilities

Kawagama Lake is home to a few resorts and private cottage rentals are available. Inquire for availability. Basic supplies can be picked up in nearby Dorset.

Lake Definition

Mean Depth: 34.3 m (112.8 ft)
Max Depth: 67 m (220 ft)
Way Point: 45° 18' 00" Lat - N
78° 45' 00" Lon - W

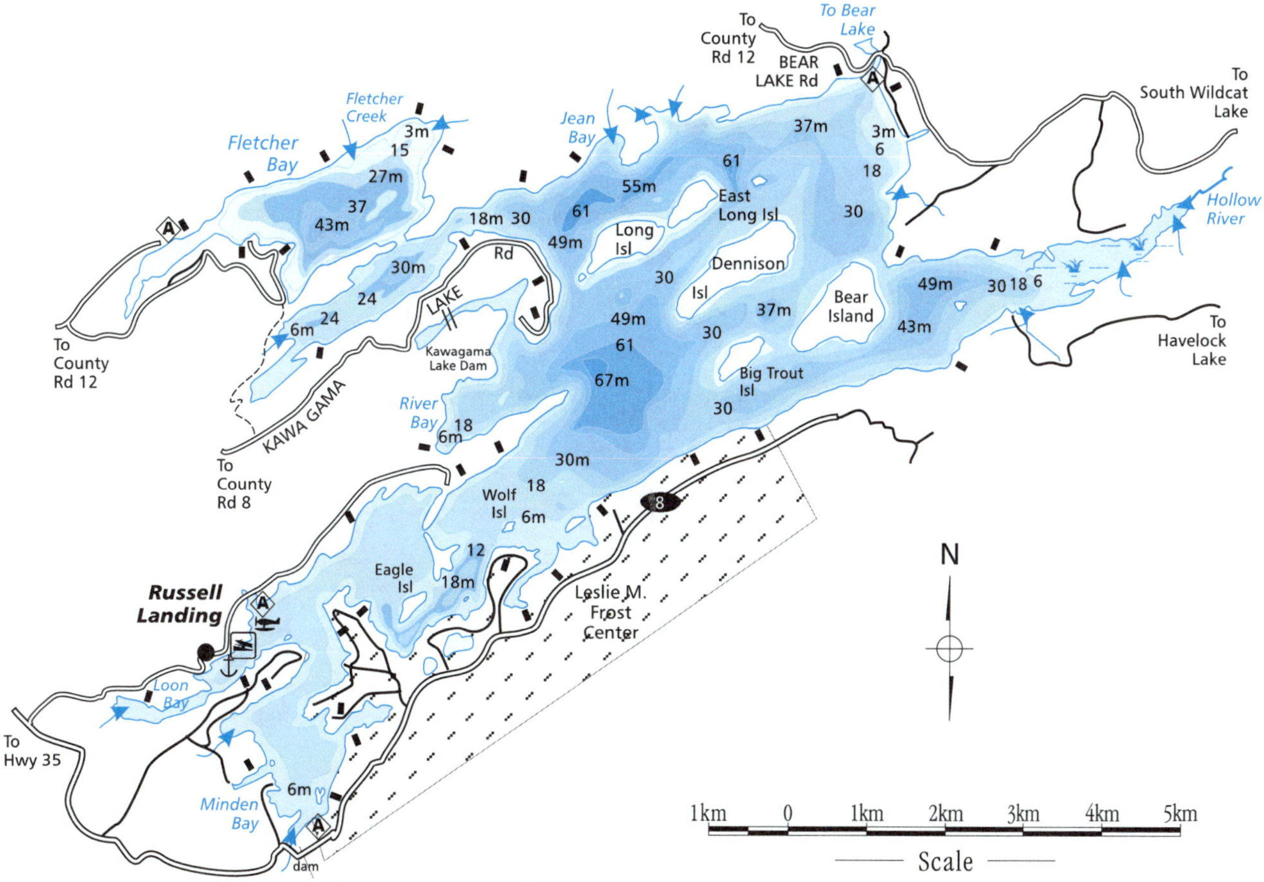

Access

This long shaped lake is one of the focal points of activity in the area and is located south of the town of Haliburton. The two main access areas are found off Highway 121. One launching site is located along the northern end of the lake, while the other access is found near the middle of the lake along its northwestern shore. There is also an access point onto the smaller Grass Lake, which is adjoined to the northern end of Kashagawigamog Lake.

Fishing

Anglers visiting this lake have a variety of sportfish to focus on including bass, lake trout, walleye and muskellunge. Lake trout and walleye are the two most sought after species and as a result fishing for either fish can be hit and miss. Ice fishing seems to be one of the more productive periods as ice huts dot the lake in the winter. A small population of muskellunge also inhabits Kashagawigamog Lake. Despite often-slow fishing, there are reports of consistent success in the northern end of the lake at times. With a little luck and a lot of patience, the odd musky will hit a well-presented ice fishing set up.

Lake trout slot size restrictions are in place on this lake to help preserve the natural lake trout population. For ice fishing, only one line is permitted to help reduce winter pressure on both lake trout and walleye.

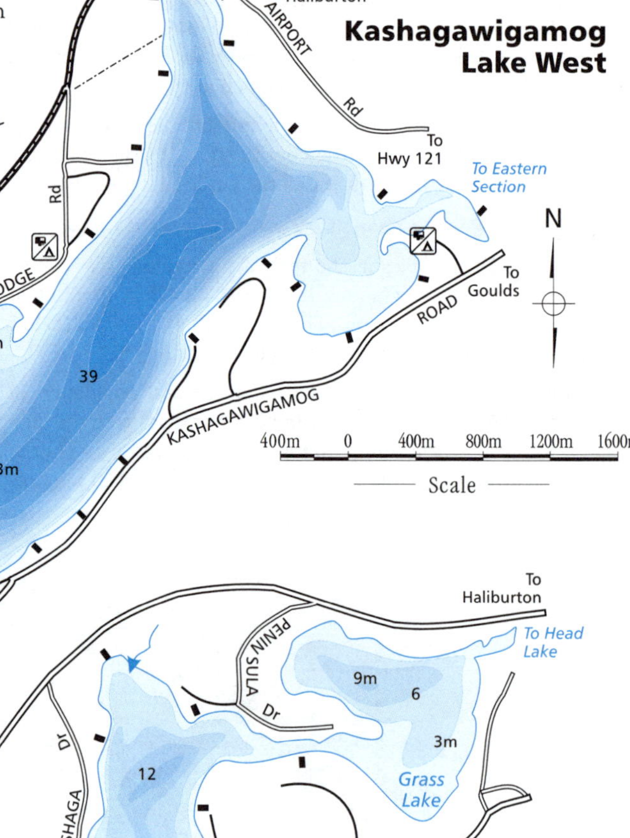

To Minden
21m
9m12
15m
SOUTH
Canning Lake
Ingoldsby
To Haliburton
PENINSULA Dr
To Head Lake
9m
6
3m
Grass Lake
12
KASHAGA Dr
12
9m
ROAD
To Minden
KASHAGAWIGAMOG
ROAD
To Lochlin
12
15m
21
To Hwy 121
NORTH
9m
3m
15m 12
21
6
To Western Section
SOUTH
Bonnie View Inn
Halimar Resort
KASHAGAWIGAMOG
To Ingoldsby

Kashagawigamog Lake East

Lake Definition

Elevation:	313 m (1,043 ft)
Surface Area:	81 ha (202 ac)
Mean Depth:	12.7 m (42.5 ft)
Max Depth:	39 m (130 ft)
Perimeter:	34 km (21 mi)
Way Point:	44° 59' 00" Lat - N 78° 36' 00" Lon - W

Facilities

Visitors flock to the Haliburton area in search of the rural enjoyments of the area. Facilities abound on and around Kashagawigamog Lake with a number of resorts, lodges and rental cottages in the area.

Hurst Lake

To find Hurst Lake follow County Road 15 north from Wilberforce to the Kenneway Road. The Kenneway Road can be followed by snowmobile west to Holland Lake. Hurst Lake lies just north of Holland Lake. The secluded lake is stocked every few years with brook trout. Fishing for brook trout to 30 cm (12 in) can be good during ice fishing season or in spring just after ice off.

Isabella Lake

Isabella Lake can be accessed via the Blackwater Road north of Orrville. Some big northern pike are caught annually and walleye fishing is best in winter through the ice. The lake has also been stocked with rainbow trout in the past. Fishing success has been sporadic and it is unclear if rainbow will be planted in the lake again.

Jack Lake

Jack Lake is a remote lake that offers good fishing at times for small northern pike. The pike are usually in the 1-2 kg (2-5 lb) range. There is also a small population of walleye in the lake. Jack Lake borders the Massasauga Provincial Park and is accessible by snowmobile north of Three Legged Lake. To access Three Legged Lake Road, follow the Otter Lake access road south past Otter Lake.

Kabakwa Lake

Kabakwa Lake lies partially within the southwestern corner of the Leslie M. Frost Centre. Access to the lake can be found via the Shang Ra La Road off Highway 35 north of Carnarvon. This small lake has a number of camps and cottages along its shoreline and is stocked regularly with lake trout. The lake has also been stocked with rainbow trout in the past. Fishing success can be good at times for lake trout, although catches of rainbow trout seem to be slowing. Ice fishing is productive for trout and success remains steady into the spring.

Kahshe Lake

See Pages 28-29

Kashagawigamog Lake

See Page 32

Kawagama Lake

See Page 31

Ketch Lake

This lake is stocked almost annually with brook trout that provide for good fishing through the ice and in the spring. The lake is best accessed in the winter by snowmobile. Look for the parking/access area off the south side of Highway 118 west of the village of Carnarvon.

Klaxton Lake

Lake trout are stocked almost annually in Klaxton Lake. Anglers can expect fair to good fishing for average sized lake trout that is best through the ice or in spring. Winter fishing is the predominant method on these lakes due to the easier access that is provided by snowmobile. Klaxton Lake is located just off the west side of Kennisis Lake Road (County Road 7) north of Highway 118.

Koshlong Lake

See Page 36

Lake Joseph

See Pages 38-39

Lake Muskoka

See Pages 40-41

Lake Rosseau

See Pages 42-43

Langford Lake

Langford Lake is found just outside the Village of Novar off Long Lake Road and offers slow to fair fishing for average sized brook trout. Brookies are best fished through the ice or in spring with a small shiny lure.

Lasseter Lake

This small, hidden lake contains the elusive brook trout. Look for the lake off the north side of Millar Hill Road, which is found off the north side of Highway 60 east of Huntsville. The lake offers fair fishing for small brookies.

Lee Lake

Lee Lake can be reached via snowmobile from along the Lost Road. Lost Road can be picked up off Millar Road east of Huntsville. The lake provides good fishing at times for brook trout to 35 cm (14 in) in size. Ice fishing can be productive for brook trout.

Liebeck Lake

The Seguin Trail passes right by the northern end of Liebeck Lake providing good snowmobile access. The lake has been regularly stocked with splake and fishing is generally better in the winter through the ice.

Limburner Lake

Limburner Lake is a small lake off the west side of County Road 12 between Clinto and Crozier Lakes. The small lake is stocked every two years with brook trout that average 20-30 cm (8-12 in) in size. Fishing can be good through the ice or in spring just after ice off.

Go Home Lake

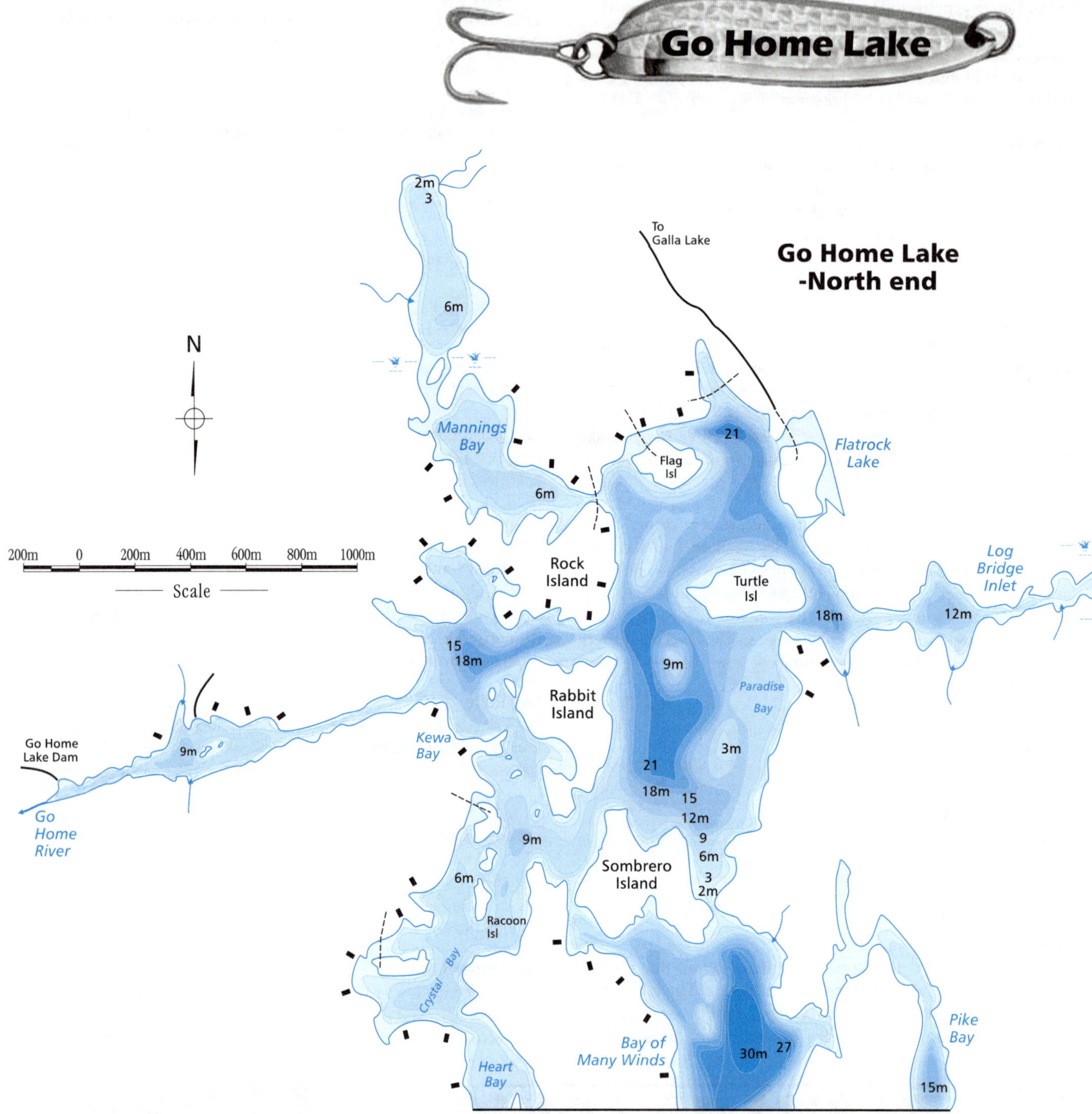

Access

To find Go Home Lake, follow Highway 400 north over the Gibson River to Go Home Lake Road (County Road 32) off the west side of the highway. There are two access areas found off the south side of the road. The first access area lies along the north bank of the Gibson River, while the second access is found on the southeast shore of Go Home Lake.

Fishing

Go Home Lake is a large odd shaped lake that is riddled with hundreds of bays and inlets just waiting to be fished. The lake is part of the drainage system into the Georgian Bay and is the mid point between the Muskwash River and the Go Home River.

Walleye and northern pike inhabit the lake in fair to good numbers and can reach decent sizes. Northerns are caught annually in the

6 kg (13 lb) range, while walleye average about 0.5-1 kg (1-2 lbs) although can be found much bigger. Pike can be found cruising any of the many bays throughout the lake, especially in the evening period during winter. A couple of prime walleye holding areas are just south of the Haunted Narrows, near the shallow shoal area or just off the west side of Turtle Island. These shoal areas often attract good numbers of walleye and big northern pike.

During summer, the action heats up with smallmouth bass being the most active sportfish.

Facilities

The two boat launch areas double as snowmobile access points. The big, sprawling nature of the lake makes a snowmobile an essential tool to properly explore the lake.

Lake Definition

Mean Depth: 15 m (49.5 ft)
Max Depth: 30 m (98.5 ft)
Way Point: 45° 00' 40" Lat - N
79° 50' 45" Lon - W

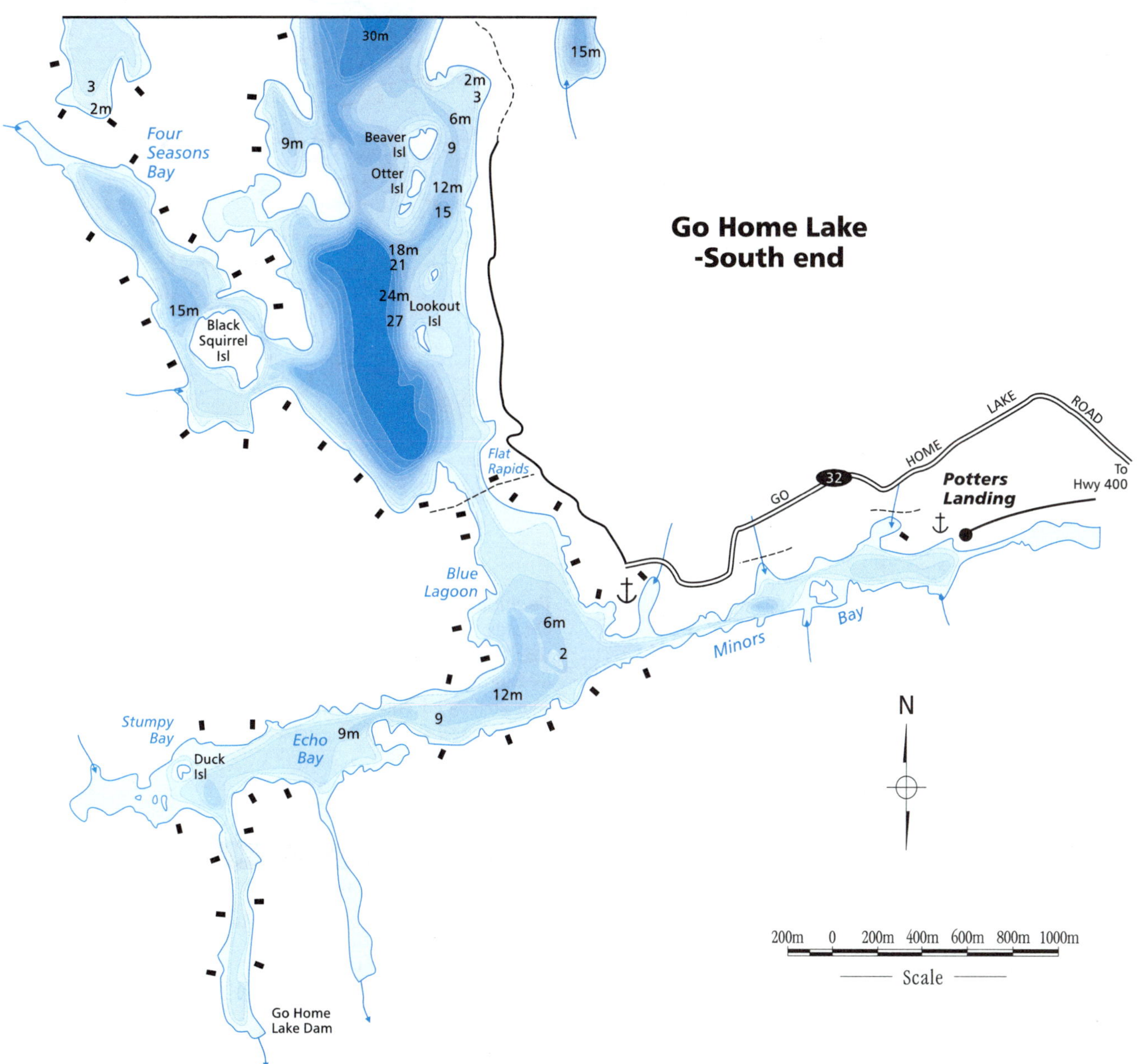

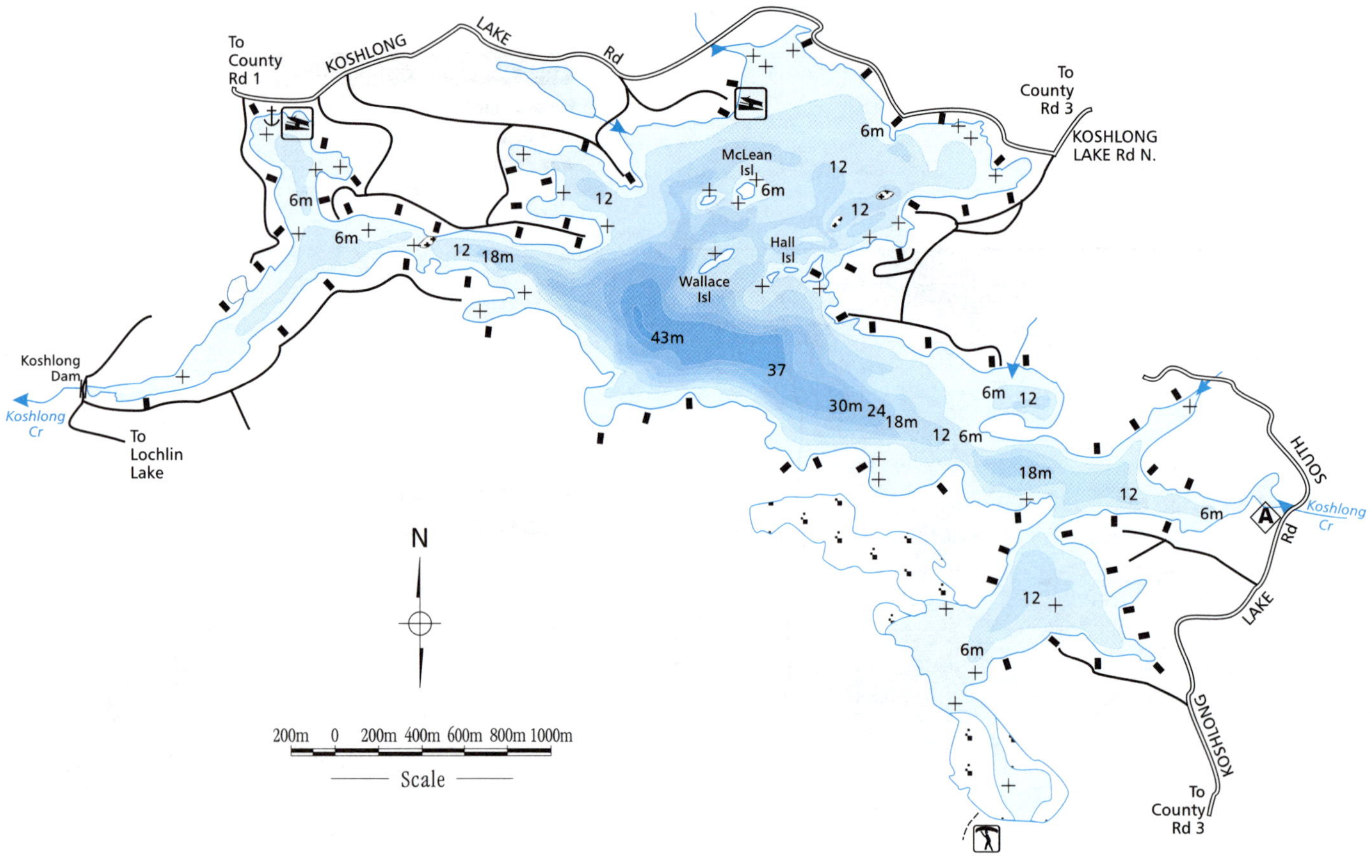

Access

South of Haliburton, Koshlong Lake is accessible by following County Road 1 south from Haliburton to the Koshlong Lake Road. Take the Koshlong Lake Road east and you will soon find a boat launch along the northwestern shore of the lake. Continuing further east will lead to another access point on the north shore.

Fishing

Koshlong Lake has had several different names over the years, such as Kokwayong Lake, and Cockweong Lake, before receiving its current name just after the turn of the 19th Century. Koshlong Lake was originally inhabited by only smallmouth bass, however in 1956 the lake was stocked with lake trout. Since the initial stocking, lake trout have been stocked almost annually and are now the fish of choice for visiting anglers. Ice fishing is one of the more effective times to find one these lake trout.

Before fishing, please check the fishing regulations for special restrictions on Koshlong Lake.

Facilities

Outside of the two launch areas on the north shore of the lake, there are no facilities available to visitors in the winter. If you are looking for a little adventure and some exercise before or after your angling adventure, the Victoria Rail Trail passes to the west of Koshlong Lake and is a great spot for cross-country skiing or snowmobiling.

Lake Definition

Elevation:	341.1 m (1,137 ft)
Surface Area:	40 ha (100 ac)
Mean Depth:	10.2 m (34 ft)
Max Depth:	42 m (140 ft)
Perimeter:	11.3 km (7.1 mi)
Way Point:	44° 58' 00" Lat - N 78° 29' 00" Lon - W

Lipsy Lakes

Lake trout are stocked almost annually in each of these lakes and anglers can expect fair to good fishing for average sized lake trout. Winter fishing is the most active time on these lakes due to the easier access that is provided by snowmobile. The access trail follows what is a rough 4wd road in the summer and can be picked up off the Kennisis Lake Road (County Road 7) just after it passes Burdock Lake.

Little Birchy Lake

Located just south of the Haliburton Forest Reserve, the lake can be accessed by short trails off Redkin Drive. The lake is stocked every few years with brook trout that average 25-35 cm (10-14 in) in size. Fishing is good through the ice or in spring just after ice off.

Little Bob Lake

Little Bob Lake is found just to the north of Gooderham Lake near the village of Gooderham. The small lake has been stocked periodically with brook trout that provide generally fair fishing for small trout. The best action comes through the ice or in the spring by using worms with a float.

Little Clear Lake

Little Clear Lake is stocked with brook trout about every two years. Ice fishing is the most productive method on this lake, although just after ice off with a fly or worm can also be good. The lake can be found by snowmobile just west of the larger Picard Lake. Picard Lake is accessible off Baker Road from Highway 507 west of Catchacoma Lake.

Little Otter Lake

Little Otter Lake can be reached by snowmobile from along the power line trail northwest of Minden. Follow the Scotch Line west off Highway 35 to reach the power line trail. The lake is stocked about every two years and the brookies are quite aggressive at times through the ice. Small spoons can produce trout over 30 cm (12 in) in size.

Livingstone Lake

There are a number of cottages on Livingstone Lake, which was once stocked with lake trout to supplement natural populations. Today, the lake relies on natural regeneration and fishing for lakers is slow to fair through the ice or by trolling in spring. There is also a small population of brook trout in the lake. The lake is found on the east side of County Road 12 northeast of Dorset. Watch for slot size restrictions on lake trout and special ice fishing regulations.

Long Lake

Southeast of Bracebridge, Long Lake can be found by snowmobile south of Highway 118, east of the Uffington Line. The lake offers slow fishing for small brook trout that are more active during ice fishing season and in spring just after ice off. Heavy fishing and the lack of catch and release have diminished this precious brook trout population.

Long Lake

This Long Lake is quite easy to find as it lies off the south side of Highway 169 at the town of Bala. You can reach Highway 169 from the town of Gravenhurst to the east or from Highway 69 to the west. The access point to the lake lies off the south side of the highway near the southern end of the lake.

Fishing in Long Lake has improved dramatically over the past several years due to the rainbow trout stocking program on the lake. Rainbow are stocked into Long Lake about every two years and provide for some good fishing at times for decent sized trout.

Longline Lake

Longline Lake can be easily accessed off Highway 117 west of Dorset. The lake is stocked with splake every few years and fishing is fair through the ice and during spring. There are also rumours of brook trout being caught in the lake. The jury is still out on whether these are misidentified splake or not.

Loon Call Lake

To reach Loon Call Lake, follow Highway 28 north from Lakefield and look for the Anstruther Lake Road off the west side of the highway past Burleigh Falls. Following this side road west will take you right past the boat access to Loon Call Lake. From the highway to the launch site on Loon Call Lake is approximately 3 km (2 miles).

Some cottages dot the shoreline of Loon Call Lake, although the lake can be quite peaceful, especially during winter. The lake is stocked with the hybrid trout species splake about every two years. These splake can reach good sizes in Loon Call Lake and are best caught through the ice. Try jigging a spoon or even a white jig along the shoal areas beside the deeper portions of the lake.

Louie Lakes

The Louie Lakes are two small lakes that can be accessed from either side of County Road 12 just north of Livingstone Lake. The lakes offer slow fishing for brook trout. The larger Louie Lake, which is found on the east side of the road, is also stocked every few years with splake. Fishing for splake can be good at times through the ice or in spring.

Mary Lake

See Page 46

McCoy Lake

McCoy Lake is stocked semi-annually with lake trout and fishing for small lakers can be good through the ice and in spring. While fishing for lake trout, anglers often hook into panfish or even a big northern pike. The lake borders The Massasauga Provincial Park and is accessible by snowmobile north of Three Legged Lake and the access area for the park.

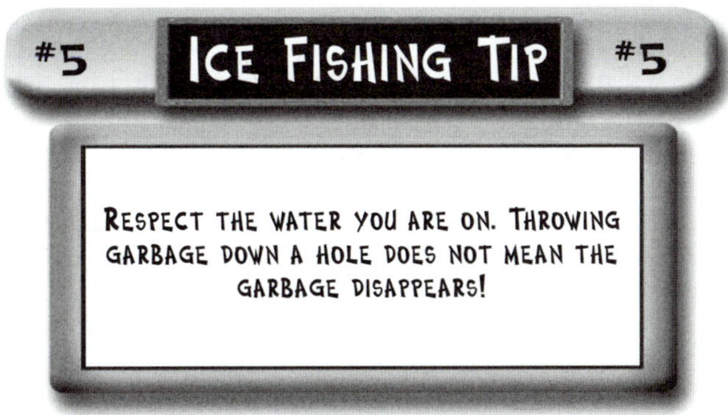

Lake Joseph -North end

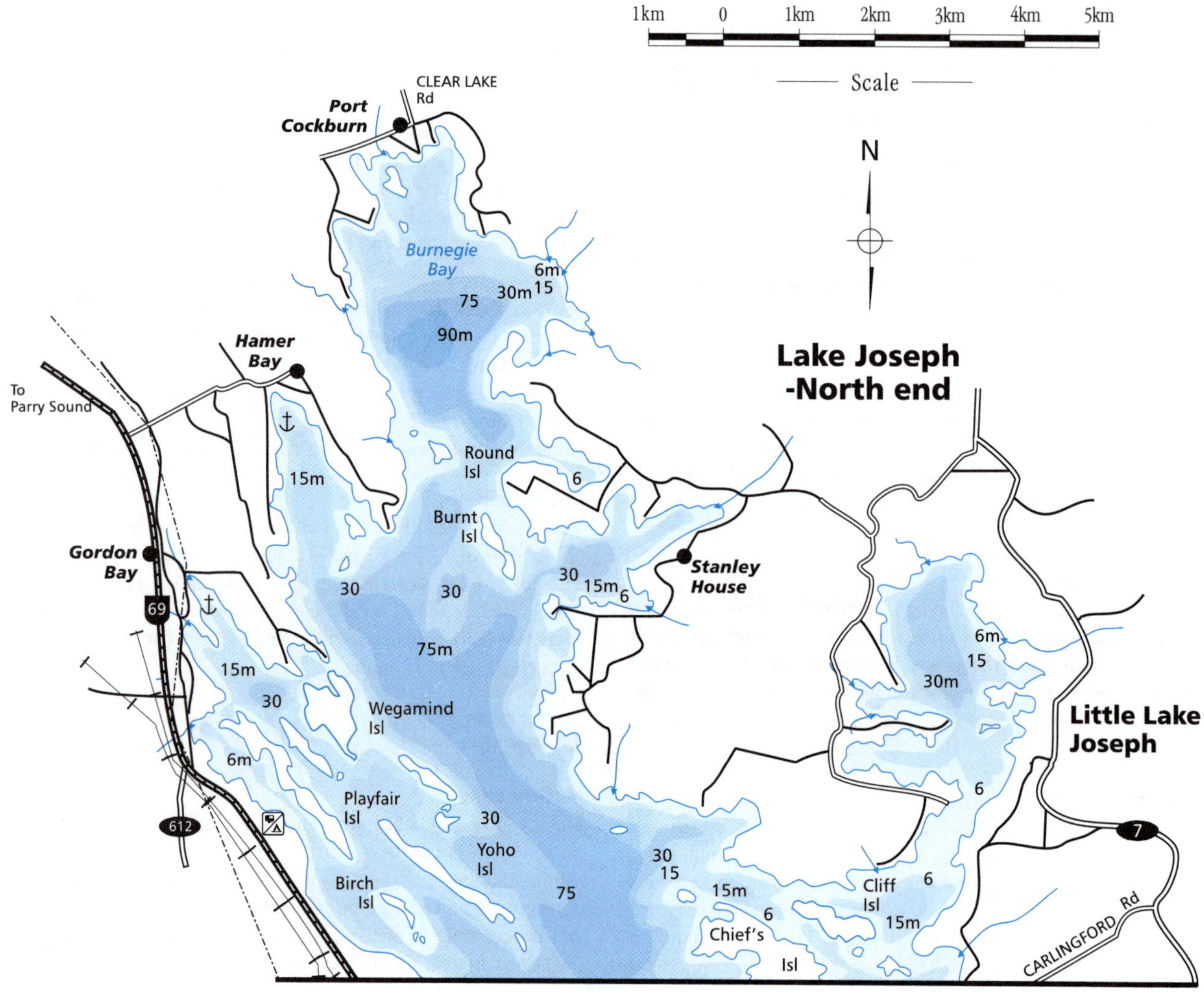

Access

Lake Joseph is located north of the larger Lake Muskoka not far off Highway 69. There are a number of access points to the lake, including the two main boat launch areas just off Highway 69. The main southern access to the lake is found on Foot's Bay, just east of the junction of Highway 69 and Highway 169. Another access area can be found further north on Hamer Bay. Hamer Bay is a short drive east off Highway 69.

Fishing

The two most sought after sportfish in the winter at Lake Joseph are lake trout and walleye. Both species receive heavy fishing pressure throughout the season, although they still sustain self-reproducing populations. Fishing for walleye can be fair at times, although it is generally slow. Look for shoal areas throughout the lake for a good hint on where walleye could be. Lake trout fishing is generally slow, although some nice sized lakers are caught in Lake Joseph annually. More and more anglers are realizing that lakers have to be released to sustain the fishery.

For something a little different, anglers can also find lake whitefish in Lake Joseph. Although most of these fish are caught by accident, they put up a good fight when hooked. To find these feisty fish all you need to figure out is the depth they are holding at. They will hit most spoons presented in their range.

There is a limited ice fishing season on Lake Joseph to help reduce pressure on ailing lake trout and walleye stocks. Be sure to check the regulations before heading out for the specifics on this restriction and any other restrictions in place on the lake.

Facilities

Along with the many public access areas there are a number of full service amenities such as marinas, lodges and resorts on Lake Joseph. Inquire locally for more details.

Lake Definition

Mean Depth: 43.2 m (141.7 ft)
Max Depth: 93.8 m (308 ft)
Way Point: 45° 11' 00" Lat - N
79° 47' 00" Lon - W

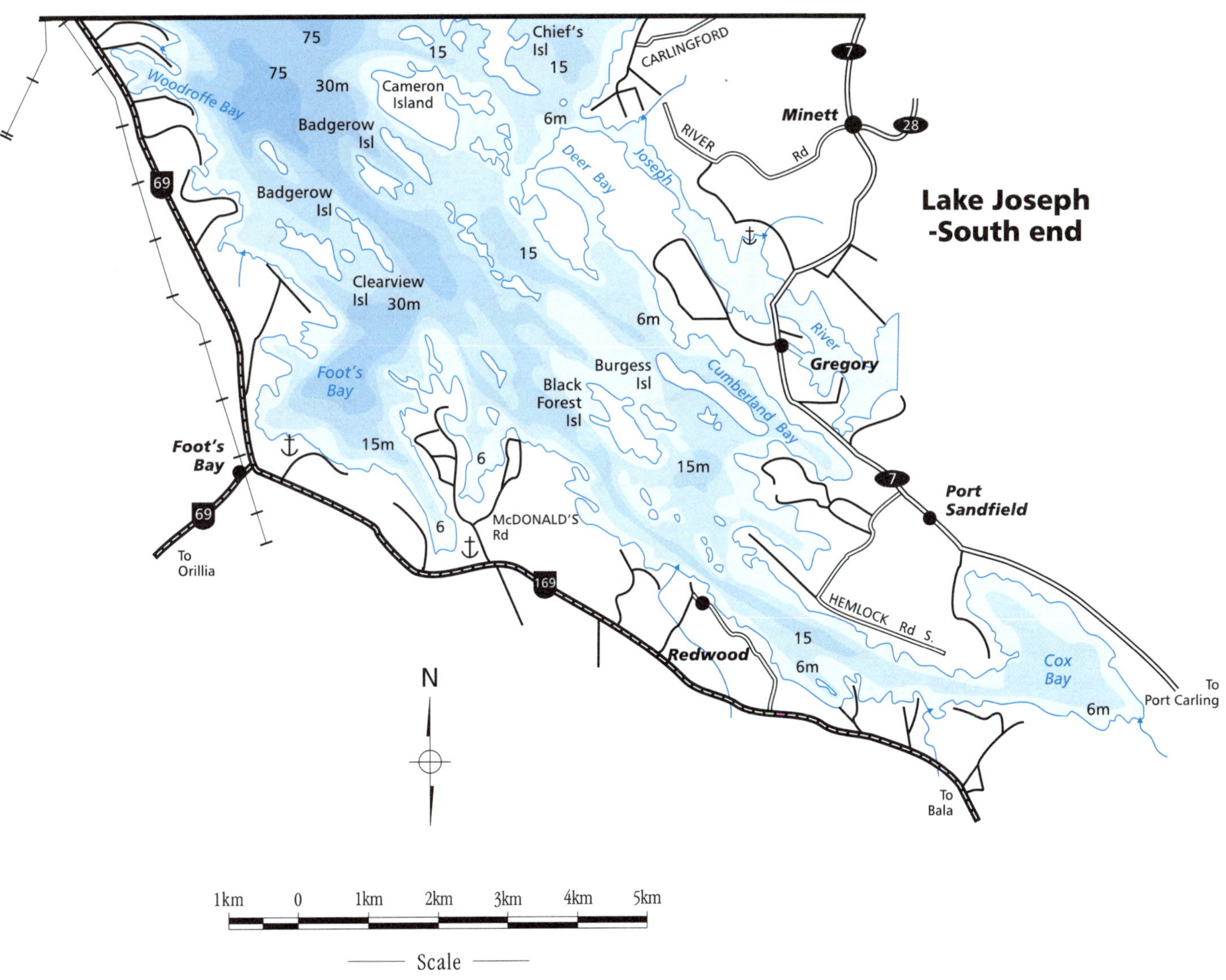

Lake Muskoka -North end

1km 0 1km 2km 3km 4km 5km

Scale

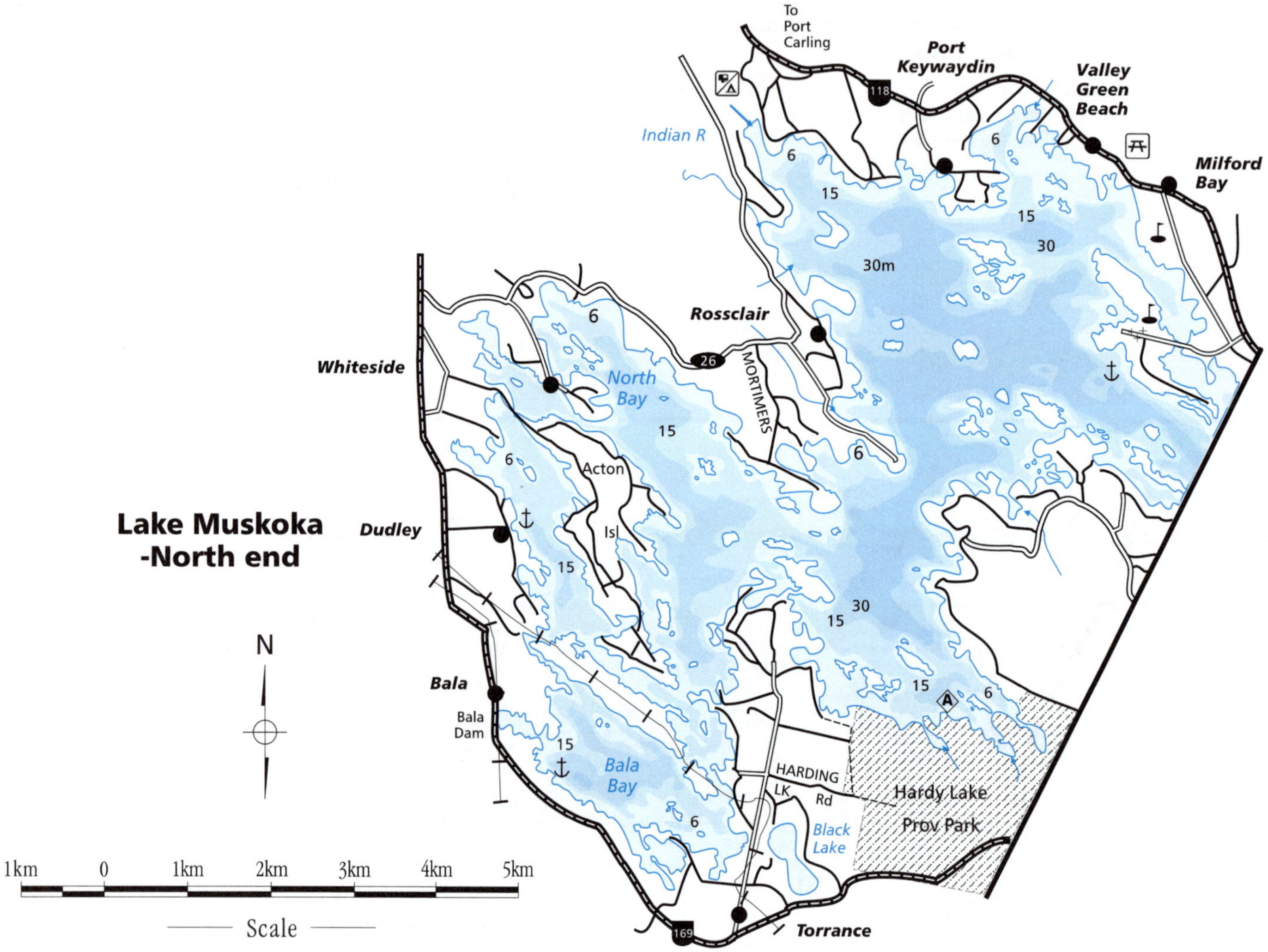

Access

Lake Muskoka is one of the larger inland lakes in southern Ontario and is perhaps the most famous cottage destination in Southern Ontario. Many famous people own property on this lake and a cruise down 'Millionaire Row' is well worth the effort. Despite the development around the area, the lake remains a beautiful destination.

The big lake can be reached from a number of different ways. One of the easiest routes is to take Highway 11 north to Gravenhurst. In the north end of the town, there is a public launch area and a small marina available for visitors. Another popular access area can be found near the village of Bala. Bala can be reached by following Highway 169 northwest from Gravenhurst. The access area lies along the shore of Bala Bay just south of the village. Port Carling also provided a good access point. People can launch a snowmobile near town and follow the Indian River south to the northern end of Lake Muskoka.

Fishing

Despite all of its fame and fortune, Lake Muskoka is not revered as a great fishing lake. Regardless, the big lake continues to be quite productive and can be surprisingly good at times. The two most popular sportfish in the winter are lake trout and walleye. Both species are heavily fished through their seasons and anglers are encouraged to practice catch and release to help protect the quality of fishing in the lake.

Lake trout have suffered over the years due to over fishing and shore development. As a result, the natural stocks are aided by an annual stocking program. The fishing for these lake trout is fair through the ice. Walleye average about 1-2 kg (2-5 lbs) in size and are most often found off shoal areas such as the 15 metre shoal found just off the west side of Browning Island.

Northern pike are the biggest predator species found in Lake Muskoka and can reach sizes in excess of 12 kg (21 lbs), although average about 3 kg (7 lbs) in size. Look for pike in the quiet bays of the lake during dusk or off deeper shoal areas throughout the day.

Facilities

There are a number of public facilities available on Lake Muskoka including several different access areas around the lake. The towns of Bracebridge and Gravenhurst, along with the villages of Bala and Port Carling all offer full service amenities such as lodging, food and supplies. The big lake is also home to a number of thriving recreation lodges and resorts that can help make your Muskoka Lake adventure a comfortable and enjoyable experience.

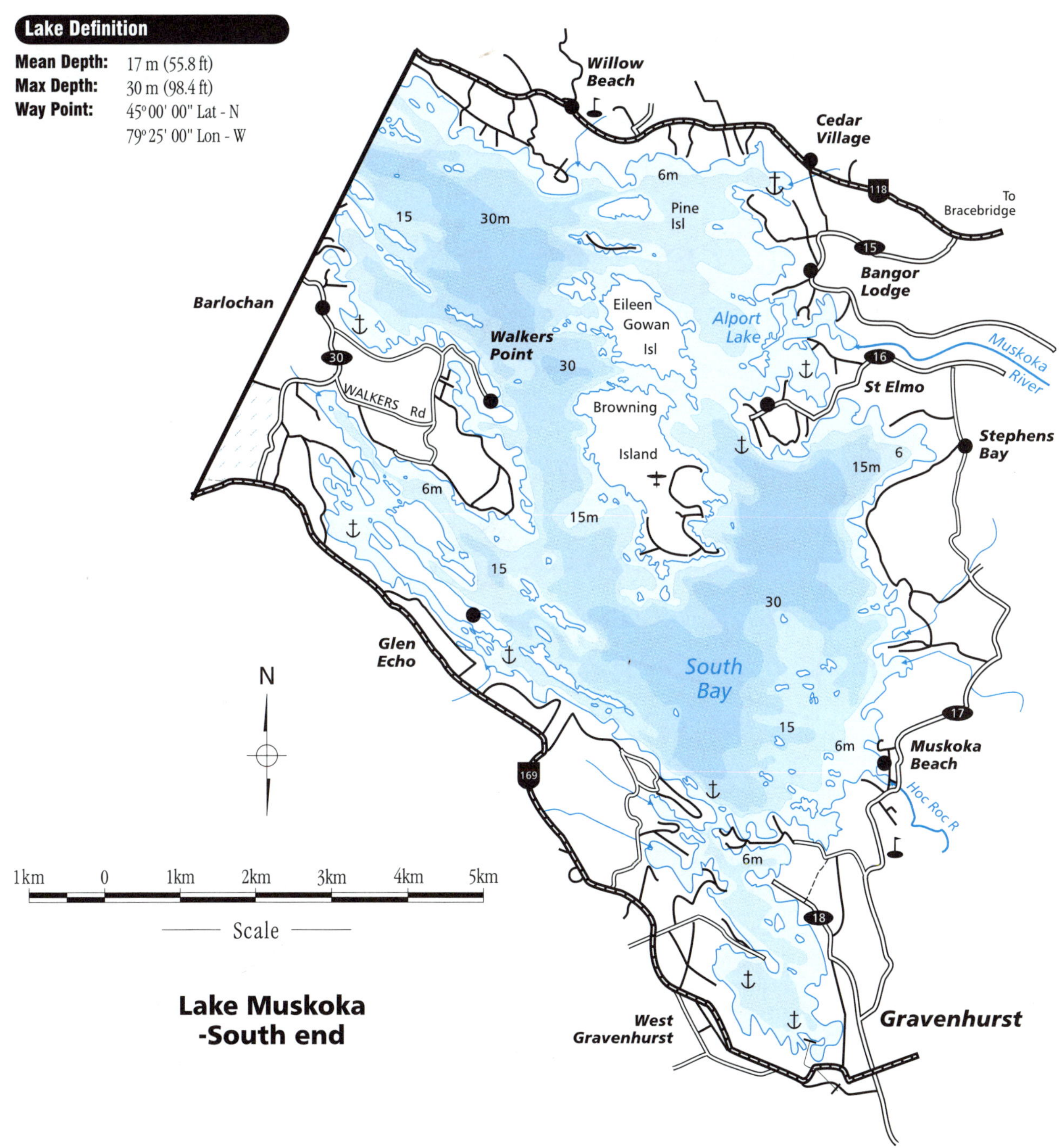

Lake Rosseau -North end

To Parry Sound
Rosseau
6m
15 30m
45
camp
Sucker Bay
Rosseau Falls
Rosseau Falls
15
6
Sandy Bay
75m
Gull Rock
Wileys Bay
Rosseau Lake Rd
To Bracebridge
15
6m
Rosseau Lake 1 Rd
Penman Isl
45
30m
Juddhaven
Juddhaven Rd
Morinus
Rest Harbour
Highlands Isl
N

1km 0 1km 2km 3km 4km 5km
Scale

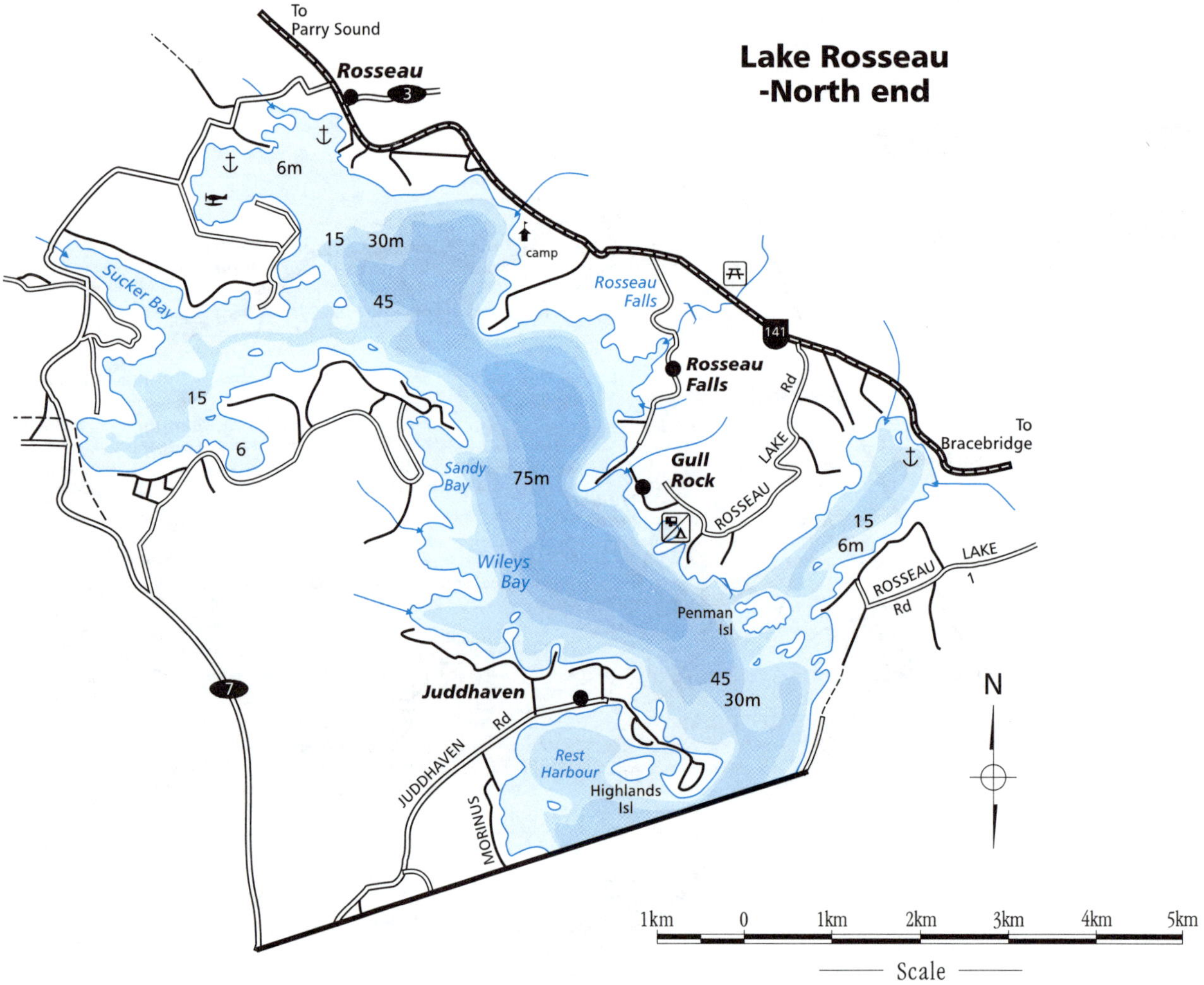

Access

Lake Rosseau is a large lake found southeast of the town of Parry Sound and north of Lake Muskoka. The lake is accessible from two main access areas, one from the north end of the lake and one from the south. The south access can be found in the village of Port Carling off County Road 118. To reach County Road 118, you can either take Highway 11 from the east or follow Highway 69 and Highway 169 from the west. The main northern access point to Lake Rosseau is located in the village of Rosseau just south of Highway 141.

Fishing

Lake Rosseau is another big Muskoka area lake that is a popular spot for recreation and cottage owners. The lake can be particularly busy throughout the summer months. However, the fishing remains consistent, producing decent results year after year.

Lake trout and walleye are the prized species of Lake Rosseau and are the most heavily fished sportfish in the winter. Walleye fishing used to be legendary on this lake; however, increased fishing pressure has reduced the angling quality. Look for weed lines and shoal areas to find cruising walleye. Lake trout are best fished by jigging small spoons or even jigs through the ice.

The largest predator fish found in Lake Rosseau is the muskellunge. Muskie anglers come from afar to fish for this fabled species and can get into some fine action for muskie at times. Unfortunately, these big fish are not very active in the winter. To ensure the future of all the species in this popular lake, be sure to practice catch and release whenever possible.

Facilities

Along with the two main boat launch areas there are a number of other access areas available on the lake. For lakeside accommodation, Lake Rosseau is home to a few great lodges and resorts. Alternatively, the villages of Rosseau and Port Carling offer all the amenities needed for a trip, such as lodging, food, and other basic supplies.

Lake Rosseau -South end

Lake Definition

Mean Depth: 34.2 m (112 ft)
Max Depth: 75 m (246 ft)
Way Point: 45° 10' 00" Lat - N
79° 35' 00" Lon - W

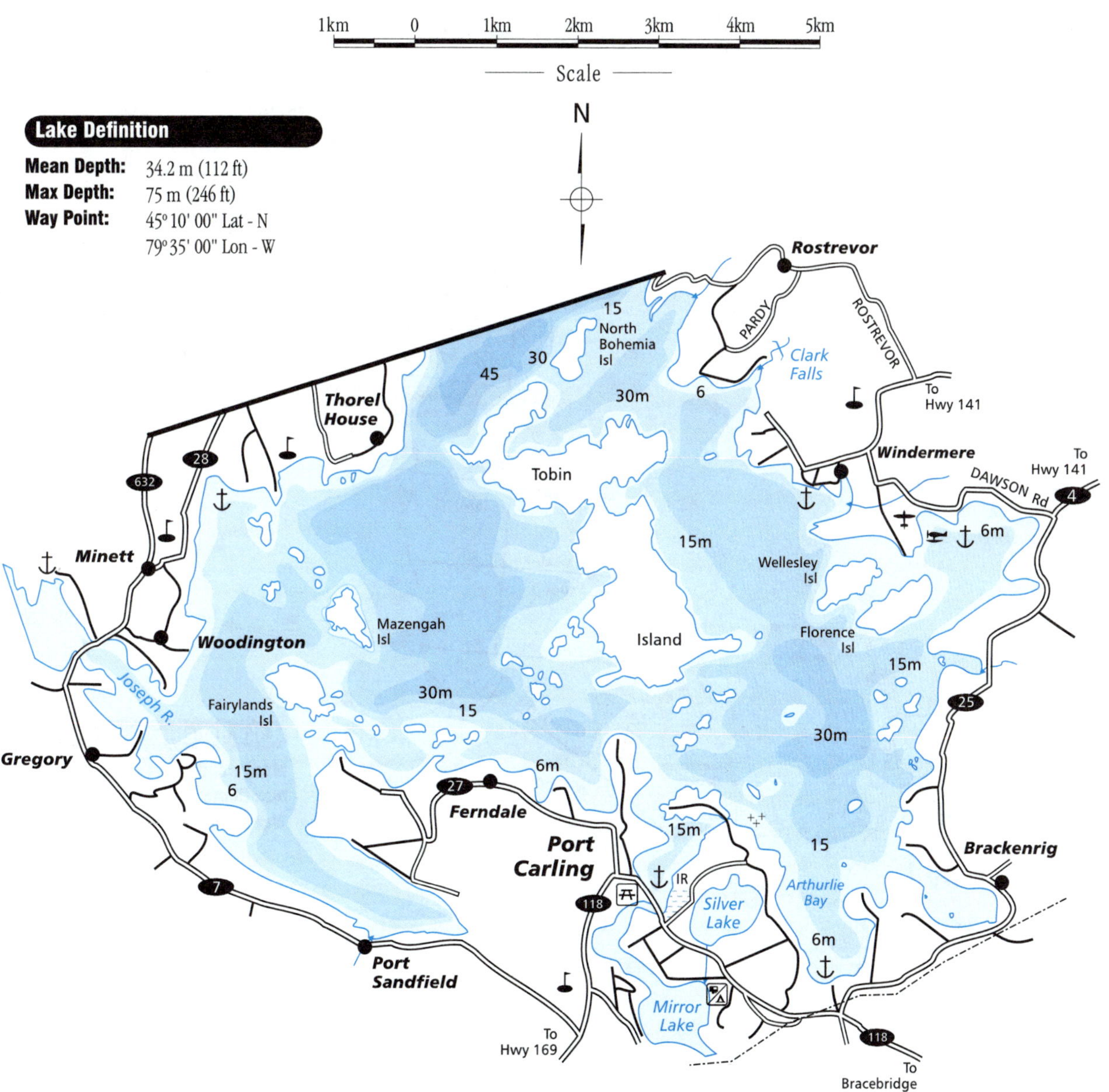

Access

You will find Lake Scugog in the midst of a low-lying wetland region northeast of Greater Toronto. The lake is considered as one of the main Kawartha Lakes, although unlike the other lakes, Scugog is not a part of the Trent Severn Waterway. The lake is easily found by following Highway 7A to the town of Port Perry. Port Perry is situated along the southwest shore of the lake and provides one of the main access points onto the big lake. Other boat launch and access points are scattered around the lake.

Facilities

Port Perry is a scenic lakeside community offering all the essentials, such as motels, groceries and other retailers. Anglers can rent ice huts (see ad below) or if your luck is a little slow, why not visit the charity casino located on Scugog Island. Outside of town, there are several other access areas and marinas that can be used to access the lake.

Fishing

Lake Scugog continues to be a decent provider of sport fishing opportunities despite the increased pressure the lake continues to experience. The weedy nature of the lake makes for lush habitat for all the sportfish species that inhabit its waters. Similar to other Kawartha Lakes, walleye and muskellunge are the main attraction for anglers and fishing for both species can be good at times. For both predators, look for weed areas where there will be an abundance of baitfish. However, perch are also readily available and seem to hang out in these areas, too. Although smaller, the feisty fish can be a lot of fun to catch through the ice. But if you want to concentrate on walleye, try jigging along the drop offs near the deeper portions of the lake.

Before heading out on the lake, be sure to check the regulations for any special restrictions on this lake.

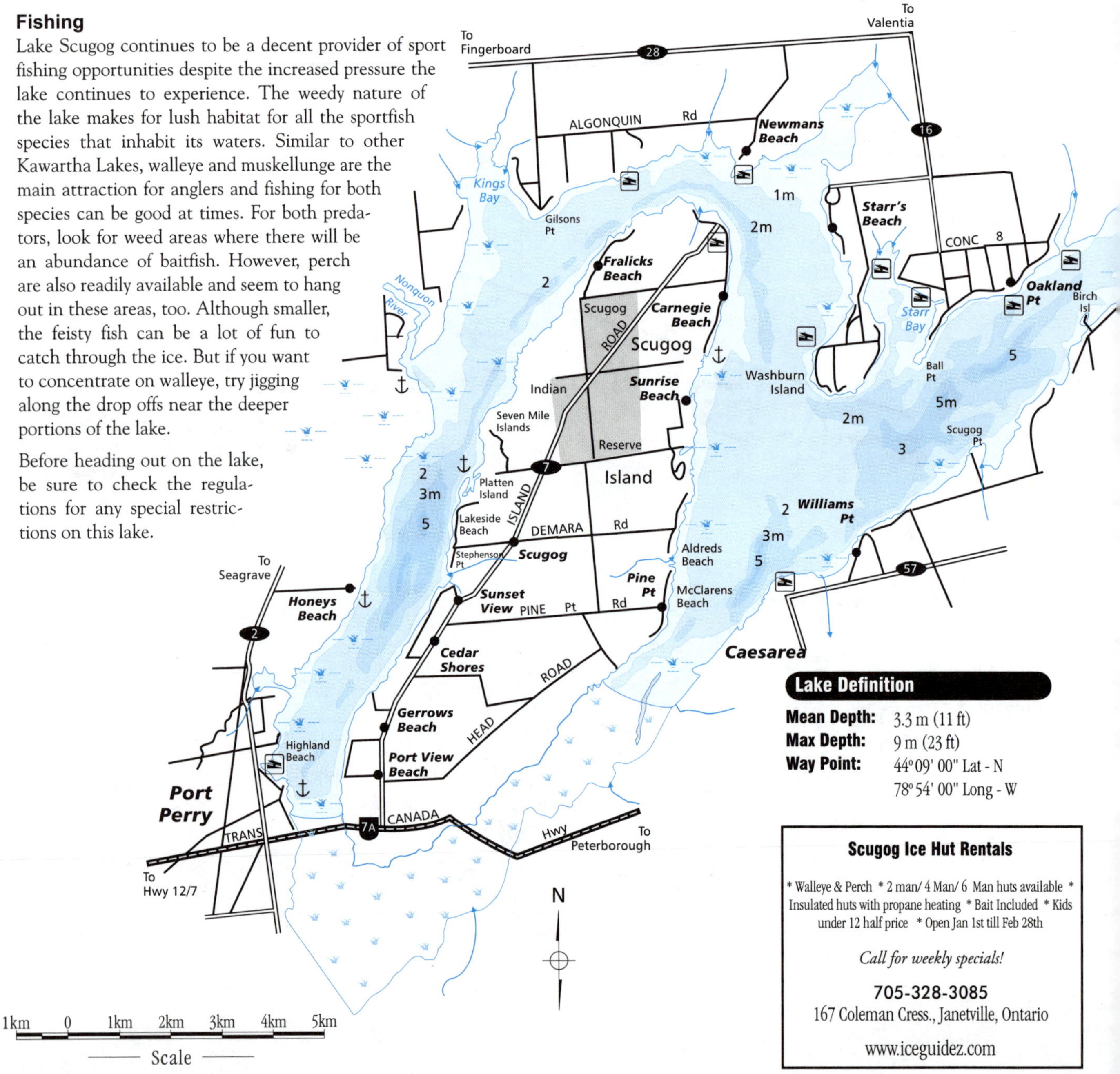

Lake Definition

Mean Depth: 3.3 m (11 ft)
Max Depth: 9 m (23 ft)
Way Point: 44° 09' 00" Lat - N
78° 54' 00" Long - W

Depth Chart Not Intended for Navigational Use

McEwen Lake

McEwen Lake lies between Dan and Horse Lake of the Leslie M. Frost Centre. The lake is accessible by snowmobile via established trails that can be picked up off Highway 35. The lake is stocked with splake about every two years and offers good fishing at times for nice sized splake. Small spoons or jigs can be productive during ice fishing season.

McGee Lake

McGee Lake is actually a remote access lake that does not have any established roads or trails leading to it. As a result, the main method of access to the lake is via snowmobile during the winter. From Highway 28 it is a short snowmobile ride west to the lake. The lake is fairly popular and you may be able to find an established snowmobile route during winter.

McGee Lake is stocked about every two years with lake trout, which provide for decent action mainly through the ice. Look for lakers along shoal areas off the deeper holes of the lake. Jigging small silver spoons can be effective, but some anglers swear by the white jigs. Lake trout are not very big in McGee Lake, but they can be a lot of fun to catch during the winter.

Meach Lakes

These are two brook trout lakes that can be accessed by snowmobile along a maze of unplowed logging roads. Fishing in the lakes can be good through the ice or in spring for brook trout to 40+ cm (16+ in) in size. The lakes lie near Lake St. Peter and the village of Maynooth. Inquire locally for directions or consult the Backroad Mapbook for Cottage Country.

Merdie Lake

Merdie Lake is a small, remote lake that is rarely visited except by the odd ice fisherman in winter. Anglers can expect good fishing for average sized brook trout. Snowmobilers can take County Road 12 to the gated Bear Lake Road and follow this road to the Hollow River crossing. On the west side of the crossing there is a rough trail that leads northeast to the lake.

Mink Lake

Mink Lake is a secluded lake that is most often visited by snowmobilers via an unplowed road that can be found just west of Paint Lake near Dorset. Mink Lake offers slow to fair fishing for small brook trout that are best caught through the ice or in spring just after ice off.

Mohan Lakes

The Seguin Trail passes by the southern shore of Mohan Lake providing good snowmobile access in winter. The trail can be picked up behind the Parry Sound Visitor Centre off Highway 69. Mohan Lake has been regularly stocked with splake and fishing is generally fair in the winter months.

Monck Lake

Monck Lake can be found to the north of Highway 118 southeast of the village of Wilberforce. The lake is stocked periodically with splake and fishing for average sized splake is fair. This hybrid fish seems to be more readily caught through the ice than in open water.

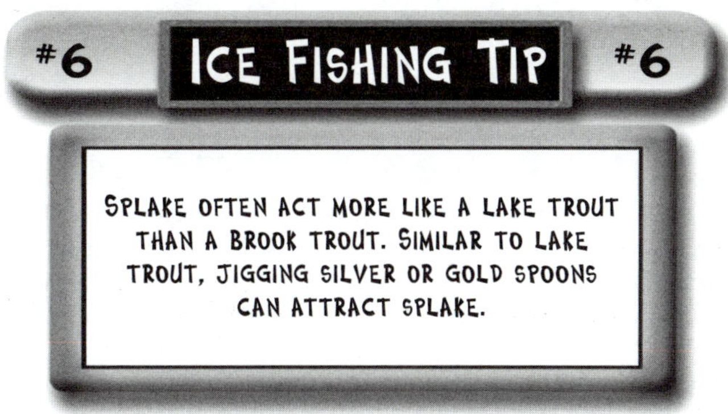

Monmouth Lake

To find Monmouth Lake, follow Highway 121 east from Tory Hill to Highway 648. Take Highway 648 south to the West Eels Lake Road. The West Eels Lake Road travels west, eventually passing by the southern tip of Monmouth Lake.

Lake trout are stocked annually in Monmouth Lake and provide for good fishing at times for average sized lakers. Ice fishing for lake trout is one of the most popular times of the season to try for lakers; however, the spring just after ice off can also be productive. Through the ice, try jigging small silver spoons. Further to the west, visitors will find Lower Monmouth Lake. Lower Monmouth Lake is similar in size to Monmouth Lake but only offers angling opportunities for smallmouth bass and largemouth bass in the summer.

Moore Lake

See Page 47

Morrow

Morrow Lake is stocked every two years with splake that provide fair to good fishing at times for average sized fish. Access to the lake is via snowmobile trail west off Haliburton Lake Road.

Moose Lake

Located north of the town of Haliburton, Moose Lake can be reached by taking Eagle Lake Road (County Road 14) north off Highway 118. Just past Eagle Lake, Eagle Lake Road passes by the north end of Moose Lake. While it is possible to access the lake at the north end, Moose Lake is best accessed by snowmobile from Eagle Lake.

With shoreline development and the subsequent fishing pressure over the years, it is surprising that natural lake trout still survives in Moose Lake. The trout fishing in Moose Lake is usually slow, although it can be fair at times. Ice fishing is a popular winter activity on the lake and is one of the best ways to find lakers. If you do happen to hook into a lake trout, be sure to release it unharmed as the species could benefit greatly if catch and release is practiced regularly. Be sure to check your regulations before heading out onto Moose Lake as there are special size and ice fishing restrictions in effect to help preserve lake trout stocks.

Mountain Lake

See Page 48

Access

You will find Mary Lake just south of the town of Huntsville. The large lake has a few different access areas, but the most popular access point is from Port Sydney at the southern end of the lake. To find the access near Port Sydney follow Highway 11 to County Road 10. Take County Road 10 east into Port Sydney and to the access to Mary Lake.

Another maintained access point is found at the north end of the lake. From Huntsville follow County Road 2 south to the Chub Lake Road. This road leads to the North Mary Lake Road and the much quieter north end of the lake.

Fishing

Mary Lake is a popular cottage destination lake as it lies in the heart of Cottage Country just south of Huntsville. The lake is very scenic and lake trout are stocked annually. Trout can be found in the 75+ cm (30+ in) range and are best fished through the ice in winter or in the early spring just after ice off. The typical minnow and jig is one of the more productive ice fishing methods used on the lake for trout. Whitefish are also found in Mary Lake and can provide for some fun action if hooked.

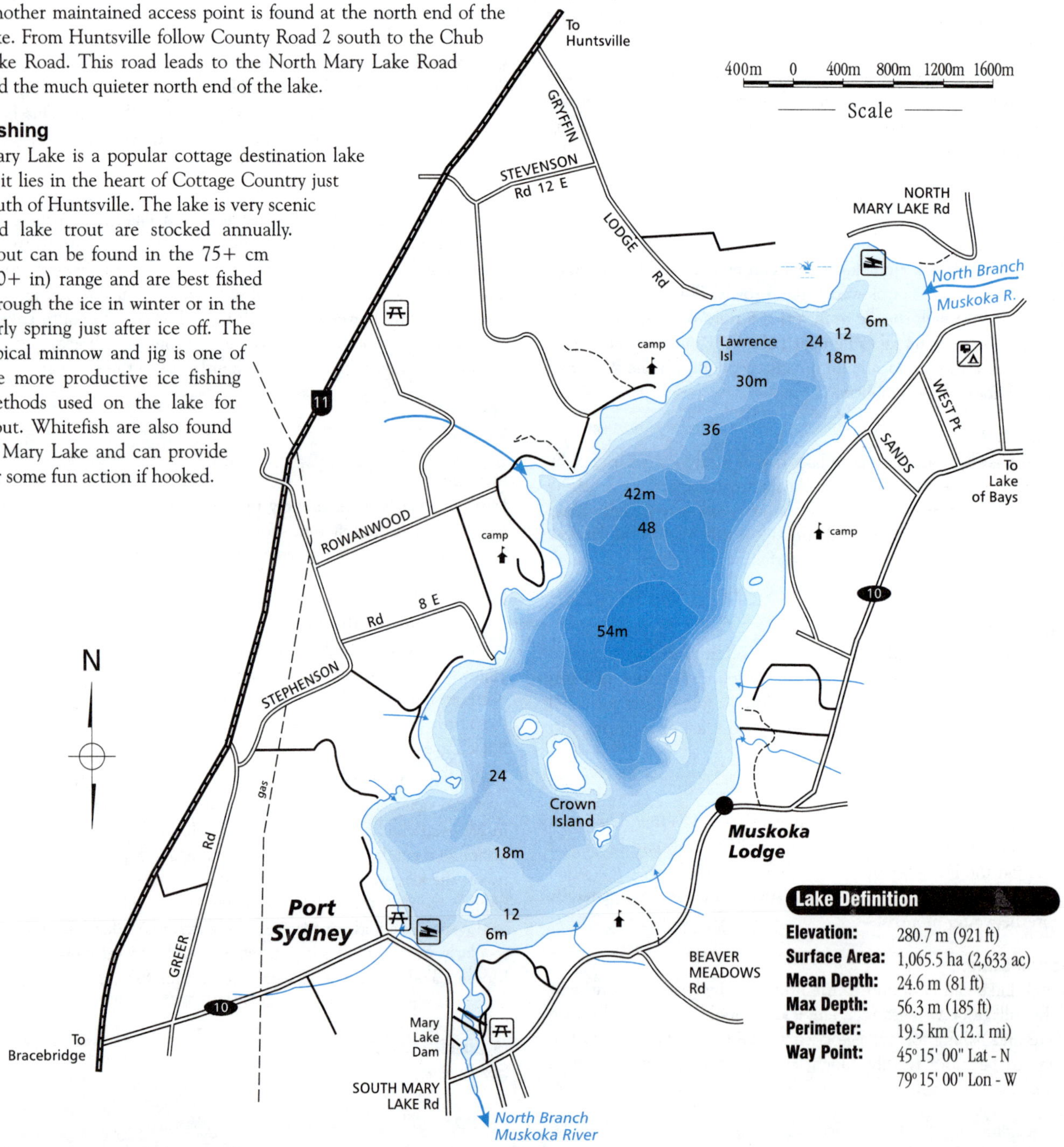

Facilities

In addition to the two maintained access areas, there are a number of full facility lodges available on Mary Lake. Inquire locally for more details. Alternatively, the city of Huntsville will provide visitors a wider range of accommodations, services and retailers to choose from.

Lake Definition

Elevation:	280.7 m (921 ft)
Surface Area:	1,065.5 ha (2,633 ac)
Mean Depth:	24.6 m (81 ft)
Max Depth:	56.3 m (185 ft)
Perimeter:	19.5 km (12.1 mi)
Way Point:	45° 15' 00" Lat - N 79° 15' 00" Lon - W

Access

Moore Lakes are located just north of the village of Norland off the east side of Highway 35. The lakes are accessible via a small marina available in the settlement of Moore Falls.

Facilities

Outside of the small marina in Moore Falls, there are no facilities on Moore Lakes. The village of Norland is found to the south and provides basic amenities for area visitors.

Fishing

Moore Lakes are part of the Gull River system and the close proximity of the lakes to Highway 35 makes this a popular year round destination. As a result, the lakes receives a lot more angling pressure compared to some of the more out of the way lakes in the area.

Although stocked in the past, the lakes now relies on natural reproduction to sustain the fishery. In turn, anglers are asked to practice catch and release to help maintain the fishery. Success for lake trout is usually slow with the best times being in the winter through the ice or in the early spring just after ice off.

Be sure to consult your regulations before heading out on Moore Lakes, as there are special ice fishing and lake trout regulations in place.

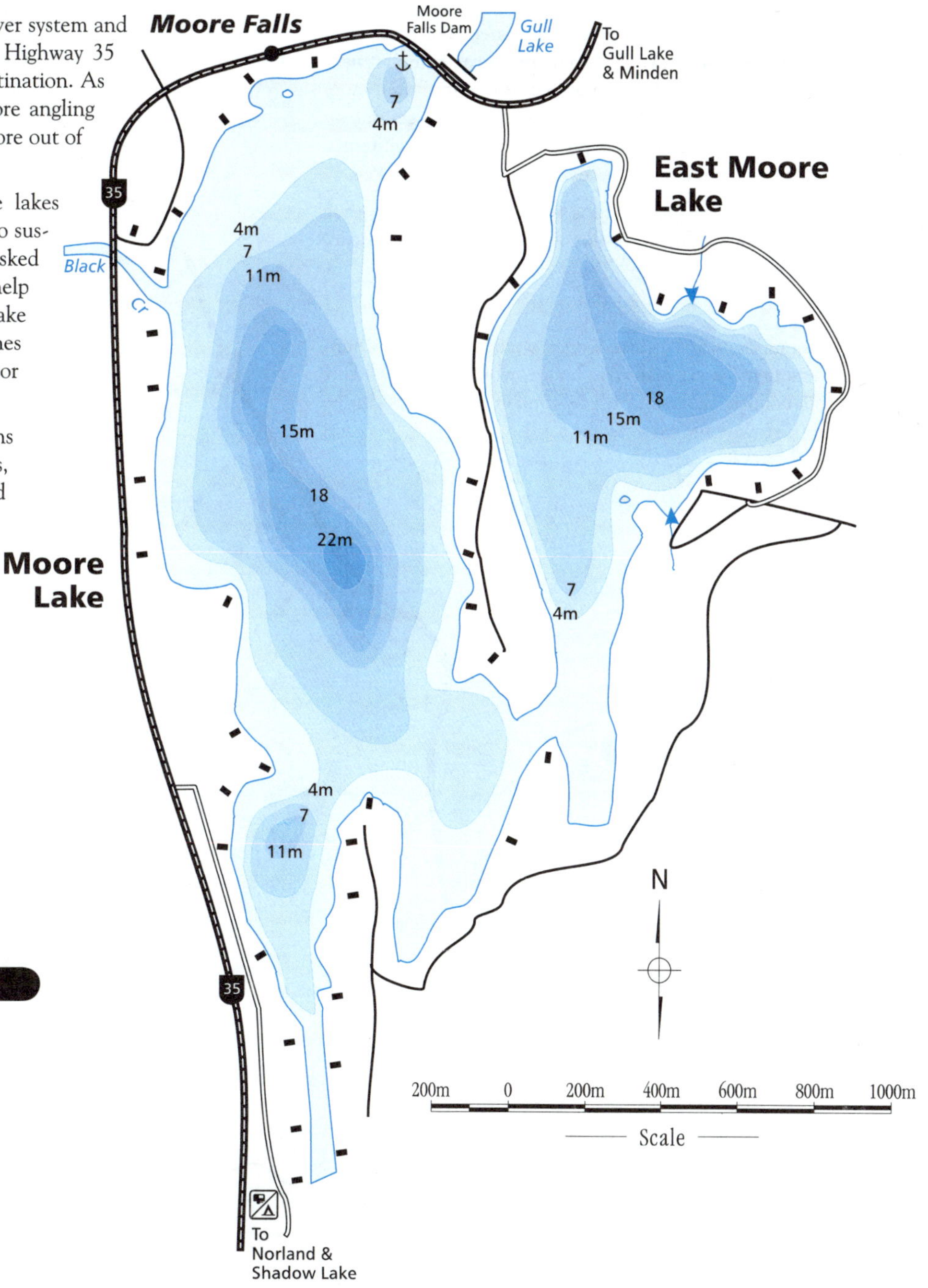

Lake Definition

Elevation:	241 m (803 ft)
Surface Area:	117 ha (390 ac)
Mean Depth:	6.9 m (23 ft)
Max Depth:	22 m (73.3 ft)
Perimeter:	11.2 km (7 mi)
Way Point:	44° 48' 00" Lat - N 78° 48' 00" Lon - W

Access

North of the town of Minden, Mountain Lake can be reached by following Highway 35. The highway passes right along the western shore of the lake. The main public access area is found just off the highway near the middle of the lake.

Fishing

This clear lake is quite deep with a maximum depth of over 31 m (103 ft). A natural strain of lake trout remains in the lake, but fishing for these lakers can be slow at times. Ice fishing is often a more productive time and visitors will find numerous ice anglers out on the lake in the winter. Ice fishing also produces catches of whitefish, which make for fine table fare and an even better fight if hooked.

Be sure to check the provincial fishing regulations before heading out on Mountain Lake. There are slot size and ice fishing restrictions in place.

Facilities

There are a number of resorts and lodges available around Mountain Lake including the popular Hart Lodge, which provides a fine series of cross-country ski trails. Supplies and all necessities can be picked up in the town of Minden to the south.

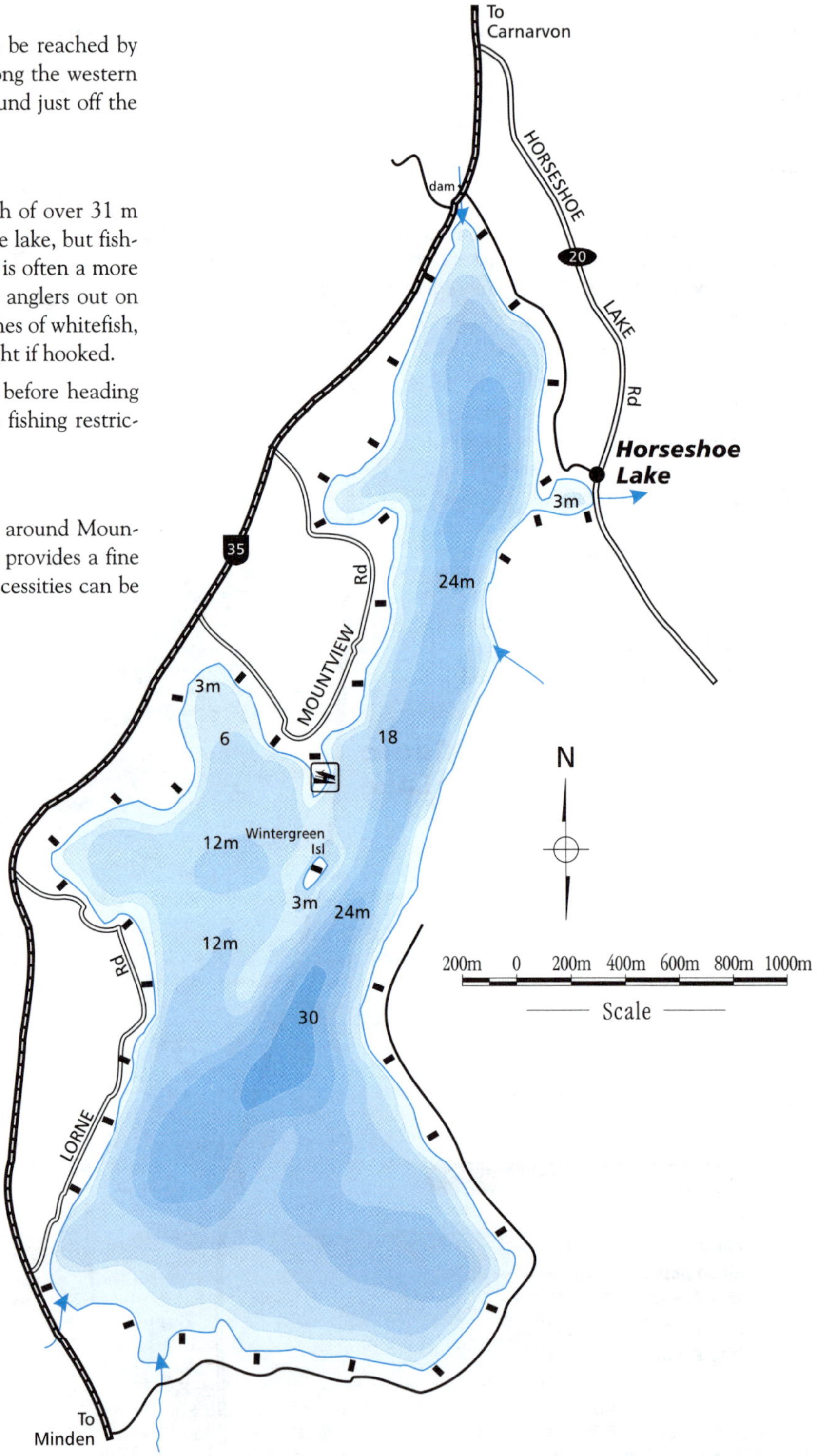

Lake Definition

Elevation:	274 m (920 ft)
Surface Area:	27 ha (68 ac)
Mean Depth:	12 m (40 ft)
Max Depth:	28.2 m (94 ft)
Perimeter:	14 km (9 mi)
Way Point:	44° 59' 00" Lat - N 78° 43' 00" Lon - W

To Carnarvon
HORSESHOE LAKE Rd
20
dam
Horseshoe Lake
3m
35
MOUNTVIEW Rd
24m
3m
6
18
N
Wintergreen Isl
12m
3m
24m
12m
200m 0 200m 400m 600m 800m 1000m
Scale
LORNE Rd
30
To Minden

Depth Chart Not Intended for Navigational Use

Nehemiah Lake

This small, secluded lake is found in the Leslie M. Frost Centre off the north side of the Sherborne Access Road. The small lake is stocked ever few years with brook trout that average from 20-25 cm (8-10 in) in size. Fishing can be good through the ice and in spring just after ice off.

North Muldrew Lake

North Muldrew Lake is connected to South Muldrew Lake and can be reached off the North Muldrew Road just west of Gravenhurst. The lake receives heavy fishing pressure resulting in fair fishing for bass and walleye. Walleye action is best through the ice or during late spring for fish that average 0.5-2 kg (1-45 lbs).

Orley Lake

This small Leslie M. Frost Centre lake is stocked with splake every few years. Fishing for average sized splake can be good through the ice or in spring just after ice off. Try small spoons through the ice and streamer patterns in the spring. The lakes can be reached by snowmobile off the Sherborne Access Road to the east of Highway 35.

Oxtongue Lake

See Page 50

Paint (Deer) Lakes

Paint Lake is an easily accessed lake southwest of Dorset. The Paint Lake Road branches south from County Road 112 and leads to the southern shore of the lake. Paint Lake has been stocked with splake, which provide fair fishing through the ice and in the spring.

Partridge Lake

Brook trout are stocked in this lake every few years and fishing is good at times for generally small brookies. Try ice fishing or casting small spoons or spinners in the spring. The small lake can be accessed right off the side of Highway 35 north of Halls Lake.

Pencil Lake

Pencil Lake offers fair fishing for stocked lake trout to 2 kg (4.5 lbs) and good fishing for smallmouth bass to 2 kg (4.5 lbs). Ice fishing for lake trout is sometimes productive. There is a public boat launch at the north end of the lake.

Percy Lake

Currently, there is no public right of way into Percy Lake and while there are roads around the lake they are private and off limits to the public. Short of asking permission to use private roads in the area, one public access into Percy Lake is via a short 600 m (1,973 ft) trail from Haliburton Lake to the west.

Percy Lake was named after an official of the historic Canada Land and Emigration Company. In the mid 1800's, the British company was a major player in helping develop the Haliburton area through the development and sale of land parcels in the region. Visitors to Percy Lake can expect to find a beautiful Haliburton Lake with a few cottages and camps along its shoreline. Beginning as far back as 1964, Percy Lake has been stocked every few years with lake trout. Angling success for lake trout is usually fair for trout that can be found up to 75 cm (30 in) in size on occasion. Ice fishing provides consistent results each year.

Rabbit Lake

Rabbit Lake is a small, hidden lake that can only be found by a 170 m (557 ft) portage from the southern shore of Nunikani Lake. Nunikani Lake lies in the middle of the Leslie M. Frost Centre property just west of the larger Red Pine Lake. Rabbit Lake is stocked every two years with brook trout and fishing for average sized brookies is good through the ice.

Rebecca Lakes

See Page 51

Ronald Lake

This secluded lake is found in the Leslie M. Frost Centre just north of the much smaller Nehemiah Lake. Ronald Lake is stocked ever few years with brook trout. Fishing for brookies that average 20-25 cm (8-10 in) is good at times in the winter. Nehemiah Lake can be accessed via the Sherborne Access Road west of Highway 35 and a 455 m (1,493 ft) trail can take you to Ronald Lake.

Ross Lake

Ross Lake is stocked every few years with splake, which provide for fair to good fishing at times for average sized splake. Ice fishing for splake is popular on this lake. To find the lake, look for the Ross Lake Road at the northwest end of Haliburton Lake.

Rustyshoe Lake

South of the small village of Gooderham, Rustyshoe Lake can be found off the west side of Highway 507. A small boat/snowmobile access area is available just off the highway along the eastern shore of the lake. Due to the easy access, the lake does receive significant angling pressure throughout the year. Fishing remains fairly productive since anglers can try their luck for smallmouth bass and largemouth bass in the summer or splake and the odd muskellunge in winter. Splake are stocked in Rustyshoe Lake every few years and are most readily caught in the winter while ice fishing.

Scraggle Lakes

These two secluded lakes are stocked every few years with brook trout. Fishing for brook trout to 30 cm (12 in) can be good during ice fishing season. The lakes lie within the privately owned Harcourt Park.

Shoe Lake

Lake trout are stocked in Shoe Lake periodically and provide for slow to fair fishing on occasion. Fishing for these small lakers is best through the ice in winter or in the spring just after ice off. Try a small silver spoon through the ice. The lake is accessible by the Shoe Lake Road on the west side of Highway 35 south of Dorset.

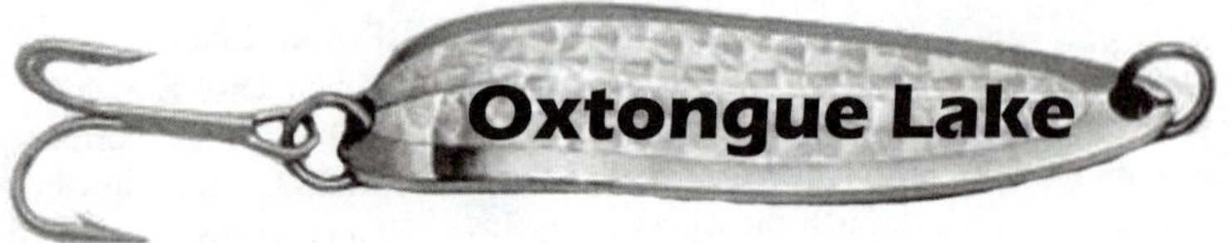

Access

Oxtongue Lake is located just outside of Algonquin Provincial Park and can be reached off the south side of Highway 60. There are a number of access points to the lake including places to launch a snowmobile from the side of the highway.

Fishing

Oxtongue Lake has a long history and was an intregal part of the first log drives in the area. Today it is a popular year round retreat.

A natural strain of lake trout is found in the lake and they provide generally slow fishing, even in the winter. Ice fishing is probably the best way to find lake trout, however, trolling in the spring is also a popular method. In order to protect the natural strain of lake trout in Oxtongue Lake, slot size and special ice fishing restrictions have been established.

A natural population of brook trout once thrived in the lake and rainbow trout were once stocked in the lake. Unfortunately, both species are now extinct. While there is the odd report each year that brook trout have been caught in Oxtongue Lake, it is thought that they are most likely misidentified lake trout.

Facilities

Nearby Algonquin Park is a fantastic place to visit throughout the year and several resorts, motels and other accommodations are established in the area. Oxtongue Lake, itself, is home to a couple of resorts. Alternatively, the town of Huntsville can be found to the west along Highway 60 and the village of Dorset is located minutes to the south.

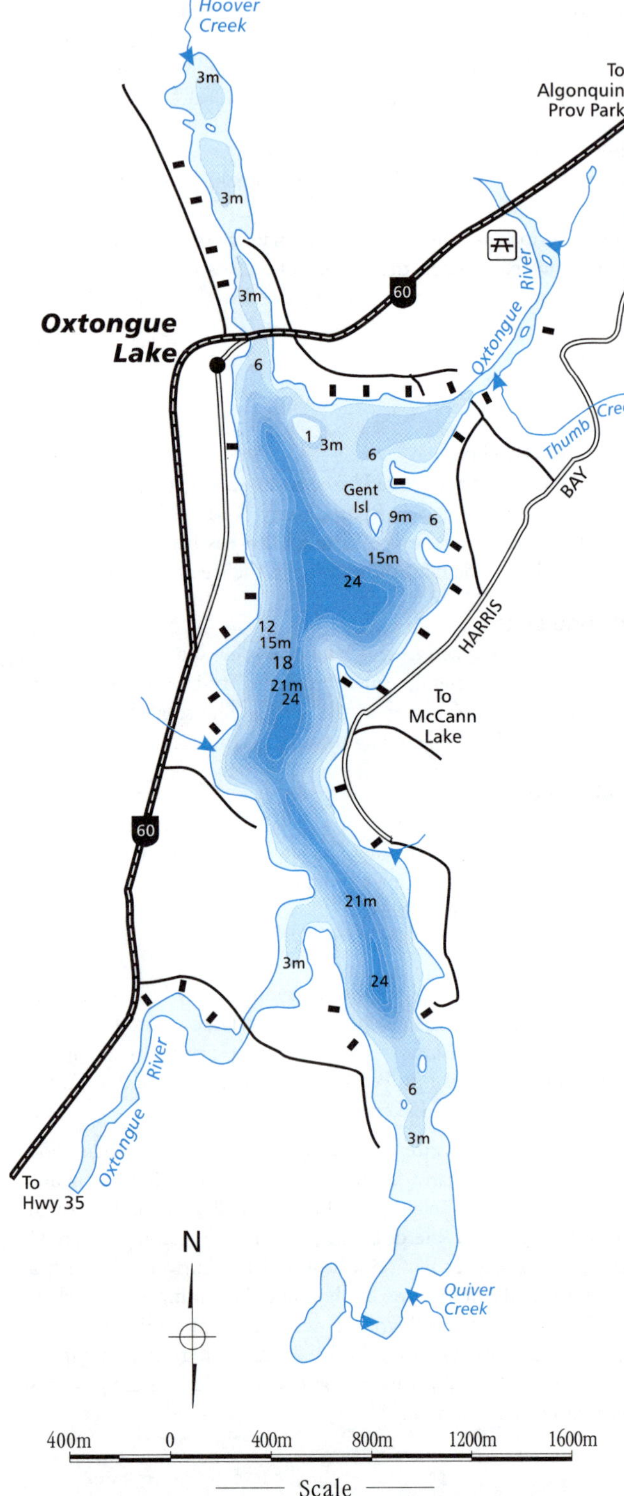

Lake Definition

Elevation:	364 m (1,193 ft)
Surface Area:	249 ha (616 ac)
Mean Depth:	8.9 m (29.2 ft)
Max Depth:	26.8 m (88 ft)
Perimeter:	19 km (11.8 mi)
Way Point:	45° 22' 00" Lat - N 78° 55' 00" Lon - W

Depth Chart Not Intended for Navigational Use

Access

To find Rebecca Lake, take Highway 60 east from Highway 11 near Huntsville to County Road 8. Follow County Road 8 north to Fieldale Road, which leads to the northern shoreline of Rebecca Lake and eventually a rustic access point.

Fishing

Rebecca Lake is stocked with lake trout, which provide for fair fishing throughout the year. Lakers are not very big in this lake, although the action can be decent, especially compared to some of the other lake trout lakes in the area. Ice fishing is productive for lakers, although lake trout are also quite active during the spring just after ice off. Try a small spoon to attract the fish. On occasion, you may even luck into a good-sized whitefish when angling for lake trout.

Facilities

Since Rebecca Lake is not very developed, there is only the possibility of renting a private cottage for an intimate weekend or week on the lake. To find out more information on cottage rentals, contact the Huntsville Chamber of Commerce or a local real estate office.

Lake Definition

Mean Depth: 13.5 m (108 ft)
Max Depth: 28.9 m (95 ft)
Way Point: 45° 26' 00" Lat - N
79° 02' 00" Lon - W

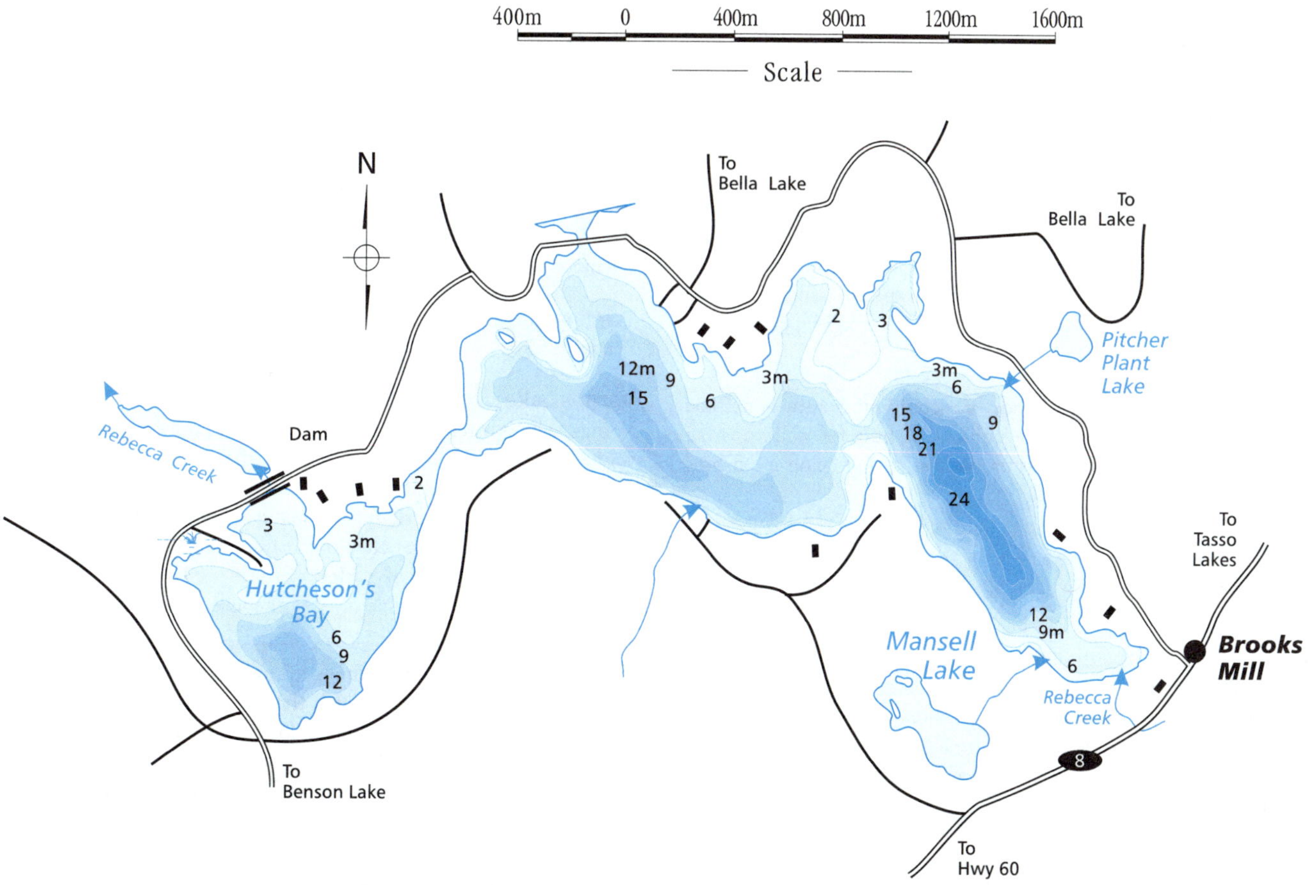

400m 0 400m 800m 1200m 1600m
Scale

N
To Bella Lake
To Bella Lake
Pitcher Plant Lake
Dam
Rebecca Creek
Hutcheson's Bay
To Tasso Lakes
Brooks Mill
Mansell Lake
Rebecca Creek
8
To Benson Lake
To Hwy 60

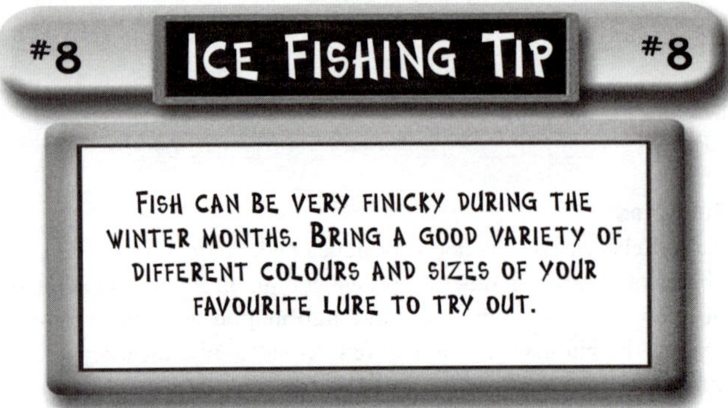

Shoelace Lake
Shoelace Lake is stocked every few years with brook trout and fishing can be good at times for brookies to 35 cm (14 in). Ice fishing season is one of the better times to visit this remote lake that is found in the heart of the Leslie M. Frost Centre property. For a detailed map of the area, pick up a copy of the Backroad Mapbook for Cottage Country.

Silver Buck and Silver Doe Lakes
Found within the Leslie M. Frost Centre, these are snowmobile accessible lakes that offer fair to good fishing for stocked brook trout. Fishing is best through the ice or in the spring for brook trout that can be found in the 30+ cm (12+ in) range. The lakes lie south of Sherborne Lake.

Skeleton Lake
See Page 53

Soaking Lake
Soaking Lake is a small, secluded lake that can be found via snowmobile trail northwest of the village of Maynooth. The lake offers fair fishing for small brook trout. Ice fishing is popular and if you can get down the soggy roads in the spring, you should have fair to good success. The access road to the lake may be difficult to find due to the maze of logging offshoot roads in the area. Inquire locally or consult a copy of the Cottage Country Backroad Mapbook.

South Muldrew Lake
This lake has a few access roads branching off Southwood Road (County Road 13) west of Gravenhurst. Fishing for walleye is fair during the year with the most productive period being ice fishing season.

St. Nora Lake
See Page 54

Star Lake
Star Lake is found south of the village of Orrville via the Star Lake Road. The lake receives heavy fishing pressure throughout the year and has a number of cottages along its shoreline. Northern pike and lake trout fishing is slow to fair at times for less than average sized fish. Lakers are stocked every few years and are best fished through the ice and in spring.

Sucker Lake
Sucker Lake is a busy summer cottage lake that is stocked semi-annually with lake trout. Fishing for lakers is fair through the ice and by trolling in spring just after ice off. Watch for slot size restrictions on lake trout. To find the lake, take Highway 632 west from Rosseau, the highway passes by the eastern shore of the lake.

Surprise Lake
Surprise Lake can be accessed by snowmobile east of the village of Novar. The lake is stocked periodically with brook trout, which provide good fishing at times for average sized brookies. Success is best through the ice.

Sward Lake
This is a small, remote lake that can be accessed by snowmobile trail east of Livingstone Lake. The lake offers fair fishing at times for small brook trout. Try small silver spoons through the ice and worms or nymph fly patterns in spring.

Tedious Lakes
To reach Tedious Lake, follow Highway 118 to the Kennisis Lake Road (County Road 7) and head north. The Kennisis Lake Road soon passes by the western shore and a boat launch onto Tedious Lake. The lake is stocked annually with lake trout that provide for good fishing at times during the winter months. Ice fishing off shoals with small spoons or light coloured jigs can work quite well. Presenting these lures in the upper level of the lake is your best bet for a lake trout strike through the ice.

Triangle Lake
Triangle Lake is stocked with lake trout every few years and provides slow to fair action during the winter months. The lake is accessible by snowmobile within the heart of the Kawartha Highlands Provincial Park. A GPS unit and a good map such as the Backroad Mapbook for Cottage Country is helpful in locating such a remote lake.

Twelve Mile Lake
See Page 55

Verner Lake
Verner Lake is a remote lake that can be found by following Highway 11 to Highway 592. Just north of the junction, look for the Savage Settlement Road leading east. Continue past Foote Lake Road until you reach a sharp turn about 3 km past the Foote Lake Road. A rough road branches south from this point and leads to the west side of Verner Lake. Most of these roads are not plowed in the winter and a snowmobile is a definite asset to access the lake.

Verner Lake is stocked every few years with brook trout, which provides for good fishing at times for average sized brookies. Fishing is best for brook trout through the ice. Verner Lake is the ideal brook trout lake. It has deep areas for trout to retreat into during the summer solstice as well as plenty of prime shallows for trout to cruise in the winter. Ice anglers should concentrate on the 6 m (20 ft) level for cruising lakers.

Access

Skeleton Lake lies off the north side of Highway 141 between Port Sydney to the east and Lake Rosseau to the west. There are two main access points to the lake, which are both located along the southern shore of the lake. The first is found at the end of Skeleton Lake Road 2, about 2 km north off the highway. The second site can be found right off Highway 141 along the most southerly bay of the big lake. Both access points can be used by snowmobilers in the winter.

Fishing

This big lake is not the most popular lake of the big Muskoka area lakes, but it is very scenic and a pleasure to visit. The lake is home to many cottages as well long stretches of undisturbed shoreline that helps maintain that wilderness feeling when out on the lake.

Fishing pressure over the past few decades has certainly affected the walleye fishery. However, ice fishing can still be fair for the nocturnal fish, as they are best found in winter. Try jigging off one of the many shoals found throughout the lake. To find these shoals, look on the lake depth chart for a significant bottom irregularity in the lakes contour to help increase your success. Often baitfish will congregate near structure, which in turn attracts sportfish such as walleye.

Rainbow trout were stocked in the lake, although there have been few (if any) reports of catches over the past many years. However, there is still a natural population of lake trout found in the lake. Fishing is usually quite slow for this slow growing species. Due to the increased pressure on lake trout in Skeleton Lake, there are special slot size restrictions to help improve spawning success. Other restrictions include only one line being permitted when angling through the ice.

Facilities

Along with the two main public access areas, Skeleton Lake does have a few other areas from which to access the lake. During the summer there are a couple of tent and trailer parks as well as a few cottages for rent. For something different, why not visit the old fish hatchery or Skeleton Lake Trails found at the southwest corner of the lake.

Lake Definition

Elevation: 280 m (920 ft)
Surface Area: 2,155.5 ha (5,326.4 ac)
Perimeter: 36.4 km (22.6 mi)
Way Point: 45° 15' 00" Lat - N
79° 27' 00" Long - W

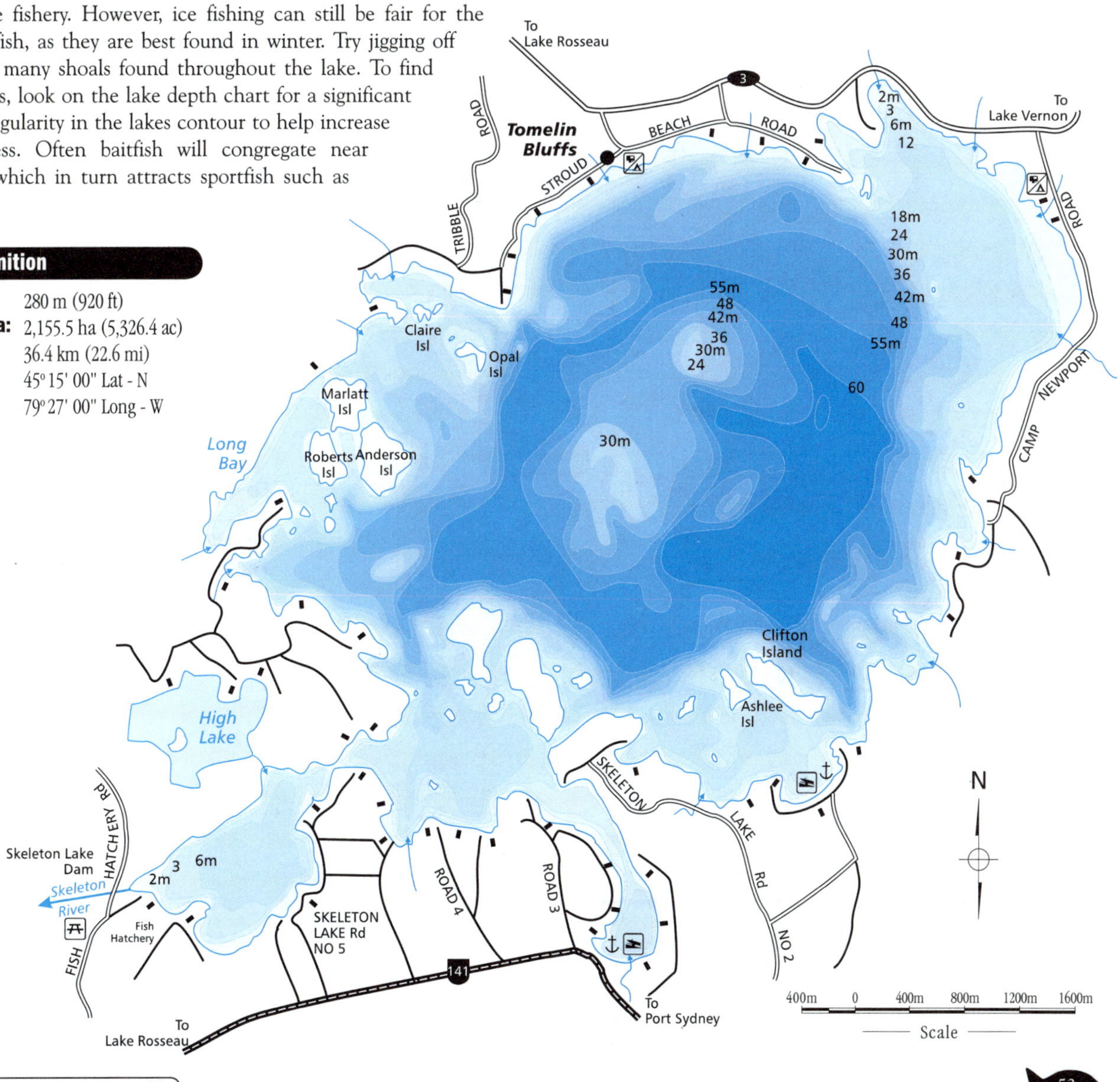

Depth Chart Not Intended for Navigational Use

Access

Highway 35 travels right past the main buildings of the Leslie M. Frost Centre property, which are located along the western shore of St. Nora Lake. It is still possible to access the lake from this area but this may change in the near future if the Frost Centre area is sold. Be sure to check our updates page through www.backroadmapbooks.com for this and any other updates to this book.

Fishing

Anglers visiting St. Nora Lake can expect slow to fair success for natural lake trout. Ice fishing is the most productive method for finding lakers, although early spring just after ice off can also be decent.

Before you head out on St. Nora Lake, please check the provincial fishing regulations as there are slot size restrictions for lake trout and ice fishing limits.

Facilities

St. Nora Lake is a rustic lake that has maintained its wilderness feel despite its close proximity to the highway and the hub of the Frost Centre. Outside of washrooms at the main building and a rustic launching area, there are no facilities available. Supplies can be picked up in the village of Dorset to the north.

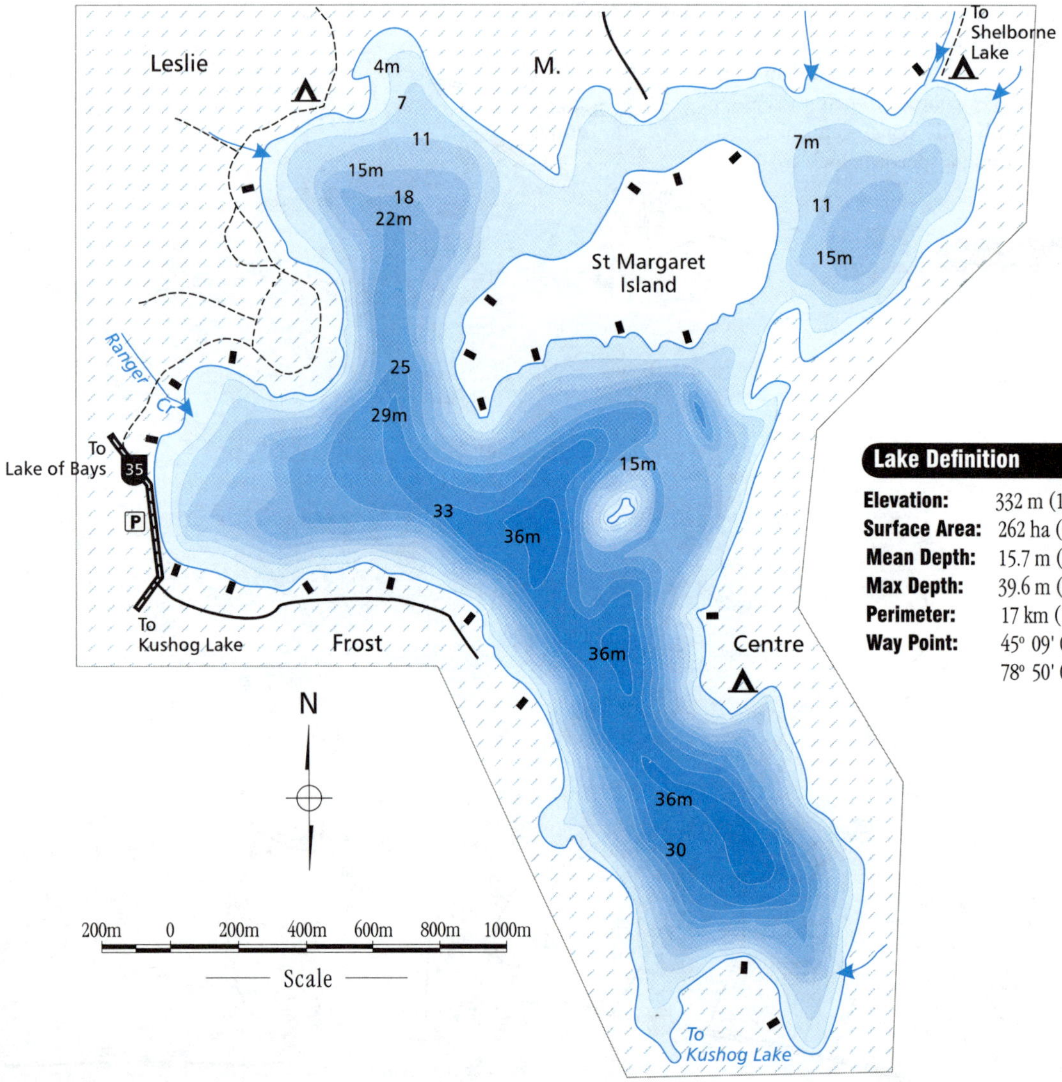

Lake Definition

Elevation:	332 m (1,090ft)
Surface Area:	262 ha (647 ac)
Mean Depth:	15.7 m (51.5 ft)
Max Depth:	39.6 m (130 ft)
Perimeter:	17 km (11 mi)
Way Point:	45° 09' 00" Lat - N 78° 50' 00" Lon - W

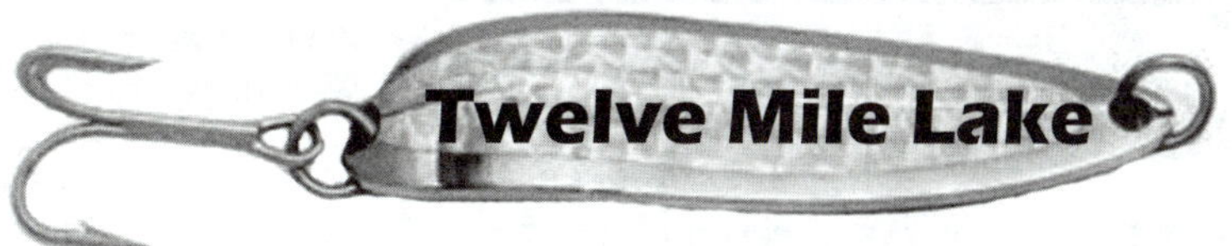

Access

Twelve Mile Lake is found a few minutes north of the town of Minden at the south end of Carnarvon. There are two main access points to the medium size lake, one on its southern end and one along the eastern shore. Both access sites can be reached off Highway 35.

Facilities

Since most of the facilities around this lake close down in winter, area visitors are best to visit the nearby town of Minden for supplies and accommodations. The town is found a short distance to the south and is home to the local Ministry of Natural Resources office.

Fishing

Being so close to the highway, Twelve Mile Lake does receive plenty of angling attention throughout the year. Fishing quality has decreased over the past decade or so but the lake continues to provide consistent results, especially for bass.

Lake trout make up the bulk of the winter fishery and fishing can be fair at times. It is best to focus efforts off shoals in the upper portion of the lake to find lakers. Slot size and special ice fishing restrictions are in place on these lakes to help the natural lake trout species survive. Be sure to check the regulations for details.

Little Boshkung Lake, which is connected to the northwest end of Twelve Mile Lake, offers mainly a summer bass fishery. The odd lake trout is caught in the channel connecting the two lakes in the winter.

Lake Definition

Elevation:	303 m (1,010 ft)
Surface Area:	33 ha (82 ac)
Mean Depth:	11.8 m (39.4 ft)
Max Depth:	27 m (90.0 ft)
Perimeter:	12 km (8 mi)
Way Point:	45° 01' 00" Lat - N 78° 43' 00" Lon - W

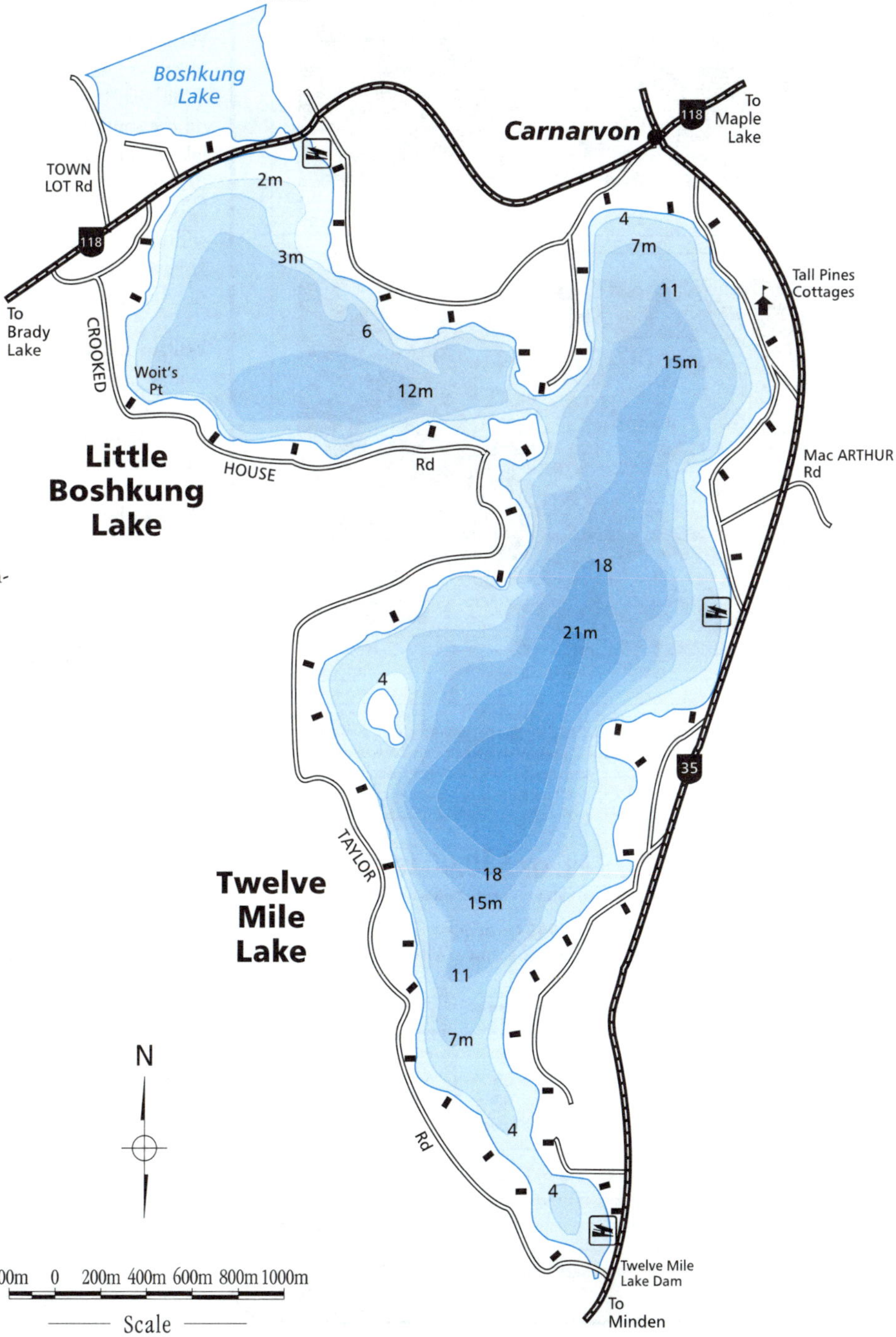

Walker Lakes

Walker Lakes can be found off the Limberlost Road (County Road 8) east of the town of Huntsville. The lake is thought to have a small population of lake trout still available, but there have been few successful reports over the last few years. The lake is now stocked with rainbow trout, which provide for fair fishing at times during the winter.

Weeden Lake

A main snowmobile trail travels between the Seguin Trail and Highway 141 east of Parry Sound. The trail passes by the southern end of Weeden Lake allowing access to this secluded lake that has been stocked over the past few years with brook trout. There are reports of decent fishing success, especially through the ice.

Whitefish Lake

North of Lake Joseph and west of the town of Rosseau, you can find Whitefish Lake just off Highway 141. An access point is available off the southwest side of the highway. Despite the name of the lake, lake trout remain the fish of choice in Whitefish Lake. Although fishing success is quite slow, it is a natural strain of lake trout. Your best bet at catching one of these elusive lakers is to try during winter. Be sure to check the regulations before fishing Whitefish Lake as there are slot size restrictions and special ice fishing regulations on the lake.

Wilbur Lake

Wilbur Lake is accessible by snowmobile south of Oxtongue Lake and east of Huntsville. The lake is stocked every few years with brook trout. Fishing for brookies to 30 cm (12 in) is good through the ice in winter.

Wolf Lake

Wolf Lake is found in the Haliburton Forest Reserve and is a nice place to wet a line. The lake is stocked with splake periodically and fishing for stocked splake can be good during the winter. For directions to the lake, inquire with the Haliburton Forest Reserve. The reserve also offers overnight accommodations such as rooms at their lodge or cabin rentals.

Wood Lake

Wood Lake is a popular Cottage Country lake that can be accessed from a few different 2wd roads off Highway 118 east of Bracebridge. In winter, the lake offers slow to fair fishing for walleye and panfish. Walleye average 0.5-1 kg (1-2 lbs), although can be found up to 3.5 kg (8 lbs).

Wren Lakes

Wren Lake lies within the Leslie M. Frost Centre and can be reached by following Highway 35 north past the Frost Centre administration buildings. The lake lies off the west side of the highway and it is possible to launch a snowmobile at the side of the highway.

Wren Lake was originally named Three Mile Lake, although with the popularity of the 'Three Mile Lake' name, the name of the lake was changed to Wren Lake in 1939. Over the past few decades, fishing quality has improved significantly on this lake. Splake are heavily stocked and provide for good fishing at times. The brook trout/lake trout hybrid is quite active during winter. Spoons and flashy spinners are the best choice for finding splake through the ice.

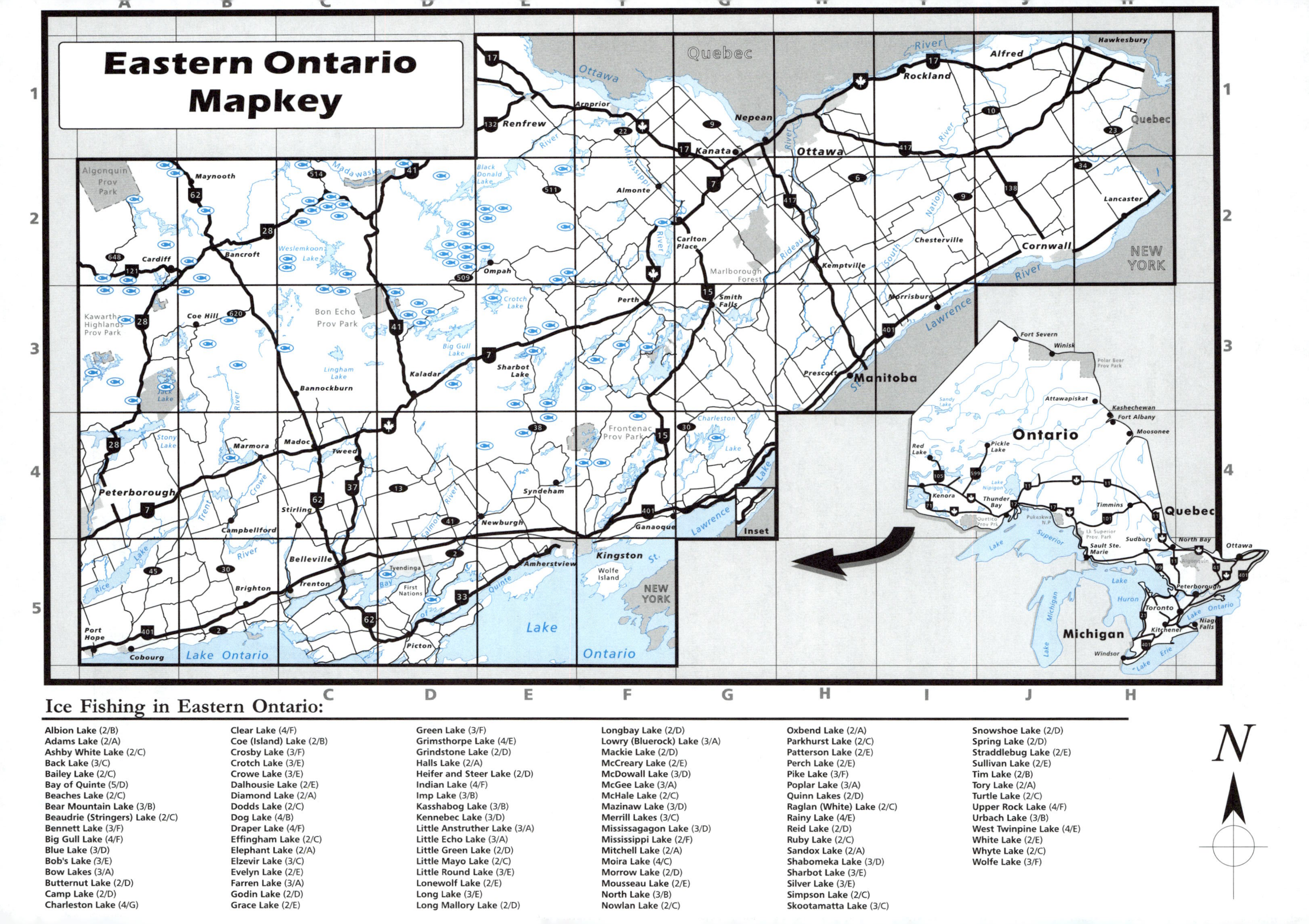

Ice Fishing in Eastern Ontario:

Albion Lake (2/B)
Adams Lake (2/A)
Ashby White Lake (2/C)
Back Lake (3/C)
Bailey Lake (2/C)
Bay of Quinte (5/D)
Beaches Lake (2/C)
Bear Mountain Lake (3/B)
Beaudrie (Stringers) Lake (2/C)
Bennett Lake (3/F)
Big Gull Lake (4/F)
Blue Lake (3/D)
Bob's Lake (3/E)
Bow Lakes (3/A)
Butternut Lake (2/D)
Camp Lake (2/D)
Charleston Lake (4/G)
Clear Lake (4/F)
Coe (Island) Lake (2/B)
Crosby Lake (3/F)
Crotch Lake (3/E)
Crowe Lake (3/E)
Dalhousie Lake (2/E)
Diamond Lake (2/A)
Dodds Lake (2/C)
Dog Lake (4/B)
Draper Lake (4/F)
Effingham Lake (2/C)
Elephant Lake (2/A)
Elzevir Lake (3/C)
Evelyn Lake (2/E)
Farren Lake (3/A)
Godin Lake (2/D)
Grace Lake (2/E)
Green Lake (3/F)
Grimsthorpe Lake (4/E)
Grindstone Lake (2/D)
Halls Lake (2/A)
Heifer and Steer Lake (2/D)
Indian Lake (4/F)
Imp Lake (3/B)
Kasshabog Lake (3/B)
Kennebec Lake (3/D)
Little Anstruther Lake (3/A)
Little Echo Lake (3/A)
Little Green Lake (2/D)
Little Mayo Lake (2/C)
Little Round Lake (3/E)
Lonewolf Lake (2/E)
Long Lake (3/E)
Long Mallory Lake (2/D)
Longbay Lake (2/D)
Lowry (Bluerock) Lake (3/A)
Mackie Lake (2/D)
McCreary Lake (2/E)
McDowall Lake (3/D)
McGee Lake (3/A)
McHale Lake (2/C)
Mazinaw Lake (3/D)
Merrill Lakes (3/C)
Mississagagon Lake (3/D)
Mississippi Lake (2/F)
Mitchell Lake (2/A)
Moira Lake (4/C)
Morrow Lake (2/D)
Mousseau Lake (2/E)
North Lake (3/B)
Nowlan Lake (2/C)
Oxbend Lake (2/A)
Parkhurst Lake (2/C)
Patterson Lake (2/E)
Perch Lake (2/E)
Pike Lake (3/F)
Poplar Lake (3/A)
Quinn Lakes (2/D)
Raglan (White) Lake (2/C)
Rainy Lake (4/E)
Reid Lake (2/D)
Ruby Lake (2/C)
Sandox Lake (2/A)
Shabomeka Lake (3/D)
Sharbot Lake (3/E)
Silver Lake (3/E)
Simpson Lake (2/C)
Skootamatta Lake (3/C)
Snowshoe Lake (2/D)
Spring Lake (2/D)
Straddlebug Lake (2/E)
Sullivan Lake (2/E)
Tim Lake (2/B)
Tory Lake (2/A)
Turtle Lake (2/C)
Upper Rock Lake (4/F)
Urbach Lake (3/B)
West Twinpine Lake (4/E)
White Lake (2/E)
Whyte Lake (2/C)
Wolfe Lake (3/F)

Albion Lake

Albion Lake is found west of Bancroft and offers good fishing at times for decent sized splake. Splake are stocked in the lake every few years and are best found through the ice. Try jigging small silver spoons for productive results. Inquire locally in Bancroft for more detailed directions to the lake.

Adams Lake

This semi-secluded lake can be found on foot or snowmobile south off Highway 121 west of Cardiff. The lake is stocked periodically with brook trout and offers good fishing at times in winter for nice sized brook trout.

Ashby White Lake

Visitors will find a few camps along the shoreline of this lake, which is found just south off Highway 28 west of Denbigh. The lake is stocked every few years with lake trout, which provide for fair fishing at times through the ice.

Back Lake

Back Lake is a small lake that is mainly accessed during the winter via snowmobile. The lake is stocked every few years with splake and fishing is often quite good through the ice for nice sized splake. The lake lies west of the boundary of Bon Echo Provincial Park. Please consult the Backroad Mapbook for Eastern Ontario to find the best route into the lake.

Bailey Lake

This small, secluded lake is stocked every few years with brook trout. Fishing is good through the ice for average sized brook trout. Look for the lake south of Ashby White Lake.

Bay of Quinte

See Pages 60-61

Beeches and Beaudrie (Stringers) Lake

Best accessed by snowmobile or on foot from Highway 28 east of Bancroft, these lakes are stocked every few years with brook trout. Be sure not to trespass, as some areas near these lakes are private lands. Some big brookies are caught regularly, especially at Beaudrie Lake. Ice fishing close to shore or other shallow structure can be very effective.

Bear Mountain Lake

As a remote access lake, Bear Mountain Lake is probably never visited except during winter by snowmobilers. The small lake is stocked every few years with brook trout and offers very good fishing through the ice. The lake lies south of the small village of Coe Hill. A Backroad Mapbook for Eastern Ontario is recommended to find access details to the lake.

Bennett Lake

Bennett Lake is a long, narrow lake that lies just west of the town of Perth. From Highway 7 west of Perth, look for County Road 36. Follow County Road 36 north to County Road 19 (Bennett Lake Road). Bennett Lake Road travels east passing by numerous cottage access roads along the northern length of the lake.

Ice fishing is a popular winter activity on Bennett Lake as numerous huts are found on the lake each year. Walleye, perch and northern pike can be found through the ice. Try a small jig, tipped with a minnow or worm. If you plan to keep your walleye, there is a minimum length limit of 41 cm (16 in) in place on Bennett Lake to help aid reproduction rates. Always consult the regulations for current restriction information.

Big Gull Lake

See Page 59

Blue Lake

Blue Lake is found just to the east of Mississagagon Lake and is stocked every few years with splake. To reach the lake, take Highway 506 east off Highway 41 and look for the Blue Lake Road off the north side. Fishing for splake can be good at times, especially through the ice. Some nice sized splake are regularly caught in this lake.

Bob's Lake

To reach the eastern basin of Bob's Lake, travel along Highway 7 to County Road 36 near the village of Maberly. Head south along County Road 36 to the village of Balingbroke, where you can find the far eastern tip of the lake. Branching west are the Crowe Lake and the Long Bay Roads. Crowe Lake Road provides access to the northern portion of the east basin, while the Long Bay Road has numerous branches that lead to the southern shore of the east basin.

Bob's Lake is inhabited by smallmouth bass, largemouth bass, northern pike, walleye and lake trout. Since bass are inactive in the winter, the primary species ice anglers are after are walleye and lake trout. Fishing for both species is regarded as fair to slow throughout the season. This is despite the aggressive stocking program in place for lake trout. Northern pike fishing can be a little better for fish that can be found to 3.5 kg (8 lbs) on occasion.

Bow Lakes

The Bow Lakes are two very small lakes that are stocked with splake every few years. Fishing for splake can be fairly consistent in the winter for generally small fish. Access to the lakes is limited to snowmobile just east of Jack Lake south of the town of Apsley.

Butternut Lake

A small, secluded lake, Butternut is found at the end of a snowmobile accessible road northwest of the village of Ompah. The lake is stocked every few years with brook trout that can result in good fishing, especially through the ice.

Camp Lake

This remote lake is only accessible by snowmobile trail from Mackie Lake north of the village of Plevna. Fishing for stocked lake trout is fair through the ice. Try jigging a small spoon or even a white jig for active lakers during the winter.

Fishing

Sometimes referred to as Clarendon Lake, Big Gull Lake is found to the southeast of Bon Echo Provincial Park. It is a popular cottage destination lake that is inhabited with smallmouth bass, largemouth bass, northern pike and walleye. The big lake is quite scenic and it receives significant angling pressure throughout the year.

Ice Fishing is one of the more productive times of the year to fish with northern pike and walleye roaming the big lake. Some large pike and on occasion walleye are caught through the ice. Anglers will more often find both species in the shallower sections of the lake as well as cruising along island areas at times. Jigging along these structure areas can entice some big strikes.

Access

To reach the lake, follow Highway 7 to the Harlowe Henderson Road located at the yellow flashing light near Arden. Head north along this side road and look for the Veley Road off the east side. Veley Road leads to a couple of public launching areas. If you continue west along the Harlowe Henderson Road, you will pass by the access road to Earls Bay where another boat launching area and small marina are located.

Visitors wishing to access the east side of the lake can follow the Coxvale Clarendon Road to a launching area near the dam at Coxvale. Following Highway 509 can reach the Coxvale Clarendon Road north from Highway 7 at Sharbot Lake. Snowmobilers use the various launch areas in winter.

Facilities

A number of cottages and tourist operators are located around Big Gull Lake. However, most of them close down for the winter. The lake is also home to four public boat launches that provide good access to different bays on the big lake.

Lake Definition

Elevation:	253.3 m (831 ft)
Surface Area:	2,364.4 ha (5,840 ac)
Mean Depth:	4 m (12.9 ft)
Max Depth:	26 m (85 ft)
Perimeter:	88.5 km (55 mi)
Way Point:	44° 50' 00" Lat - N 76° 58' 00" Lon - W

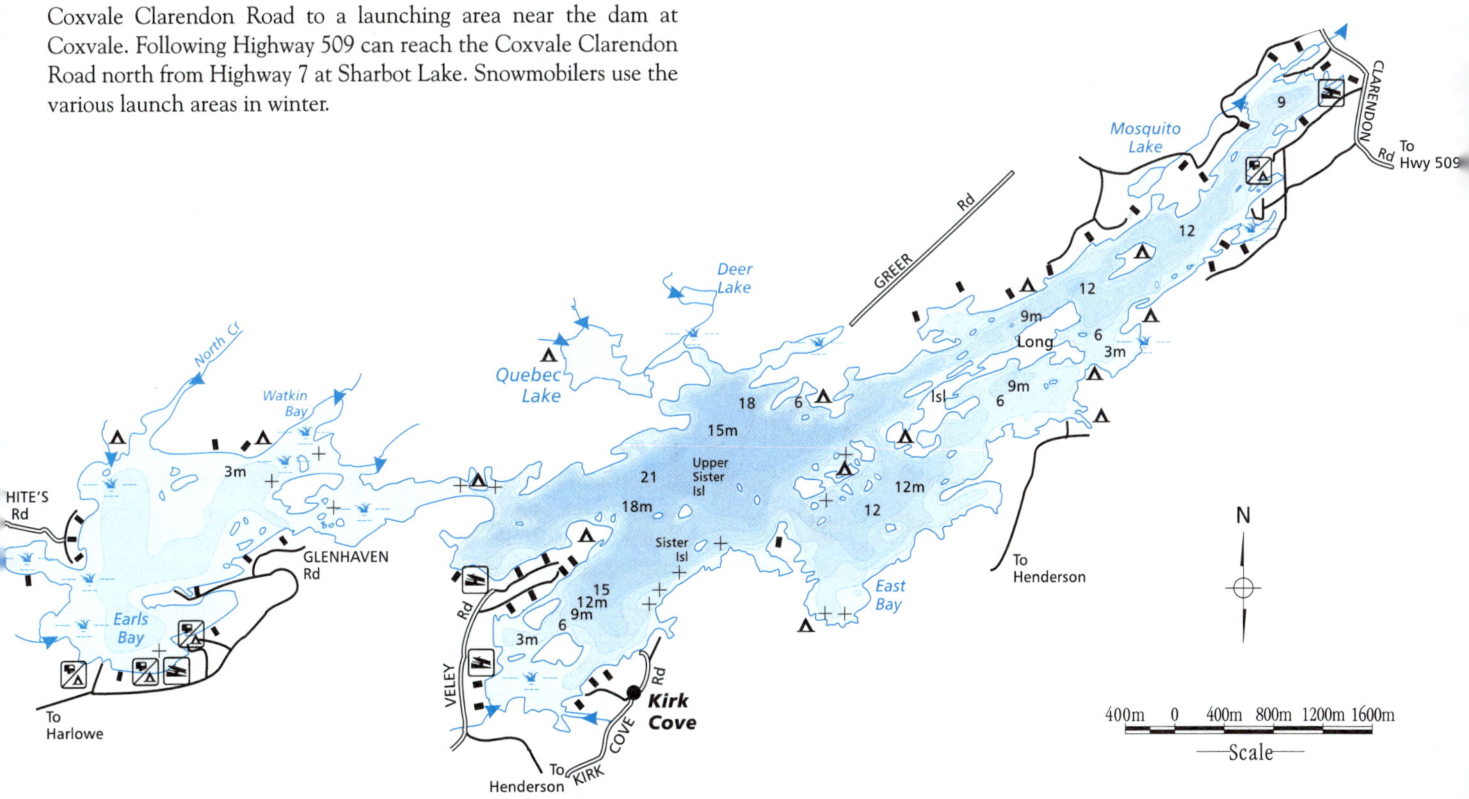

Access

Forming the start of the fabled Trent Severn Waterway, the Bay of Quinte is a large, inland portion of the much bigger Lake Ontario. One of the most scenic portions of the bay is found around the town of Picton. Picton is an original loyalist community that is easy to find along Highway 33 southwest of Belleville. Highway 33 is essentially the eastern extension of Highway 62, which begins in Belleville.

Closer to Highway 401, the northern stretch of the bay can be found around the town of Trenton or the city of Belleville. The launching area in Belleville is near the northwest side of the Bay Bridge in the southern core of the city. The main access areas in Trenton are located south of the town off the east side of County Road 33.

Further to the east you will encounter what is known as the Big Bay, this portion of the Bay of Quinte is also accessed from the city of Belleville. There are also other access areas around Big Island and near the settlements of Northport.

Lake Definition

Mean Depth:	7.8 m (25.7 ft)
Max Depth:	15.2 m (50 ft)
Way Point:	44° 09' 00" Lat - N 77° 15' 00" Lon - W

Fishing

The Bay of Quinte is synonymous with sport fishing. The bay has long been home to fine catches of everything from panfish and bass to northern pike. But every year anglers flock to the bay in search of the fabled walleye fishing. Since so many anglers visit the Bay of Quinte for its walleye, species such as pike and panfish are often overlooked and can be a lot of fun to catch.

The bay around the Picton area is not as popular as some of the other regions despite the fact that the fishing remains productive. Fishing for walleye can be good at times, but success is usually better for panfish such as crappie and perch. Northern pike are also readily available and are often picked up when fishing for walleye.

Due to the easy access to the Trenton portion of the Bay of Quinte, this area is probably the most popular section of the bay. Fishing for walleye can be productive throughout the season, as the shallow, weedy nature of this portion of the Bay of Quinte provides a good source of habitat. Some big northern pike can also be found almost

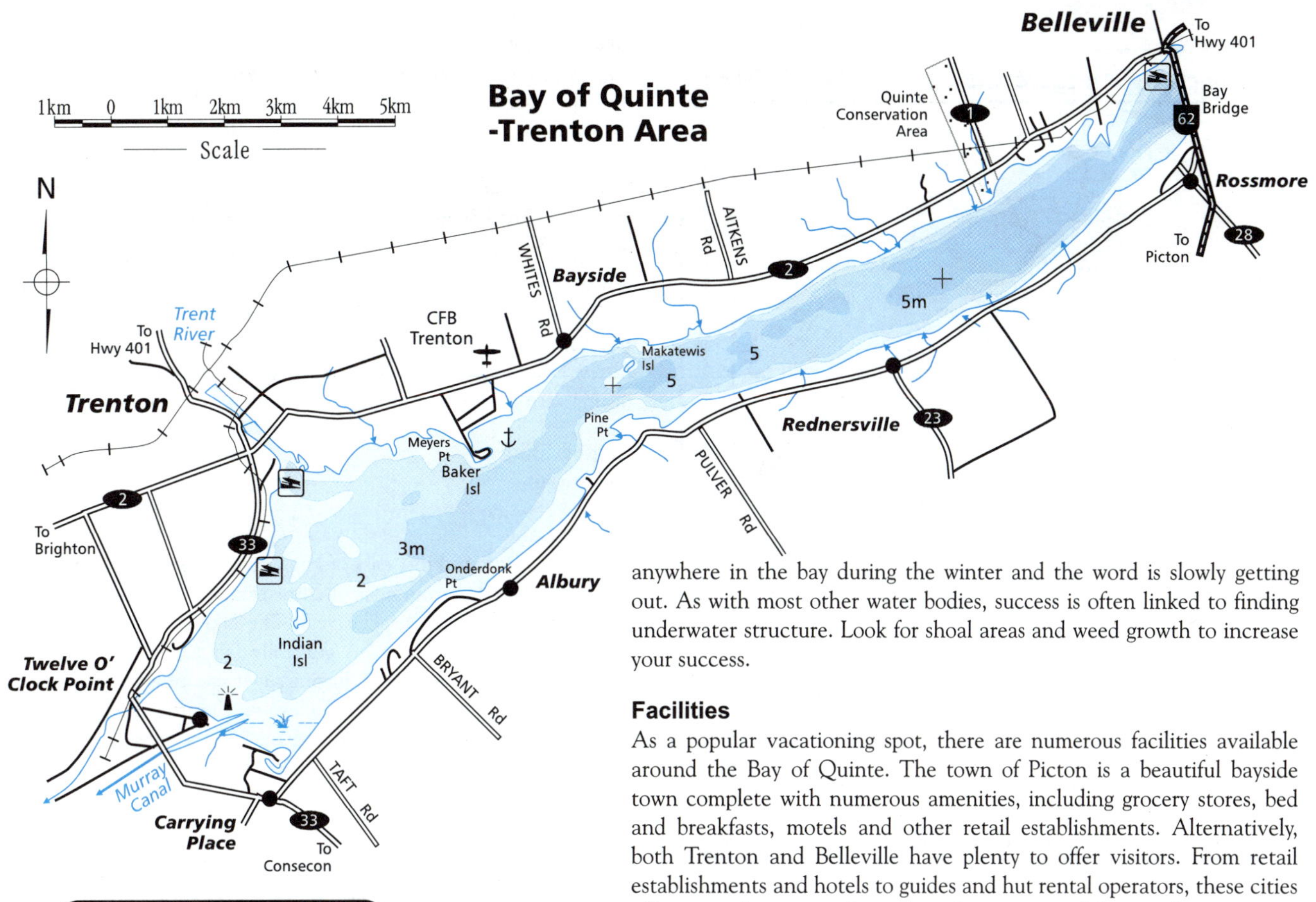

Bay of Quinte -Trenton Area

Lake Definition

Mean Depth: 3.3 m (11 ft)
Max Depth: 4.5 m (15 ft)
Way Point: 44º 09' 00" Lat - N
77º 26' 00" Lon - W

anywhere in the bay during the winter and the word is slowly getting out. As with most other water bodies, success is often linked to finding underwater structure. Look for shoal areas and weed growth to increase your success.

Facilities

As a popular vacationing spot, there are numerous facilities available around the Bay of Quinte. The town of Picton is a beautiful bayside town complete with numerous amenities, including grocery stores, bed and breakfasts, motels and other retail establishments. Alternatively, both Trenton and Belleville have plenty to offer visitors. From retail establishments and hotels to guides and hut rental operators, these cities offer everything an angler will need to enjoy ice fishing in the area.

Those visitors looking to get away from the cities will find a few other areas and marinas that provide access to the big bay. Snowmobiles can usually be launched from the boat launch areas outside of the city.

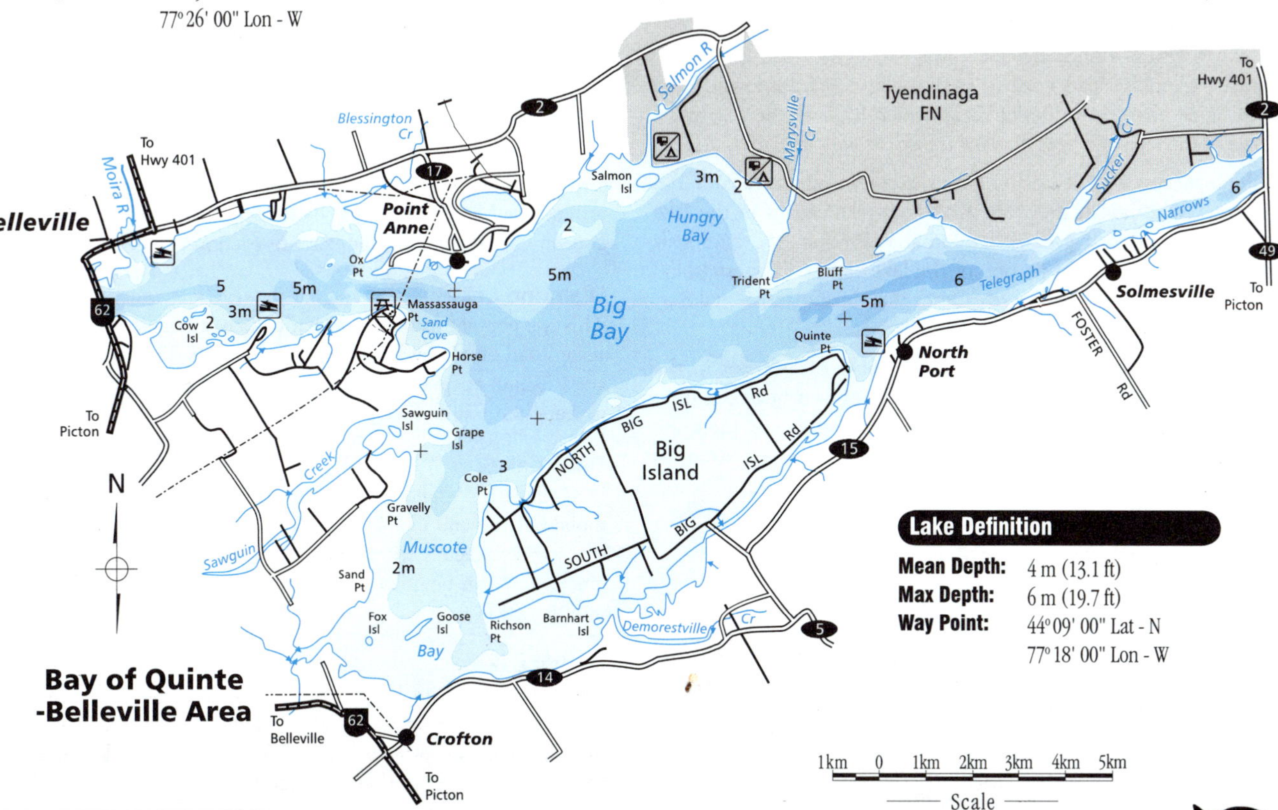

Lake Definition

Mean Depth: 4 m (13.1 ft)
Max Depth: 6 m (19.7 ft)
Way Point: 44º 09' 00" Lat - N
77º 18' 00" Lon - W

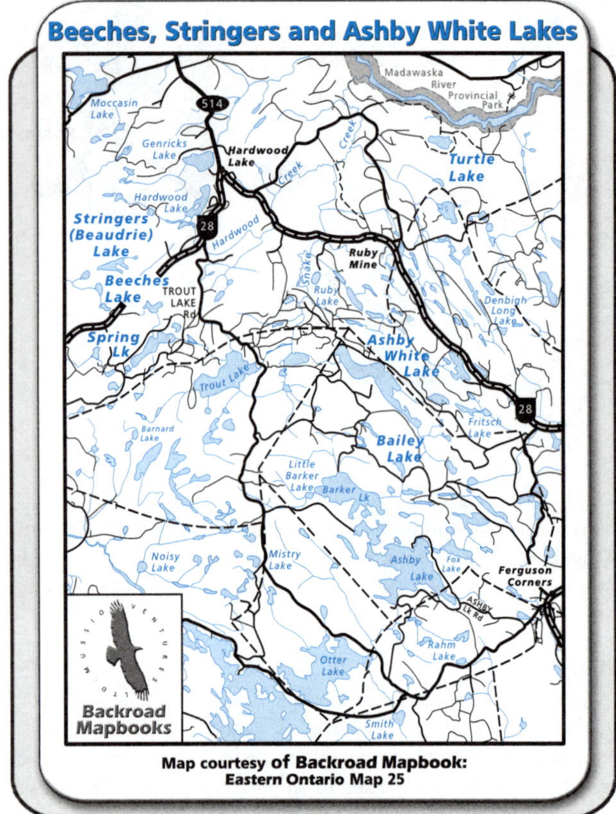

Map courtesy of Backroad Mapbook: Eastern Ontario Map 25

Charleston Lake

Located northeast of the town of Gananoque, this big lake is a popular spot during the summer months. It is not nearly as busy in the winter but the close proximity to the United States border crossing and the cities of Ottawa and Kingston still makes it worth mentioning. The easiest way to find the lake is to travel along Highway 401 to exit 659 and Prince Reynolds Road (County Road 3). Follow Prince Reynolds Road north past the village of Lansdowne. The road name changes to Outlet Road, which leads to the southwest shore of the lake and the Charleston Lake Provincial Park.

Fishing success for Charleston Lake's northern pike is regarded as fair to slow, although there are good sized pike caught in the lake annually. Jigging a bigger jig around the two 3 m (10 ft) shoals located in the southern portion of the lake east of Croziers Island can entice northern pike strikes. Other than pike, panfish make up most of the action on Charleston Lake in winter.

If you happen to hook into one of the stocked lake trout in the winter months it must be thrown back. Before you head out onto Charleston Lake, be sure to check your regulations, as there are specific restrictions on the type of baitfish that are permitted for angling use.

Clear Lake

See Page 63

Coe (Island) Lake

Coe Lake is located southwest of Bancroft not far from Highway 28. The lake offers good fishing for stocked splake. Ice fishing and early spring fishing can be quite productive for this sportfish.

Crosby Lake

Crosby Lake lies to the northwest of the town of Westport. The easiest way to access the lake is to travel along Highway 7 to County Road 36 just east of Silver Lake Provincial Park. Follow County Road 36 south past Bolingbroke to the Althorpe Road or further south to the Big Crosby Road. Both roads branch off the east side of County Road 36 and provide access to Crosby Lake.

This popular lake offers ice fishing opportunities for panfish, northern pike and walleye. For walleye seekers, there are a number of shoal areas around the lake that can attract this aggressive predator. An area in particular that is regarded as a hot spot is around the two shoal humps located in the southern tip of the lake. Try still jigging with coloured jigs for cruising walleye and northern pike.

Crotch Lake

See Page 65

Crowe Lake

Crowe Lake is found just east of Highway 38, southeast of Sharbot Lake. The lake has a number of cottages along its shoreline and is heavily fished throughout the year. The lake is stocked annually with lake trout and fishing is generally fair for lakers, especially early in the ice fishing season. Jigging silver spoons is often an effective method in finding lakers. Walleye and northern pike are also present in the lake although fishing for both species can be quite slow at times. Access to the lake is via Crowe Lake Road off Highway 38.

Dalhousie Lake

To find Dalhousie Lake, follow Highway 7 to Maberly Elphin Road (County Road 36) east of Sharbot Lake. Head north along the Maberly Elphin Road to the junction with Corners Road (County Road 12). Corners Road travels east passing by a number of local access roads to the lake.

Fishing pressure in Dalhousie Lake is consistent, however, anglers can still have decent success throughout the year. During the winter, there is currently a two month ice fishing season that enables anglers to try their luck through the ice for walleye, northern pike and other panfish. For success, try jigging a white jig tipped with a worm or even a small spoon to attract walleye or pike into striking. To help protect walleye stocks, there is a special sanctuary around the Mississippi River where it enters Dalhousie Lake. Please consult your regulations for exact restrictions.

Diamond Lake

This is a popular fishing lake that can be accessed by the Diamond Lake Road off Highway 648 north of Cardiff. The lake offers fair to good fishing at times for lake trout. Lakers are stocked in the lake and are best found through the ice.

Dixie Lake

Dixie Lake is a small, secluded lake that can be accessed via snowmobile at the end of the West Lane off Highway 648. The lake is stocked periodically with brook trout and fishing for brookies to 30 cm (12 in) can be good during ice fishing season or in spring just after ice off.

Dodds Lake

Found to the east of Ireland Road, this small lake is best accessed by snowmobile or on foot. Be sure not to trespass, as some areas near the lake are private lands. Dodds Lake is stocked every few years with brook trout that are often active during the winter.

Clear Lake

Fishing

As a part of the Rideau River Waterway, Clear Lake does experience significant boating traffic throughout the summer months. Although the lake is heavily fished, the fishing remains relatively good. The main sportfish ice fishing anglers can expect to find are northern pike and walleye.

Walleye in Clear Lake are definitely the hardest sportfish to find on a consistent basis. The best way to locate these predators is to sit off one of the many shoal humps found around the lake and jig not far off bottom. The shoal area located in the eastern middle section of the lake is a good spot to try to find cruising walleye. The shoal is shallow enough to enhance baitfish activity and eventually predatory fish activity like walleye. Many anglers looking for walleye do not even go out onto the lake during the winter until almost dark. As with most walleye producing lakes, this species is almost nocturnal in nature, with increased feeding as evening sets in.

Access

Clear Lake is part of the Rideau River Waterway and is located between Indian Lake to the south and Newboro Lake to the north. The best route to the lake by vehicle is by taking Highway 15 to Chaffey's Lock Road (County Road 9). Follow Chaffey's Lock Road southwest and look for Garrett Road off the north side. After a short trek north along Garrett Road, you will pass Clear Lake Road, which heads west to the shoreline of Clear Lake.

Facilities

There are several cottages and lodges along Clear Lake, many of which can be rented. Inquire locally for rental opportunities. For basic supplies, the village of Newboro is located to the north of Clear Lake off County Road 36.

Lake Definition

Mean Depth: 16.1 m (53 ft)
Max Depth: 33.5 m (110 ft)
Way Point: 44° 36' 00" Lat - N
76° 18' 00" Lon - W

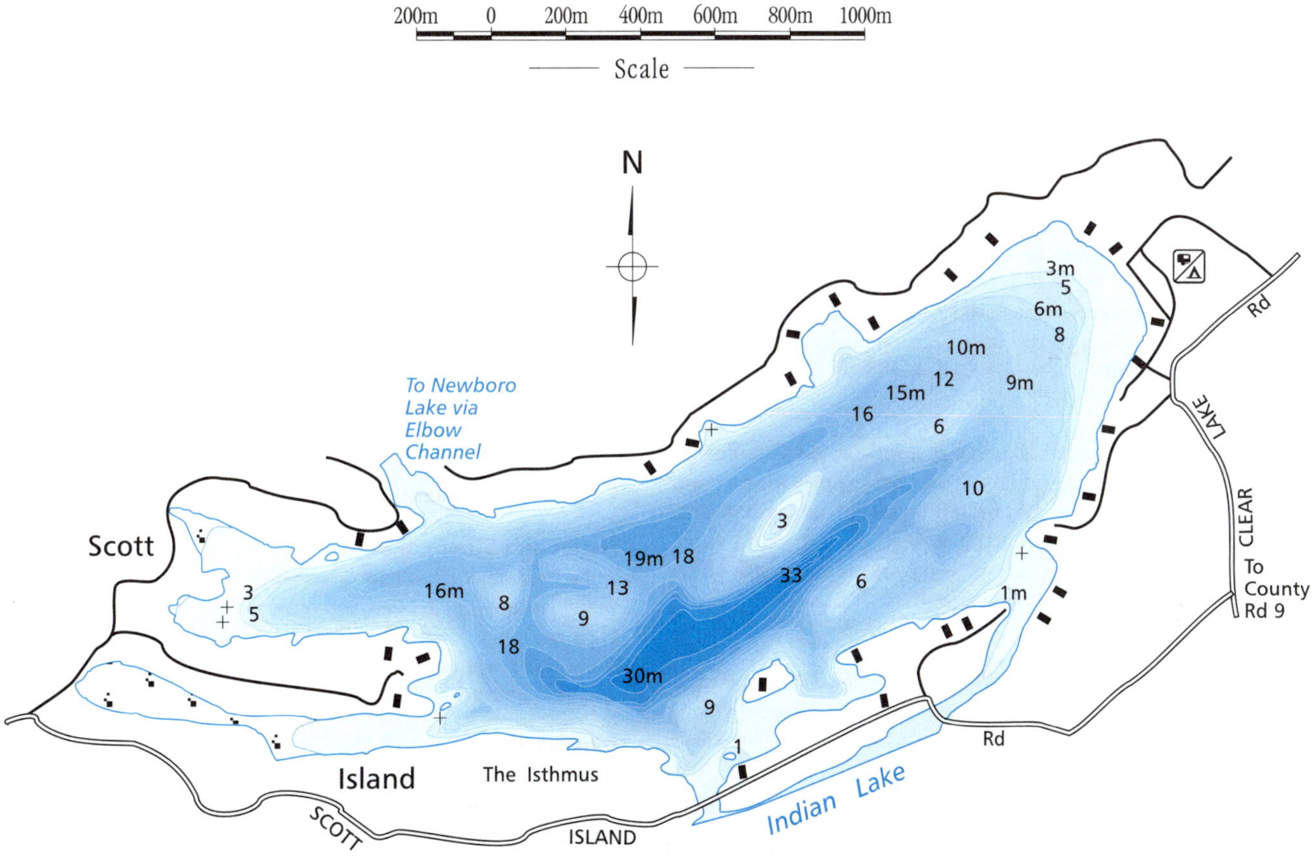

200m 0 200m 400m 600m 800m 1000m
Scale

N
To Newboro Lake via Elbow Channel
Scott Island
The Isthmus
Scott Island Rd
Indian Lake
Clear Lake Rd
To County Rd 9

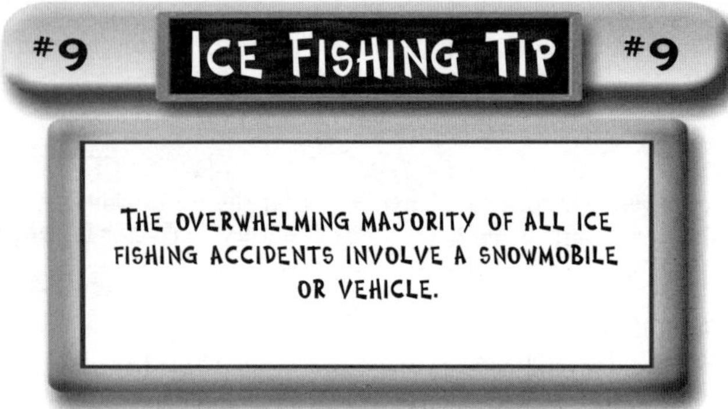

Dog Lake

Dog Lake can be found not far off County Road 11, north of the City of Kingston. The lake was once a productive lake trout fishery, although over fishing has resulted in the extinction of the species from the lake. Today, the lake is stocked annually with splake, which provide for fair fishing through the ice and in spring just after ice off. Northern pike are harder to find, however, there are some good-sized pike in the lake.

Draper Lake

Draper Lake is found not far west of County Road 10. The lake is stocked annually with splake, which provide for fair to good fishing at times through the ice. Northern pike also exist in the lake, although they can be hard to find at times.

Effingham Lake

This large lake is located north of Bon Echo Provincial Park and can be accessed by rough road/snowmobile trail west of Highway 41. A natural population of lake trout remains in the lake, although fishing is merely fair through the ice and during early spring. Watch for special restrictions on lake trout and please practice catch and release.

Elephant Lake

Elephant Lake is one of the larger lakes in the area and is a popular cottage destination lake. The lake is popular in the summer for bass fishing, but during the winter anglers can enjoy fair fishing for walleye that average 1 kg (2 lbs). Muskellunge also inhabit the lake, although finding musky through the ice can be a challenge. Access to the lake is via the Elephant Lake Road off Highway 648 north of the village of Cardiff.

Elzevir Lake

Elzevir Lake is a secluded lake that is mainly accessed during the winter by snowmobile. The lake is stocked every few years with splake, which provide for good fishing, especially through the ice in winter. Try jigging a small white jig or small silver spoon to attract hungry splake. The lake is accessible via a rustic trail south off the Lingham Lake Road east of Bannockburn.

Evelyn Lake

This small, remote lake is stocked every few years with brook trout. Fishing in the lakes is good through the ice for generally small brookies. Access to the lakes is via snowmobile north of the village of Ompah.

Farren Lake

Farren Lake is stocked annually with splake, which provide for good fishing at times, especially through the ice. A small population of northern pike is also found in the lake. Farren Lake can be reached via Highway 36 north of the village of Westport.

Godin Lake

Godin Lake can be accessed only by snowmobile in winter. The lake is stocked every year with brook trout, which results in a good fishing lake. Brookies are most aggressive in winter and spring. Try a small spoon in the shallows when ice fishing.

Grace Lake

This small, remote lake is stocked every few years with brook trout. Fishing in the lakes is good through the ice for generally small brookies. Access to the lakes is via snowmobile north of the village of Ompah.

Green Lake

This lake is stocked annually with brook trout, which provide for fair to good fishing through the ice. Trout average 20-30 cm (8-12 in) in size, although larger brookies are caught occasionally. Northern pike are rumoured to also exist in the lake, although this report seems a little odd since brookies are stocked in the lake. Access can be found off the Lavant-Darling Road south of Calabogie Lake.

Grimsthorpe Lake

Accessible by a very rough 4wd road, this lake lies west of Bon Echo Provincial Park just off the power line road south of the Merrill Lakes. The lake offers slow to fair fishing for natural lake trout. Be sure to practice catch and release for this threatened Eastern Ontario fish species. Also watch for slot size and special restrictions on these trout.

Grindstone Lake

To find Grindstone Lake, begin by travelling along Highway 7 to the junction with Highway 509 just north of Sharbot Lake. Travel north along Highway 509 past the villages of Danaldson and Ompah then look for Mountain Road off the north side of the highway. Follow Mountain Road north to the Grindstone Lake Road and turn east. The Grindstone Lake Road heads northeast all the way to the southern shore of Grindstone Lake.

Splake are stocked annually and provide for fair fishing. Jigging a small spoon or jig can be effective for brook trout/lake trout hybrid through the ice.

Halls Lake

Halls Lake is a small, secluded lake that is stocked with brook trout every few years. Fishing for small brookies can be good during ice fishing season or in spring after ice off. There is a live fish bait ban on the lake, which is accessible via snowmobile east of the settlement of Wilberforce. Using a Backroad Mapbook for Eastern Ontario will help immensely in finding this lake.

Heifer and Steer Lake

These two small lakes that are stocked with brook trout every few years. Fishing for brookies is often good for trout in the 25+ cm (10+ in) range. Ice fishing is popular. The lakes can be accessed via snowmobile just northwest of the much larger Black Donald Lake and are surrounded by Crown Land.

Indian Lake

Indian Lake is located between Kingston and Smiths Falls and is a part of the Rideau River Waterway. To reach the lake, follow Highway 15 north from Highway 401 or south from Smiths Falls to Opinicon Road (County Road 9), south of Crosby. Follow the Opinicon Road southwest and look for Indian Lake off the north

Crotch Lake

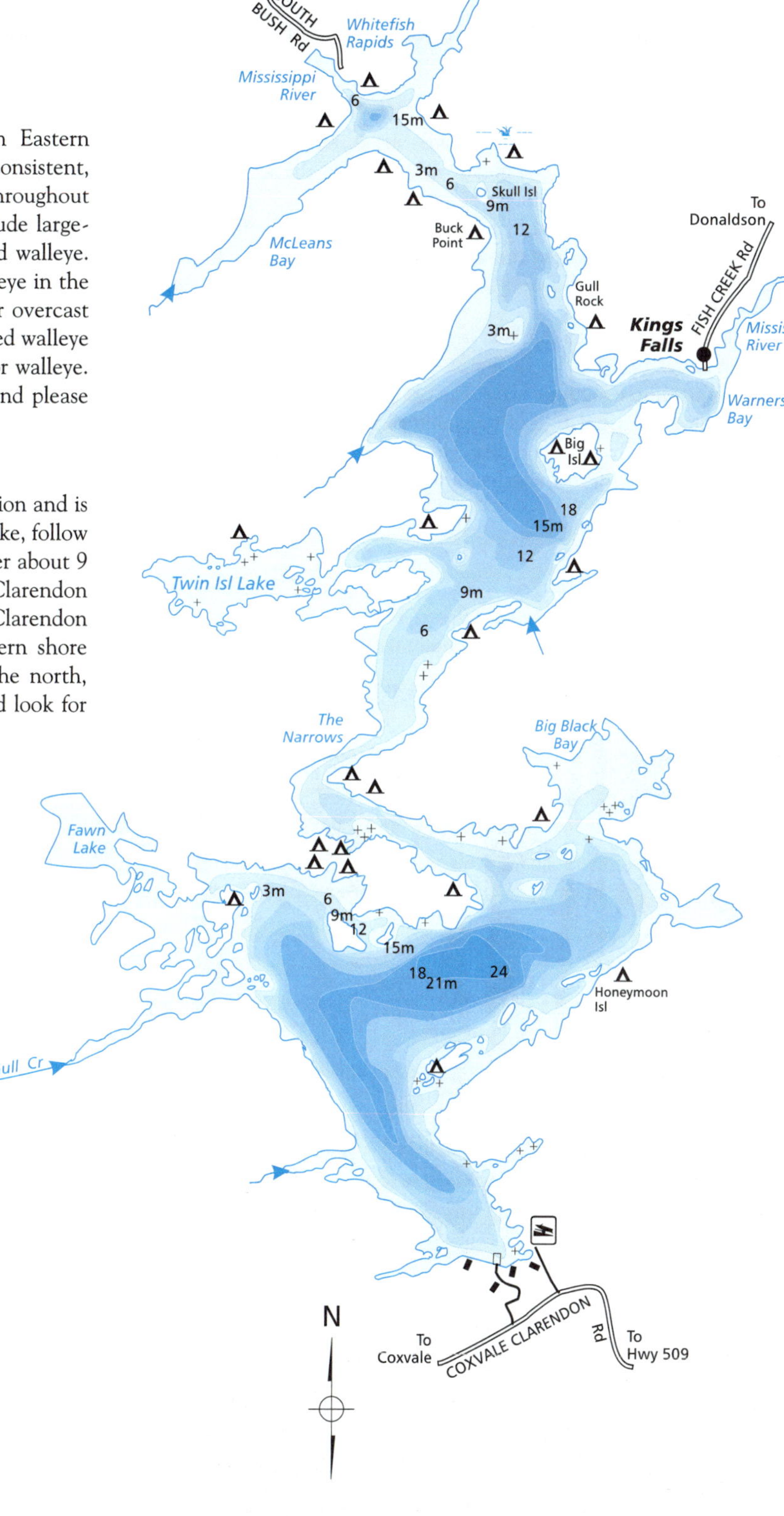

Fishing

Crotch Lake is a popular destination lake in Eastern Ontario. Fishing pressure in the lake is consistent, although anglers can still have good success throughout the year. Sportfish resident in Crotch Lake include largemouth bass, smallmouth bass, northern pike and walleye. Anglers looking to catch northern pike and walleye in the winter will have the best success during dusk or overcast periods by jigging off shoal areas. To help pressured walleye stocks, a special slot size regulation is in place for walleye. Consult your regulations for exact restrictions and please practise catch and release.

Access

Crotch Lake is one of the largest lakes in the region and is located northwest of Sharbot Lake. To find the lake, follow Highway 7 to Highway 509 and head north. After about 9 km (5.5 mi) along Highway 509, look for the Clarendon Road off the west side. Travel west along the Clarendon Road approximately 8 km (5 mi) to the southern shore of Crotch Lake. To access Crotch Lake from the north, follow Highway 509 to the village of Ompah and look for the South Bush Road. The South Bush Road is a rougher road that winds its way to the northern end of the lake.

Facilities

There are a few camps and several rustic campsites on Crotch Lake, although neither option is readily available to the ice fisher. Some anglers launch their snowmobile from the boat launch area at the south end of the lake and head out on the lake with a portable hut and supplies.

Lake Definition

Elevation:	240 m (787 ft)
Surface Area:	1,678 ha (4,145 ac)
Mean Depth:	8.4 m (27.6 ft)
Max Depth:	31.1 m (102 ft)
Perimeter:	69.7 km (43.3 mi)
Way Point:	44° 55' 00" Lat - N 76° 48' 00" Lon - W

500m 0 1km 2km 3km

Scale

side near Chaffey's Lock.

Splake are stocked in Indian Lake annually and provide for fair fishing throughout the winter months or in the spring just after ice off. During winter, try working small spoons or jigs aside drop-off areas or shoals. In the spring, trolling silver or gold spoons are the most effective angling method. Other species that anglers can expect to find in Indian Lake include northern pike and the ever-present panfish

Imp Lake

Imp Lake is stocked with splake and receives little fishing pressure based on its location. The lake is mainly fished during the winter through the ice and there are reports of good catches of nice sized splake. The lake can be reached by snowmobile about 3 km south of Lasswade Road, just outside of the village of Lasswade.

Kasshabog Lake

This popular cottage destination lake is heavily fished throughout the year and it is best known for its more productive bass fishery. During the winter months, however, fishing is slow to fair at times for walleye. A population of muskellunge inhabits the lake, although they can be hard to find through the ice. The lake offers public access from its northern and southern ends off of Country Road 46.

Kennebec Lake

Visiting anglers can find this lake by taking Highway 7 east of Kaladar to the Harlowe Henderson Road. Harlowe Henderson Road snakes north crossing the eastern end of the lake. During the winter, northern pike and walleye are the main focus for ice anglers. However, fishing success for walleye can be gruelingly slow at times. Anglers often use either minnows or jigs in this lake.

Long Lake

See Page 67

Little Anstruther Lake

Little Anstruther Lake is stocked regularly with lake trout and is mainly fished through the ice during winter. The lake can be accessed by snowmobile and fishing for small lake trout is fair during the winter. The lake is located north of the much larger Anstruther Lake not far from the village of Apsley.

Little Echo Lake

Little Echo Lake is a small, secluded lake that is stocked semi-annually with brook trout. Fishing for small brookies is good with the best action through the ice or in spring, just after ice off. The lake is accessible mainly by snowmobile about 2 km north of the Eels Lake Road, near the west end of the much larger Eels Lake.

Little Green Lake

This lake is found just east of the settlement of Plevna, sandwiched between the power line and the Mississippi River. The lake is stocked every few years with lake trout. Fishing in the lake is fair through the ice in winter or in spring just after ice off. Baitfish are not permitted for use at this lake.

Little Mayo Lake

A series of snowmobile accessible roads east of Bancroft lead to Little Mayo Lake. Anglers who make it into this lake will find fairly consistent fishing for stocked lake trout. The lake is surrounded by Crown Land making it a peaceful destination in winter.

Little Round Lake

Little Round Lake is a small lake located at the junction between Highway 7 and Highway 509. The lake is stocked annually with brook trout, which provide for fair to good fishing through the ice and in spring just after ice off. Brookies average about 25-30 cm (10-12 in) in size. Try jigging a small spoon in the 1-2 m (3-6.5 ft) depth range for active brookies during the winter.

Lonewolf Lake

This small lake lies not far off the access road that follows one of the power lines south of Calabogie Lake. The road system is part of the TOPS snowmobile trail system allowing for fairly good winter access. The lake is stocked every few years with brook trout and fishing can be good at times, especially through the ice.

Long Mallory Lake

Long Mallory Lake can be reached by snowmobile trail south of the village of Vennachar. The lake is stocked every few years with lake trout, which provide for fair fishing through the ice and in early spring. Northern pike are also found in the lake, although fishing is usually slow.

Longbay Lake

Found in the Madawaska Highlands, this secluded lake is stocked every few years with brook trout. Stocked brookies provide for good fishing in the winter and in early spring just after ice off. They average about 25-35 cm (10-14 in) in size, although rumours of larger trout surface occasionally. Access to the lake is limited to snowmobile trails found south of the large Black Donald Lake.

Fishing

Ice anglers can still expect to have some success in the winter, when the fishing pressure on the lake eases a bit. While bass are a popular attraction in the summer, northern pike and walleye are the main attractions in the winter. Fishing success for pike is better than for walleye, although success for both is generally fair to slow.

Some of the better places to look for these roaming sportfish are near the islands or even over the 3 m (10 ft) shoal area located in the middle of the lake. Working a jig off the bottom can produce some exciting action at times.

Access

Southwest of Sharbot Lake, Long Lake is a scenic lake easily found to the west of Highway 38. Highway 38 connects the two major highways in the area, Highway 7 to the north and Highway 401 to the south. Depending on which major highway you use, you will need to follow the smaller Highway 38 north or south to the village of Parham. At Parham, continue west along the Wagarville Road for a short distance to the junction with Long Lake Road. Head north along the Long Lake Road as it winds its way past the eastern shore of the lake. A boat/snowmobile launch and dock area are located just off the Long Lake Road.

Facilities

Long Lake is a scenic lake with a number of cottages and camps scattered around the shoreline. Unfortunately, many of these locations are closed during the winter. However, the nearby town of Sharbot Lake does provide accommodations and basic supplies. The boat launch area along the eastern shore of Long Lake is used as a launching point for snowmobilers in winter.

Lake Definition

Elevation:	163.8 m (603 ft)
Surface Area:	301.2 ha (744 ac)
Mean Depth:	6.1 m (20.2 ft)
Max Depth:	13.4 m (44 ft)
Perimeter:	16.8 km (10.5 mi)
Way Point:	44° 40' 00" Lat - N 76° 46' 00" Lon - W

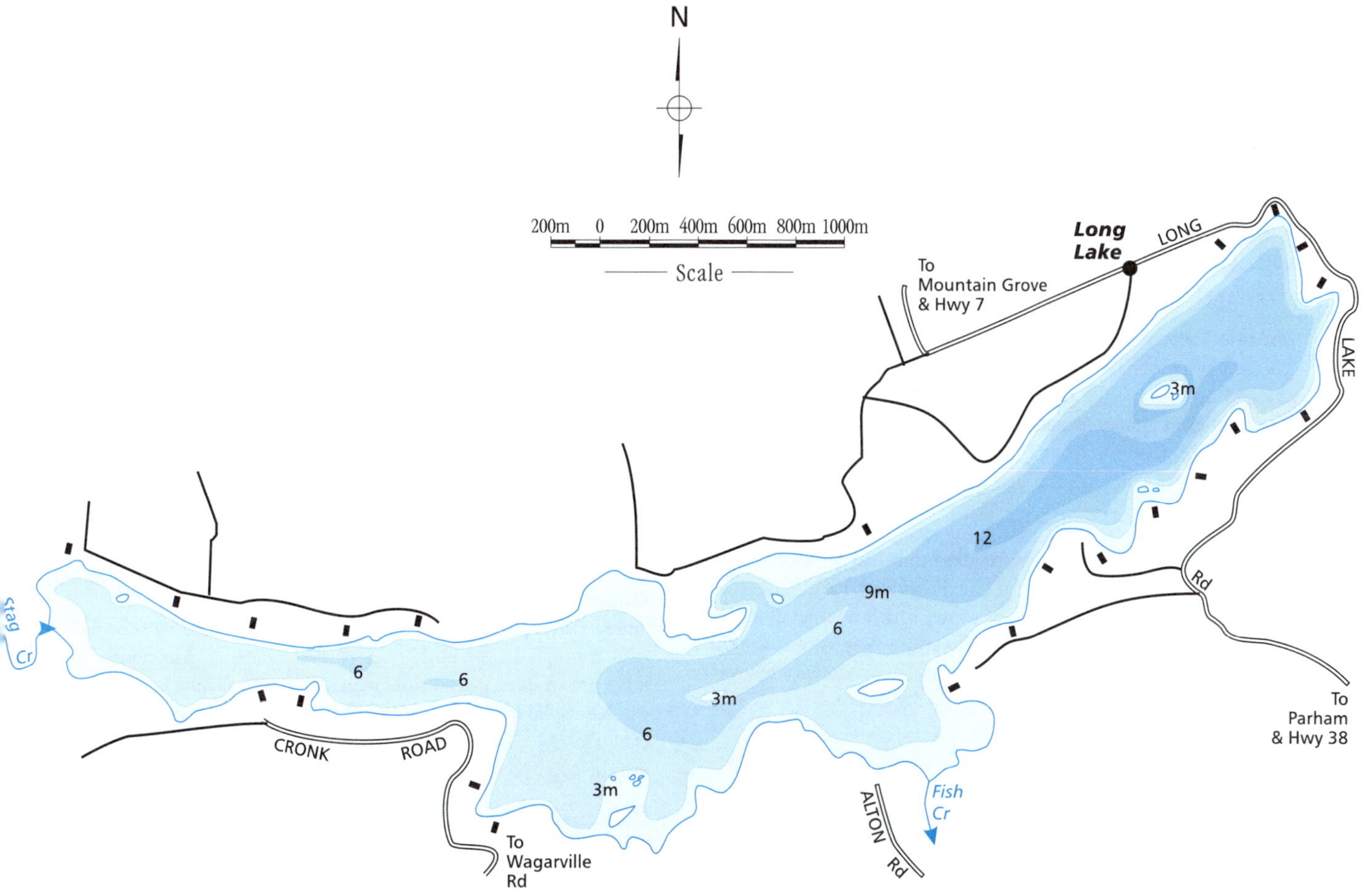

N

200m 0 200m 400m 600m 800m 1000m
Scale

Long Lake
LONG LAKE Rd
To Mountain Grove & Hwy 7
To Parham & Hwy 38
CRONK ROAD
To Wagarville Rd
ALTON Rd
Fish Cr
Stag Cr
3m 12 9m 6 6 6 3m 6 3m

Lowry (Bluerock) Lake

South of the village of Tory Hill, Lowry Lake can be accessed from the Hadlington Lake Road, which passes close by the lake. A snowmobile is definitely an asset unless you are willing to walk in. The lake is stocked almost annually with brook trout and offers fair to good fishing for brookies that can reach 35 cm (14 in) in size. One of the most productive times of year is during ice fishing season. There is a live fish bait ban on the lake.

Mazinaw Lake

See Page 69

Mackie Lake

Found north of the village of Plevna, Mackie Lake can be accessed by the rough Mackie Lake Road. The road is used mainly as a snowmobile trail in winter; simply follow the tracks in. Lake trout are stocked in the lake every few years and provide for fair fishing at times through the ice.

McCreary Lake and Mousseau Lake

These are two small, secluded lakes that are stocked every few years with brook trout. Fishing in the lakes can be quite good, especially in winter. Brook trout average about 30 cm (12 in) in size and are often found in the shallower portions of the lake. Access to the lakes is via snowmobile east of Norcan Lake.

McDowall Lake

McDowall Lake is a small backcountry access lake that is stocked every few years with brook trout. Fishing in the small lake can be good periodically for generally small trout. Try jigging a small white jig to find active brookies. The tiny lake lies in the hills between Shabomeka Lake and Lower Mazinaw Lake near Bon Echo Provincial Park.

McGee Lake

McGee Lake is stocked with lake trout regularly and is fairly productive for small lakers during ice fishing season. The only real access to the lake is by snowmobile or by bushwhacking on snowshoe. The lake lies south of the village of Apsley about 3 km west of Highway 28.

McHale Lake

Located west of the village of Griffith, this small lake can be reached by snowmobile just off the Green Lake Forest Road. The lake is stocked almost annually with brook trout. Fishing success is usually quite good for trout in the 20-30 cm (8-12 in) range. Try small spoons or white jigs through the ice.

Merrill Lakes

The Merrill Lakes are two remote lakes that can be accessed by a rough road found west of Bon Echo Provincial Park. The access road is actually a power line access route, which doubles as a snowmobile trail in winter months. The lakes are best known for their bass fishing, but Little Merrill Lake is also stocked every few years with splake. Winter ice fishing can be fair for splake.

Mississippi Lake

See Page 71

Mississagagon Lake

Mississagagon Lake is located southeast of Bon Echo Provincial Park. To reach the lake travel north along Highway 41 from Kaladar and look for the junction with Highway 506 just south of Cloyne. Highway 506 travels east soon passing along the southern shore of Mississagagon Lake. The name Mississagagon is derived from native dialect meaning 'wide mouth' or 'headwater'.

Anglers visiting the lake in winter will most likely be after its resident walleye and northern pike populations. Since 1996, local hatcheries have taken it upon themselves to attempt to re-establish the walleye fishery that was decimated by over fishing. Thousands of fingerling walleye have been stocked in the lake and the results are starting to pay off. In fact, some recent reports boast of dramatically better fishing.

Mitchell Lake

Except for a section of Crown Land on the northern shore, Mitchell Lake is surrounded by private property. However, you will still need to obtain permission from private owners to follow the access trail from Williams Lake Road. The lake is stocked every few years with brook trout, which provide fair fishing through the ice and in spring for average sized brookies. Look for the lake just north of the village of Maynooth.

Moira Lake

Moira Lake is located to the south of the town of Madoc and is a popular destination throughout the year. Even though the lake receives significant fishing pressure, it still offers fair to good fishing for walleye and northern pike. Walleye average about 1.5 kg (3.5 lbs) in size and pike average 2-4 kg (4.5-9 lbs). Although not very active in winter, there is also a fair population of muskellunge found in the lake. Watch for special restrictions on this lake.

Morrow Lake

Southeast of Griffith, look for the Morrow Lake Road heading north from the Centennial Lake Road. The road leads directly to the lake, although is only passable via snowmobile in winter. The lake is stocked annually with lake trout and fishing is usually good in winter for lakers that average 35-40 cm (14-16 in) in size.

North Lake

North Lake is stocked every few years with splake and provides good fishing in the winter and in early spring for splake in the 30-35 cm (12-14 in) range. Normal brook trout methods can be effective for splake at this lake. Found east of Boundary Road, near the village of Coe Hill, a snowmobile and a decent map are a definite asset to find this lake.

Nowlan Lake

This small, secluded lake is stocked every few years with brook trout. Fishing is good through the ice for average sized brook trout. Look for the lake south of Ashby White Lake.

Oxbend Lake and Sandox Lake

These two secluded lakes that can only be accessed by snowmobile trail through heavy bush west of the village of Maynooth. Both lakes are stocked periodically with splake and fishing is fair through the ice. Splake can grow to good sizes in these lakes and fish over 60+ cm (24+ in) have been caught more than once. Silver spoons are the most productive lure in winter.

Parkhurst Lake

East of Bancroft, there is a snowmobile trail that can be picked up near the Highway 28/Mayo Lake Road crossing. The trail heads east, passing by the lake. The lake is stocked every few years with brook trout, which provide for good fishing through the ice.

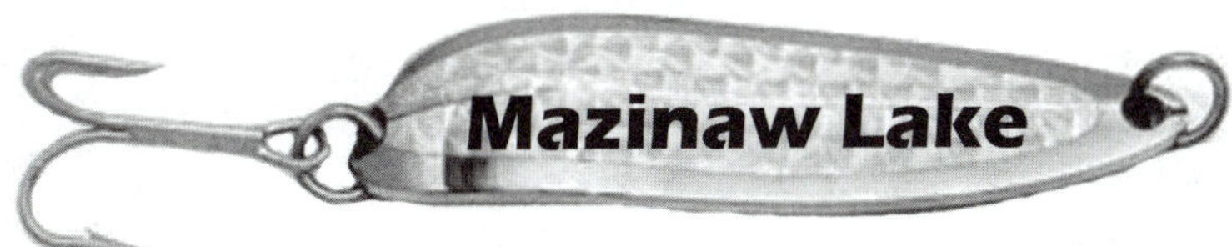

Mazinaw Lake

Fishing

The main geographical feature of Mazinaw Lake is the large rock, Mazinaw Rock, which lies along the eastern shore of the upper portion of the lake. This towering rock was the historic meeting place for local native tribes. Mazinaw Lake is named after this meeting place, as 'Mazinaw' is known in many native dialects as the word for 'meeting place'. For the adventurous and historic at heart, visitors can view the fascinating ancient native paintings or 'pictographs' located at water level along the large rock wall of Mazinaw Rock.

Mazinaw Lake has a maximum depth of 137 m (450 ft) and is one of the deepest inland lakes in Ontario. Fishing success for Mazinaw Lake's walleye and northern pike is generally slow, although there are good-sized walleye and pike caught in the lake annually. A natural population of lake trout also remains in Mazinaw Lake and the deep nature of the lake allows lakers to thrive. The best time for success with lakers in this lake is in winter through the ice or in the early spring. Jigging a small spoon or white jig through the ice can work at times.

As with all lake trout populations in Southern Ontario, special regulations have been imposed to ensure the future viability of the species. Be sure to check your regulations for the ice fishing and slot size restrictions in place on Mazinaw Lake.

Access

Mazinaw Lake is a beautifully scenic lake that is located next to Highway 41. The narrows between the upper and lower sections of the lake make up a portion of Bon Echo Provincial Park. Access is easily found by following the main highways, Highway 7 or Highway 401, to the smaller Highway 41. Once on Highway 41, head north past Kaladar and the villages of Northbrook then Cloyne. North of Cloyne, Mazinaw Lake soon unfolds along the western side of the highway.

Facilities

The main feature of Mazinaw Lake is Bon Echo Provincial Park. Bon Echo Provincial Park encompasses a good portion of land between the Lower and Upper Mazinaw Lake. The park is not open during the winter but some anglers walk through the park to access the lake from the boat launch area. For more information on Bon Echo Provincial Park, call (613) 336-2228.

There is also a marina as well as several tent and trailer parks around Mazinaw Lake that provide summer access to the lake. For supplies, the small village of Cloyne to the south offers a few retailers. Further south, Northbrook is home to a grocery store and a few restaurants.

500m 0 1km 2km 3km
Scale
Upper Mazinaw Lake
Lower Mazinaw Lake
To Hwy 28
To Hwy 7
Hungry Bay
Muggs' Mud Cr
Campbell Bay
Big Bear Isl
German Bay
Mazinaw Rock
Bon Echo Prov Park
Bon Echo
The Narrows
Bon Echo Cr
Mazinaw Heights Rd
Snyder Bay
Rekr Rock
Semicircle Cr
McCausland Lake
Dam Rd
Mazinaw
Little Marble Lake
N

Lake Definition

Elevation:	268.2 m (880 ft)
Surface Area:	1,591 ha (3,930 ac)
Mean Depth:	41.2 m (135.1 ft)
Max Depth:	137 m (450 ft)
Perimeter:	49 km (30.5 mi)
Way Point:	44° 50' 00" Lat - N 77° 12' 00" Lon - W

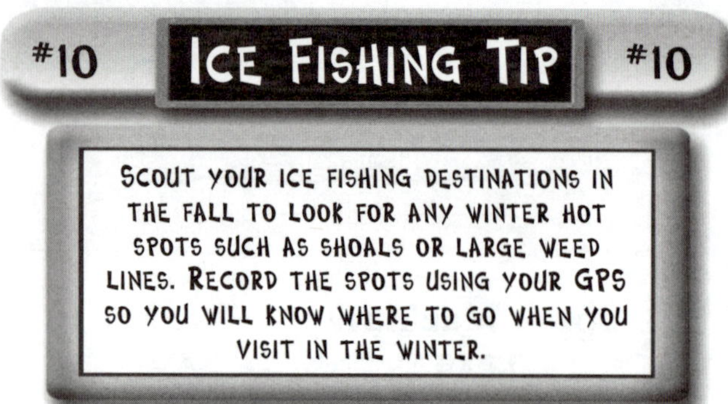

Patterson Lake

To find Patterson Lake, follow Highway 7 to the town of Perth and turn north along Highway 511. Follow Highway 511 past Balderson and Lanark to Corners Road (County Road 8). Travel west along Corners Road to Concession 8 at the Purdon Conservation Area. Trek north along Concession 8, which passes by the western shore of Patterson Lake.

Anglers visiting Patterson Lake in the winter have the opportunity to fish for walleye, northern pike and panfish. Success for walleye and northern pike can be fair although is usually slow. Many anglers still prefer to still jig for walleye, although live bait is a regular use at this lake.

Perch Lake

Perch Lake is a small, hidden lake that lies just to the east of Govan Lake north of the settlement of Ompah. The difficult access makes this a good destination for solitude seekers. The lake is stocked annually with splake, which provide for fair fishing at times. Splake average about 30 cm (12 in) in size, although can be found bigger. Consult the Backroad Mapbook for Eastern Ontario for a good map of the area.

Pike Lake

Located between the towns of Perth to the north and Westport to the south, Pike Lake is easily accessible via the Scotch Line (County Road 10). Near Perth, the Scotch Line can be found just south of town off the Rideau Ferry Road County Road 1. At Westport, the Scotch Line is located near the north end of town and crosses over a dam along the west end of Upper Rideau Lake.

Anglers visiting this lake can enjoy fishing for panfish, northern pike and walleye. Walleye fishing in Pike Lake is definitely slower than success for northern pike, although it is also the preferred sportfish species of most anglers. Walleye tend to cruise shoal areas, especially during the evening period. To help enhance the walleye fishery and reduce angling pressure, special slot size restrictions for harvesting have been imposed. Please check your regulations for specifics before heading out.

Poplar Lake

This remote lake has a fair population of stocked splake that can be readily taken by ice fishing in the winter. The hybrid fish is quite active in winter and can grow to nice sizes. The lake lies just south of the popular Anstruther Lake near the town of Apsley.

Quinn Lakes

The Quinn Lakes are a chain of three secluded lakes (West, South and North Quinn) that offer good fishing for brook trout, especially through the ice and in the early spring. All three lakes are heavily stocked with brookies every few years, which is the main reason for the quality fishery. At one time all three lakes supported natural brook trout, although over fishing has reduced them to a rarity. The lakes are found at the end of a series of snowmobile accessible roads north of the village of Ompah and Highway 509.

Raglan (White) Lake

Raglan Lake is stocked every few years with lake trout that provide fair fishing during ice fishing season. Lakers can grow to sizes exceeding 70+ cm (28+ in). Much of the shoreline is Crown Land and there is a public access at the north end of the lake. Look for the lake to the west of Highway 514, north of the settlement of Hardwood Lake.

Rainy Lake

This is a remote, snowmobile accessible lake that lies just outside the western border of Bon Echo Provincial Park. A natural population of lake trout inhabits the lake but fishing is usually slow to fair. Watch for slot size and special lake trout restrictions. Please practice catch and release if possible when fishing here.

Reid Lake

Found far from any roads, Reid Lake is most often accessed by snowmobile trail from Mackie Lake north of the village of Plevna. The lake is stocked every few years with lake trout. Fishing for lakers is fair through the ice in winter. Try jigging a small spoon or even a white jig for active lakers.

Ruby Lake

Ruby Lake is a secluded lake that is stocked every two years with brook trout. Ice fishing for brookies can be good on occasion. The lake lies not far from Highway 28 near Ashby White Lake, northwest of the small village of Denbigh.

Sharbot Lake

See Page 72

Shabomeka Lake

Shabomeka Lake is found just east of Mazinaw Lake and is best known for its bass fishing. However, the lake is also stocked every few years with lake trout that provide for fair fishing at times. From Highway 41 just south of Bon Echo Park, look for Buck Lake Road. This road leads to a dam and the south side of the lake.

Silver Lake

During the summer, Silver Lake Provincial Park is the main attraction at this lake. In the winter, ice fishing is the main draw and anglers can try their luck for stocked lake trout. Lake trout are stocked in the lake annually and fishing success is slow to fair in the winter. Northern pike are also found in the lake and fishing is fair at times for pike that can reach over 80 cm (35 in) in length. When the action for the larger sportfish is slow, panfish often provide some action.

Simpson Lake

This remote lake is mainly accessed by snowmobile. To find the lake follow Highway 28 west to the Trout Lake Road near the settlement of Hardwood Lake. The Trout Lake Road leads south to Trout Lake, which is just west of Simpson Lake. The lake is stocked every few years with lake trout. Anglers can expect fair fishing for generally small lakers.

Skootamatta Lake

See Page 74

Mississippi Lake

Fishing

This large lake lies to the south of Carleton Place, west of Ottawa. The name 'Mississippi' is another native derivation that means 'Great River'. Ontario's Mississippi River is not as grand as its American counterpart, although the river is quite large in southern Ontario standards.

Ice fishing anglers visiting Mississippi Lake can enjoy fishing for panfish, northern pike and walleye. Walleye anglers are best to try around shoal areas during darker times of the day. There are a number of shoals found around the lake, and if located can result in a flurry of activity, especially with a white or yellow jig. The lake depth chart provided will help you locate the shoals and other likely holding areas for pike.

In order to help walleye stocks, special regulations are in effect. Be sure to consult your regulations before you attempt to fish in this large water body.

Access

To find the lake follow Highway 7, as it travels right by the southern and northern ends of the lake. At the north end of the lake is the city of Carleton Place, which is home to a public boat launch. This site, which is found at the municipal park, is used by anglers in the winter. There are also several cottage roads around the lake.

lake.

Facilites

Carleton Place is a small city offering all amenities including hotels, restaurants and numerous retailers. Lodges, commercial campsites and marinas are scattered around the lake. Unfortunately, most of these locations are closed in the winter.

Lake Definition

Elevation:	268.2 m (880 ft)
Surface Area:	507.7 ha (1,254 ac)
Mean Depth:	9 m (29.8 ft)
Max Depth:	23.7 m (78 ft)
Perimeter:	35.4 km (22 mi)
Way Point:	44° 52' 00" Lat - N 77° 06' 00" Lon - W

Sharbot Lake

Sharbot Lake (West)

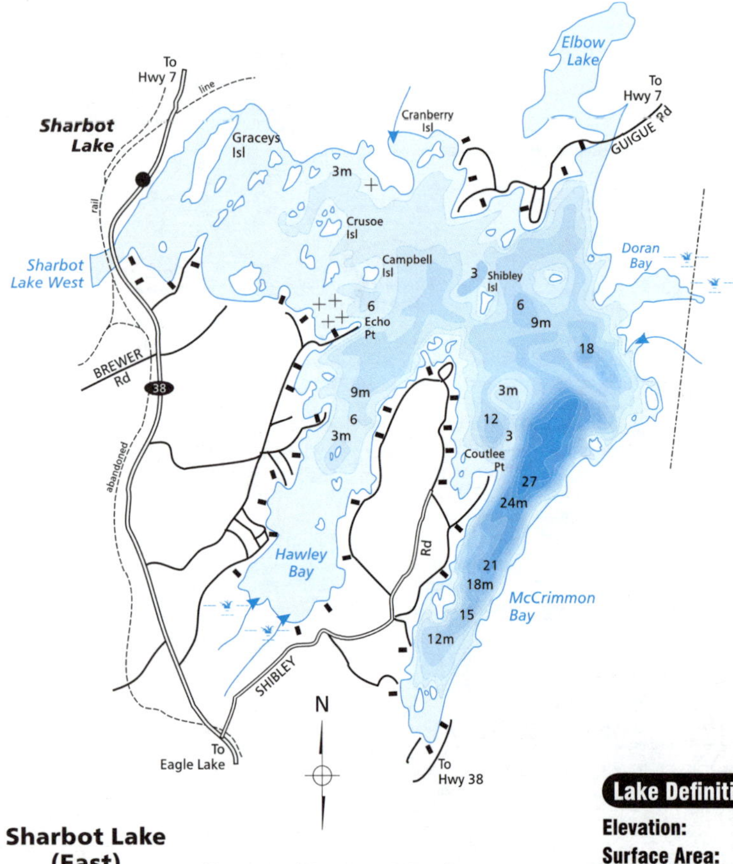

Sharbot Lake (East)

Fishing

Sharbot Lake is named after the Mohawk native settler Francis Sharbot. Sharbot built a cabin near the lake in 1826 and a few years later, European settlers arrived and named the lake after Francis. Today, the lake is a popular destination lake that receives significant angling pressure throughout the year. The lake is inhabited with smallmouth bass, largemouth bass, northern pike, walleye and a naturally reproducing strain of lake trout.

Since bass are inactive in the winter, the two most sought after sportfish in Sharbot Lake are walleye and lake trout. Walleye fishing is usually slow, although it is better than for lake trout. Jigging off underwater shoal humps or near points is a popular angling method for walleye. The lakers in Sharbot Lake are a naturally reproducing strain of trout, which are becoming increasingly rare in eastern Ontario. If you do happen to catch a laker, please practise catch and release, as these species are quite fragile.

Access

Sharbot Lake makes up the scenic backdrop for the bedroom community of Sharbot Lake. Both the town and the lake are easily accessible as they lie just off the south side of Highway 7 west of the town of Perth. Alternatively, Highway 38 cuts through the lake and town as it heads south to Kingston.

Lake Definition

Elevation:	192 m (630 ft)
Surface Area:	706.5 ha (1,745 ac)
Mean Depth:	8.1 m (26.5 ft)
Max Depth:	32 m (105 ft)
Perimeter:	22.5 km (14 mi)
Way Point:	44° 46' 00" Lat - N 76° 41' 00" Lon - W

Spring Lake

Without the aid of a good map and a snowmobile, this secluded lake is best left to the locals. Those that make it in will find good fishing for stocked brook trout. Some nice-sized brookies are caught on occasion.

Straddlebug Lake

This small lake lies not far off the access road that follows one of the power lines south of Calabogie Lake. The road system is part of the TOPS snowmobile trail system allowing for fairly good winter access. The lake is stocked every few years with brook trout and fishing can be good at times, especially through the ice.

Sullivan and Snowshoe Lakes

Found in the Madawaska Highlands, these secluded lakes are stocked every few years with brook trout. Stocked brookies provide for good fishing in the winter and in early spring just after ice off. They average about 25-35 cm (10-14 in) in size, although rumours of larger trout surface occasionally. Access to the lakes is limited to snowmobile trails found south of the large Black Donald Lake.

Tim Lake

Tim Lake is a small lake found just north of the town of Bancroft not far from Highway 62. The small lake offers fair to good fishing for stocked brook trout. Ice fishing can be quite productive. The Backroad Mapbook for Eastern Ontario is a fine resource to aid in finding a backroad lake such as Tim Lake.

Tory Lake

Found at the village of Tory Hill, Tory Lake is stocked semi-annually with splake. Fishing for splake to 35 cm (14 in) can be good at times in the winter months. Although minnows can be effective, anglers can often find larger trout by jigging small spoons.

Turtle Lake

North of the village of Denbigh, Turtle Lake can be accessed via trail near the south bank of the Madawaska River. The beautiful lake is stocked regularly with brook trout that are often quite active during the ice fishing season.

Upper Rock Lake

Upper Rock Lake is accessible off Opinicon Road, which heads east from County Road 10. The lake is stocked annually with splake, which provide for fair to good fishing through the ice. Some nice sized splake are caught in this lake. It is rumoured that small populations of northern pike and walleye also remain in the lake.

Urbach Lake

Urbach Lake is a small lake that is found south of the much larger Wollaston Lake, which in turn is found south of Coe Hill. The small lake is stocked every few years with splake that provide for good fishing at times. Try a small spoon jigged through the ice for active splake.

West Twinpine Lake

This small, semi-remote lake is found just south of the settlement of Gilmour. The lake is stocked every few years with brook trout and fishing can be good periodically. The Hastings Heritage Trail passes near the lake providing access for snowmobiles and even hardcore snowshoers.

White Lake

See Page 75

Whyte Lake

Accessible by snowmobile in the winter months, Whyte Lake is found south of Highway 28 to the east of Bancroft. The Backroad Mapbook for Eastern Ontario details how to get into the lake. The lake is surrounded by Crown Land and stocked annually with lake trout. Fishing for lakers is generally fair through the ice.

Wolfe Lake

Visitors can find Wolfe Lake just west of the town of Westport. To find the lake from the east, begin by following Highway 15 to the junction with County Road 42 at Crosby. Head west along County Road 42 to Westport and look for the Wolfe Lake Road (County Road 12/8). From Westport, Wolfe Lake is about 8 km (5 mi) west along the Wolfe Lake Road.

This popular summer cottage lake was once known for its excellent walleye fishery. Through the years, however, over fishing has reduced success for walleye to below average levels. For the best chance for walleye success, try to locate the shoal areas around the lake. A few of the known hot spots are the 3 m (10 ft) shoal in the southeast corner and the 7 m (20 ft) shoal found in the middle of the lake. These areas tend to attract plenty of baitfish, which in turn attract predators such as walleye. Still jigging off one of these areas can produce results on occasion.

Northern pike also inhabit the lake, although fishing is generally slow. Although big northerns can surprise the odd angler, most of the pike are small.

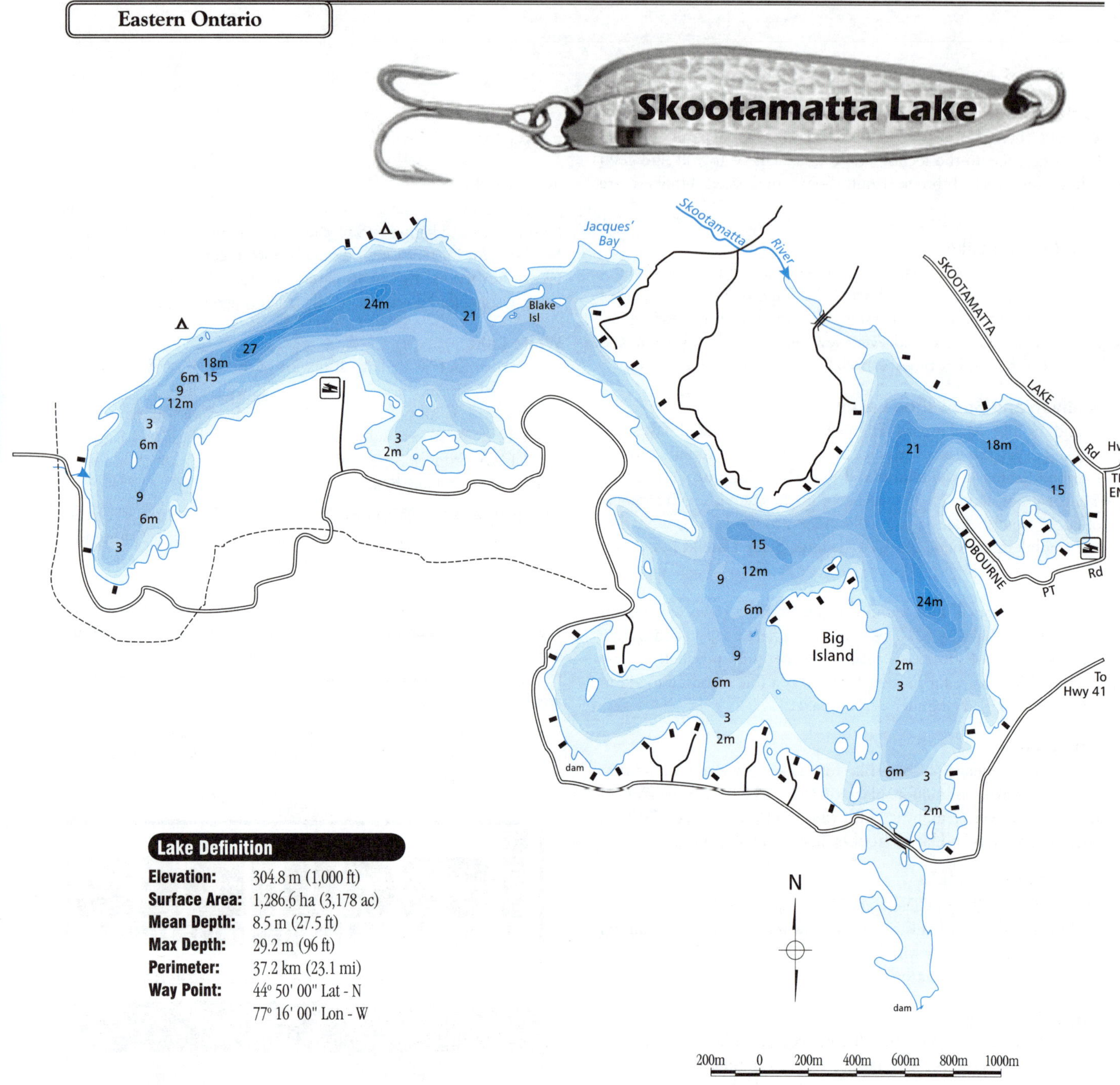

Fishing

Skootamatta Lake is an odd shaped lake that offers good bass fishing in the summer, and fair to slow fishing for northern pike and walleye in the winter. Northern pike provide for steadier action for pike that can reach 5+ kg (11+ lbs) in size. Fishing for walleye is often better during dawn and dusk periods for fish that average around 1-2 kg (2-5 lbs) in size. A few hot spots for walleye and northern pike in the lake are the two 6 m (20 ft) to 9 m (30 ft) shoal areas located just west of Big Island.

Access

South of Bon Echo Provincial Park, the large Skootamatta Lake can be found not far off Highway 41. From the village of Kaladar, head north along Highway 41 past the village of Cloyne. Just past Cloyne, look for Addington Road off the west side of the highway. Addington Road leads northwest to Trails End Road. Turn west along the Trails End Road to reach Skootamatta Lake. From Addington Road, there are a few other roads that branch off, which provide access to various other areas of Skootamatta Lake.

Facilities

A public boat launch and parking area is located off Trails End Road along the eastern shore. Another access area can be found along the southern shore of the western arm of the lake. Both areas can be used to launch snowmobiles in the winter.

Fishing

This large lake lies in a transition zone between the rolling hills of the Madawaska Highlands and the lowlands of the Ottawa Valley. Splake are stocked annually and provide for fair fishing in winter. Try jigging a small spoon like a Little Cleo near drop-off areas. Splake, similar to lake trout and brook trout, will often be attracted from a distance to the flash of the spoon. The fish will strike the spoon thinking it is a minnow in distress.

Northern pike and walleye are also residents of White Lake, although fishing success for both species is regarded as slow. Regardless, walleye are the most sought after sportfish in the lake and slot size restrictions are in place to help maintain the fishery. Still, jigging during winter can provide results for both species on occasion. For added success, try around dusk when these roaming fish begin to feed. Before you head out onto White Lake, be sure to check your regulations.

Access

White Lake is located east of Calabogie Lake halfway between the towns of Perth and Renfrew. There are a few different access points to White Lake. From the south, the easiest way to find the lake is travel north along Highway 511 to the White Lake Road located south of Calabogie. The White Lake Road travels east to the western shore of White Lake. Alternatively, Country Road 52 accesses the north end and County Road 24 the west side of the lake.

Facilities

Several cottages line the shores of White Lake and the lake is home to a few marinas. Boat launching facilities are available at the marina near the village of White Lake as well as off Bayview Lodge Road and Windy Point Road. The access area located off White Lake Road along the southeast shore is a popular launching point for snowmobiles.

Unfortunately, the tent and trailer parks and lakeside resorts are closed in the winter. The nearby towns of Arnprior and Perth offer full amenities. Visitors can choose from a full array of motels, restaurants and retailers in each of these nearby towns.

Lake Definition

Mean Depth:	6.2 m (20 ft)
Max Depth:	9.1 m (30 ft)
Way Point:	45° 18' 00" Lat - N 76° 31' 00" Lon - W

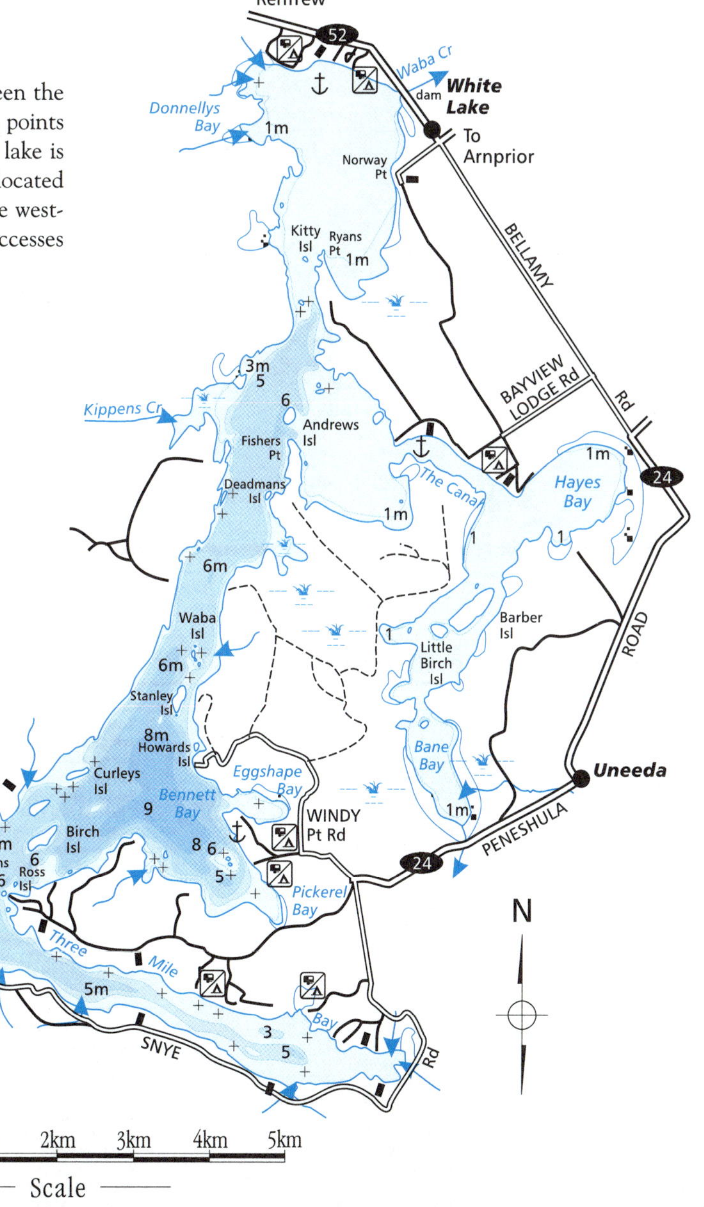

1km 0 1km 2km 3km 4km 5km

Scale

Algonquin Region Mapkey

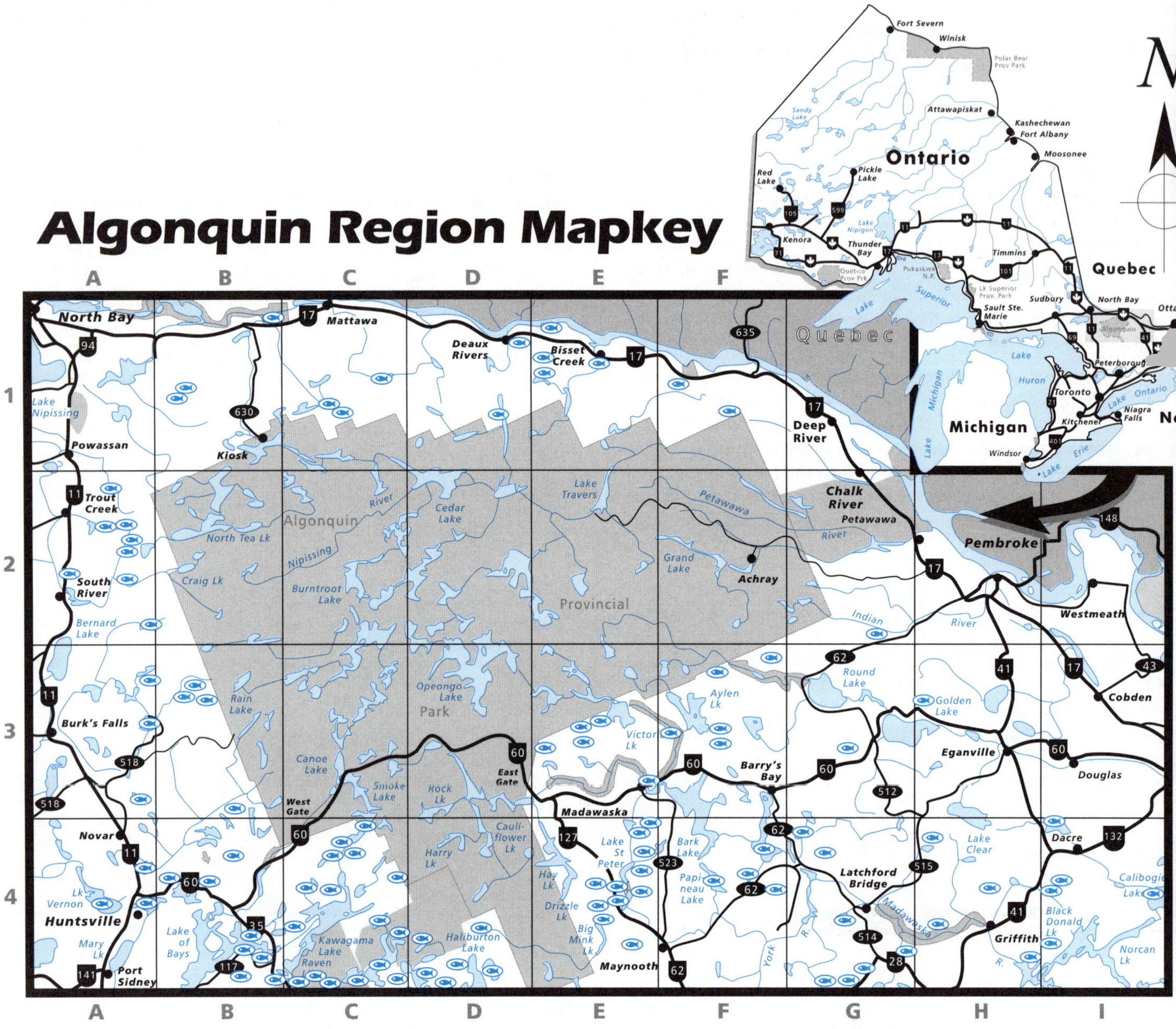

Ice Fishing in Algonquin Region Ontario:

Arrowhead and Little Arrowhead Lakes (4/A)
Back and Indian Lakes (4/E)
Bacon Lake (2/A)
Baldcoot and Littlecoot Lakes (4/F)
Ban (Band) Lake (4/C)
Barns Lake (3/E)
Bay (Bucktooth) Lake (3/A)
Big Gibson Lake (1/E)
Birchy Lake (4/C)
Bright Lake (4/C)
Buck and Raven Lakes (3/A)
Buckskin Lake (4/H)
Calabogie Lake (4/I)
Charcoal Lake (4/B)
Clara Lake (1/D)
Claradeer Lake (1/D)
Clear Lake (3/A)
Cod Lake (4/B)
Constant Lake (4/I)
Cornick Lake (2/A)
Coughlan Lake (4/E)
Crevice Lake (3/E)
Cross Lake (4/E)
Crown Lake (4/C)
Deermeadow Lake (1/D)
Diamond Lake (4/G)
Dick Lake (3/B)
Dutton Lake (4/D)
East Lake (4/D)
East Jeannie Lakes (4/C)
East Paint Lake (4/C)
Eastell Lake (4/B)
Fairy Lake (1/A)
Finger Lake (3/F)
Flat Iron Lake (2/G)
Fletcher Lakes (4/C)
Fork Lake (1/C)
Gardiner and Rattail Lake (1/D)
Genesee Lake (2/A)
Godin Lake (4/H)
Gostling Lake (4/B)
Guilford Lake (4/D)
Gun Lake (4/G)
Halfway Lake (4/G)
Hardwood Lake (4/G)
Harp Lake (4/B)
Harvey and Wylie Lakes (1/F)
Harvey Lake (4/C)
Haskins Lake (3/F)
Havelock Lake (4/C)
Hawk Lake (4/E)
Headstone Lakes (3/E)
Heifer and Steer Lakes (4/I)
James Lake (4/F)
Johnsons Lake (3/H)
Kamaniskeg Lake (4/F)
Kennisis Lake (4/C)
Lake St. Peter (4/E)
Lake Vernon (4/A)
Lasseter Lake (4/B)
Lee Lakes (4/B)
Little Clear, Long and Turtle Lakes (1/B)
Long Lake (4/I)
Long Lake (1/B)
Longline Lake (4/B)
Louie Lakes (4/C)
Loxton Lake (2/A)
Martin (Boundary) Lake (4/D)
McDonald Lake (3/F)
McHale Lake (4/H)
McKenzie Lake (4/E)
Meach Lakes (4/E)
Menet Lake (1/F)
Middle Shanty Lake (3/B)
Mink Lake (4/B)
Monkshood Lake (3/F)
Moonbeam Lake (3/E)
Morrow Lake (4/H)
Mousseau Lake (1/E)
Murphy Lake (4/I)
Nehemiah Lake (4/C)
Nelson Lakes (3/B)
Niger Lake (4/C)
Oxbend Lake (4/E)
Papineau Lake (4/F)
Pat Lake (4/D)
Pell Lake (4/D)
Percy Lake (4/C)
Peyton Lakes (2/A)
Pine Lake (3/B)
Purdy Lake (4/F)
Raglan (White) Lake (4/G)
Ronald Lake (4/C)
Ross Lake (4/C)
Sand Lake (3/A)
Sandox Lake (4/E)
Sears Lake (1/C)
Shaw Lake (2/A)
Silversheen Lake (4/D)
Smyth Lake (2/A)
Soaking Lake (4/E)
Sunken Lake (4/C)
Trout Lake (3/E)
Troutspawn Lakes (4/C)
Tub Lake (3/E)
Turtle Lake (4/G)
Twelve Lake (2/A)
Twentyseven Lake (2/A)
Valiant Lake (1/E)
Walker Lake (3/F)
Walker Lake (4/B)
Waterloo Lake (1/E)
West Aumond Lake (1/C)
Wilbur Lake (4/B)
Wish Lake (3/E)
Wolf Lake (4/C)

Arrowhead and Little Arrowhead Lakes
These two distinctly different lakes are located close to one another within Arrowhead Provincial Park. The park can be found off Highway 11 just north of the town of Huntsville. The larger Arrowhead Lake is a heavily used lake that offers slow fishing for small brook trout. Little Arrowhead Lake provides slow to fair fishing for smaller sized lake trout and brook trout.

Back and Indian Lake
Back and Indian Lakes are two small brook trout lakes that can be accessed by 4wd roads. Ice fishing with smaller spoons can be effective. Sizes of trout are relatively small with the odd 30+ cm (12+ in) trout caught. To find the lakes take Highway 217 north from Maynooth to the Cross Lake Road. Follow Cross Lake Road north for approximately 10 km and look for the rough access road off the west side of the main road.

Bacon Lake
Bacon Lake lies next to the railway line from South River to Trout Creek. A dirt road leads to the railway, which can then be followed to the lake. Fishing is slow for natural lake trout, partly because the lake receives significant ice fishing pressure.

Baldcoot and Littlecoot Lake
These are two secluded lakes that can be accessed via snowmobile through dense bush southwest of the village of Combermere. A 4wd road approaches the lakes, although ends about 1.5 km from the lakes. Baldcoot Lake has a naturally reproducing strain of brook trout, while Littlecoot is stocked every few years with splake. Success in Littlecoot can be good for splake in the 35+ cm (14+ in) range.

Ban (Band) Lake
Ban (Band) Lake is a small, secluded lake found in the Haliburton Forest and offers good fishing for small brook trout. The lake is stocked every two years and is mainly fished in the winter through the ice. For directions to the lake, please consult the Haliburton Forest Reserve gatehouse upon arrival.

Barns Lake
This lake is stocked with brook trout every few years and can be accessed by snowmobile in the winter. To find the lake from Madawaska, follow the McCauley Lake Road north to Major Lake Road. Continue north to the power line and follow the power line road south to the first branch off the north side. Brook trout average 20-30 cm (8-12 in) in size.

Bay (Bucktooth) Lake
Found southeast of the village of Emsdale, north of Huntsville, Bay Lake is also known as Bucktooth Lake. Look for Bay Lake Road off the east side of County Road 592. The lake is stocked with lake trout and offers fair fishing for small lakers as well as walleye, which can reach 4 kg (9 lbs). Ice fishing is the most productive method for lake trout.

Big Gibson Lake
Big Gibson Lake is easily accessed via snowmobile off the north side of Highway 17 west of the village of Bissett Creek. Lake trout are stocked every few years, while northern pike can also present some winter fun.

Birchy Lake
Birchy Lake is a small, secluded lake found just south of Kennisis Lake and offers slow fishing for small brook trout. Ice fishing is most effective in shallow water areas closer to shore. Try jigging a small spoon through the ice to attract active brookies. Access to Birchy Lake is via snowmobile south of the east boat launch on Kennisis Lake.

Bright Lake
Bright Lake is located south of Highway 60 via a rough road that is unplowed in the winter. The road can be found just west of the entrance to Algonquin Park. The lake is stocked periodically with brook trout and fishing for brook trout to 30 cm (12 in) can be good at times through the ice. Consult the Backroad Mapbook for Cottage Country for a good map of the area. Fishing for brook trout to 30 cm (12 in) is fair at times and can be good on occasion. Try a small jig through the ice.

Buck and Raven Lakes
The Buck and Raven Lakes are secluded lakes that can be accessed by snowmobile just northeast of Sand Lake off the west side of the Forestry Tower Road. The Lower and Upper Raven Lakes are stocked almost annually with splake, which can reach 75+ cm (30+ in) in size. The neighbouring Buck Lake continues to host a natural lake trout population. Lake trout average 45 cm (18 in), although can be found to 60 cm (24 in). Fishing in Buck Lake is generally slower than in the Raven Lakes. Be sure to practice catch and release for natural lake trout when possible.

Buckskin Lake
Buckskin Lake is a fairly large lake for brook trout and is stocked every few years. Brookies can grow to good sizes in this lake reaching up to 35+ cm (14 in). Ice fishing is often productive. Look for brookies cruising slowly in the shallower portions of the lake. The lake is accessible by snowmobile about 5 km south of the settlement of Foymount.

Calabogie Lake
Calabogie Lake us a beautifully scenic lake set in the rolling hills of Eastern Ontario. It is a popular year round destination that is home to a ski hill, resort and a number of winter cottages. The lake can be found by taking Highway 7 to Perth and then follow Highway 511 north to Calabogie.

Anglers can look forward to potentially hooking into northern pike, walleye or panfish. Northern Pike are often found to 6 kg (13

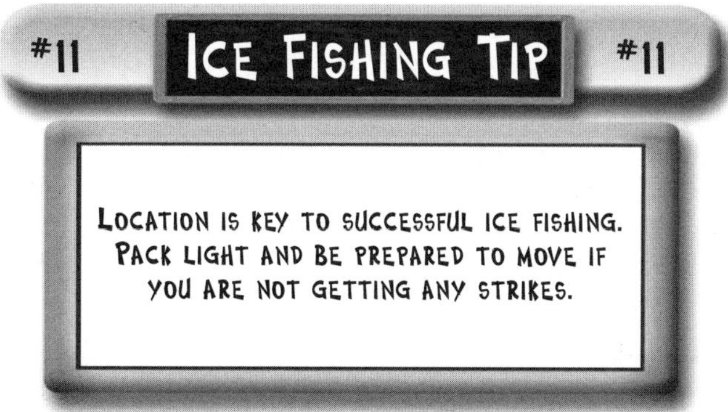

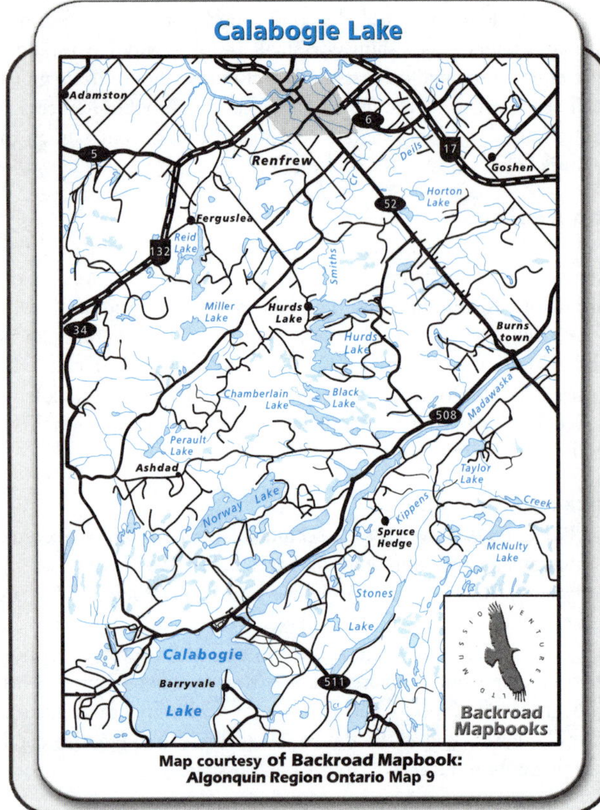

Map courtesy of Backroad Mapbook: Algonquin Region Ontario Map 9

lbs) with walleye to 3 kg (6.5 lbs) available. During winter months, walleye are the most sought after species in the lake. Fishing for walleye is generally fair but success can increase during overcast periods. A popular ice fishing spot is the bay found at the northeast end of the lake. Be sure to check provincial regulations for sanctuary areas.

Charcoal Lake

Charcoal Lake is a hidden lake located off Highway 35, just north of Dorset. The lake is stocked every few years with brook trout, which provide fair fishing for fish in the 20-30 cm (8-12 in) range.

Clara Lake

Clara Lake can be found by snowmobile via a maze of snowmobile trails about 6 km southeast of Deux-Rivieres. It is well advised to have a copy of the Backroad Mapbook for the Algonquin Region to help navigate these roads. The lake holds brook trout that can reach up to 40 cm (16 in) in size. Fishing is fair, although can be good at times. Try small white jigs through the ice.

Claradeer Lake

This lake lies south of Deux-Rivieres not far off the east side of the Brent Road. Snowmobile trails can take you to the west side of the lake, which is inhabited by natural brook trout. Ice fishing can be quite productive for brookies to 40+ cm (16+ in) in size. Try a silver spoon.

Clear Lake

Found southeast of the village of Emsdale, north of Huntsville, Clear Lake has been stocked with rainbow trout in the past. Fishing success is limited. Look for Bay Lake Road off the east side of County Road 592. Branching north from this road are a few cottage roads and the Clear Lake Road.

Cod and Wilbur Lakes

Cod and Wilbur Lake are located south of Oxtongue Lake just south of Highway 60. The lakes are stocked every few years with brook trout. Fishing for brookies to 30 cm (12 in) is good through the ice on occasion.

Coughlan Lake

Coughlan Lake is located northwest of Cross Lake and can be reached via the Cross Lake Road (Highway 523) north of Maynooth. Coughlan Lake is stocked every few years with splake and fishing is often good through the ice for nice sized splake.

Crevice Lake

To find the lake from Madawaska, follow the McCauley Lake Road north to Major Lake Road. Continue north to the power line and follow the power line road south, eventually reaching the eastern side of the lake. Crevace Lake is stocked every few years with brook trout. Brookies can reach 35 cm (14 in) in size and fishing is fair to good through the ice.

Cross Lake

The access road for Cross Lake is found off the west side of Highway 523 (Cross Lake Road) north of the village of Maynooth. Lake trout inhabit this lake and fishing can be fair through the ice. Little Cleo's and other minnow imitation lures are the most productive. Some decent sized lakers are caught throughout the winter.

Crown Lake

Crown Lake can be accessed via snowmobile and is located only a few kilometres from Algonquin Park, north of Kawagama Lake. The lake offers fair fishing for brook trout that average 25-35 cm (10-14 in).

Constant Lake

Constant Lake offers fair fishing for walleye and northern pike. Walleye can be found up to 4 kg (9 lbs) and northern pike to 5+ kg (11+ lbs). For perch enthusiasts, fishing is usually good through the ice. Many cottages line the shore of this rural lake and most of the surrounding shoreline is private land. Look for the lake on the east side of Highway 41, just north of the junction with Highway 132.

Cornick Lake

Chemical Road near Kawawaymog Lake easily accesses this lake. After crossing Smyth Creek look for the next major road branching north. Cornick Lake lies to the east of Shaw Lake and is often accessed via snowmobile. The lake supports a brook trout fishery that is fair at times in winter.

Deermeadow Lake

This lake lies south of Deux-Rivieres not far off the east side of the Brent Road. Snowmobile trails can take you to the south end of the lake, which is inhabited by natural brook trout. Ice fishing can be quite productive for bigger brookies.

Diamond Lake

Stocked every few years with lake trout, Diamond Lake was a natural lake trout lake; however, over fishing depleted natural stocks to unsustainable levels. Today the lake is stocked to maintain the lake trout fishery. Ice fishing remains a productive method on this lake.

Dick Lake

Dick Lake lies near Algonquin Park's western border and can be accessed via a rough road north of the Rain Lake Campground. In winter the road is only passable by snowmobile. Fishing can be good at times for brook trout in the 25+ cm (10 in) range. Some bigger trout (in the 35 cm/14 in range) have been caught in this lake.

Dutton Lake

Dutton Lake is stocked every few years with splake and can be found via a road in the Haliburton Forest Reserve. Fishing for splake is often fair through the ice. For directions to the lake, please consult the Haliburton Forest Reserve gatehouse.

East Lake

East Lake can be accessed via the East Lake Road found northeast of Haliburton Lake. A road branches north from the main road leading to the east end of the lake and York River. East Lake contains a self-sustaining population of brook trout that provide fair fishing through the ice. The odd trout reaches 35+ cm (14+ in) in size.

East Jeannie Lakes

The East Jeannie Lakes are two small lakes located off the Bear Lake Road from County Road 12 northwest of Dorset. The lakes are stocked every few years with brook trout. Fishing for brookies in the 20-30 cm (8-12 in) range is fair and can be good through the ice in winter.

East Paint Lake

This is one of the quieter lakes in the Frost Centre due to its remoteness. However, it does see a few visitors in winter since it is much more accessible on a snowmobile. The lake is stocked every few years with splake and offers good fishing through the ice for fish that average 30 cm (12 in) and can be found much bigger.

Estell Lake

Estell Lake is part of the J. Albert Bauer Provincial Park and can only be accessed via snowmobile through some heavy bush. The lake contains brook trout and fishing can be good on occasion through the ice in winter. To find the park, follow County Road 8 from Highway 60 to the Limberlost Road. Limberlost Road passes directly through the park.

Fairy Lake

The shoreline of this lake makes up a beautiful part of the town of Huntsville and is a busy lake year round. Ice fishing can be effective for lake trout.

Finger Lake

This small, hidden trout lake is found southeast of Aylen Lake and only accessible via snowmobile. Finger Lake is stocked every few years with brook trout. Fishing is fair for brookies to 30 cm (12 in) and is most productive in the early mornings.

Flat Iron Lake

Flat Iron Lake can be reached by snowmobile west of the settlement of Alice and is stocked every few years with splake. Splake can be found to 35+ cm (14 in) in size. The best fishing is in winter where a small white jig can be deadly through the ice.

Fletcher Lakes

These lakes can both be accessed off County Road 12 north of Dorset and are popular cottage destination lakes that are stocked every few years with lake trout. Fishing for lakers to 75 cm (30 in) is fair through the ice, but can be unbelievably slow at times.

Fork Lake

Found north of the Brain Lake access point of Algonquin Park, Fork Lake is easily accessed off a rough dirt road (snowmobile trail in winter). The lake is stocked annually with brook trout. Fishing can be good through the ice for brookies in the 25+ cm (10+ in) range.

Gardiner Lake

A 4wd road, which doubles as a snowmobile trail in winter, passes near Gardiner Lake. The lakes lie northwest of the Bissett Creek Algonquin Park access point. We have provided an inset map showing you how to find the lake. Brook trout are found to 40 cm (16 in) in size and fishing can be good through the ice.

Genesee Lake

East of the town of Trout Creek, explorers can find Genesee Lake via snowmobile. Fishing is regarded as fair to good for brook trout to 35 cm (14 in). Try a small spoon through the ice.

Godin Lake

Godin Lake can be accessed through dense bush by snowmobile in winter. The lake is about 6 km north of the village of Griffith. The lake is stocked every year with brook trout, which results in a good fishery. Brookies are most aggressive in winter and the last few weeks of the ice fishing season can be the best time of year. Try a small spoon in the shallows when ice fishing. Inquire locally at the general store in Griffith for detailed directions to the lake.

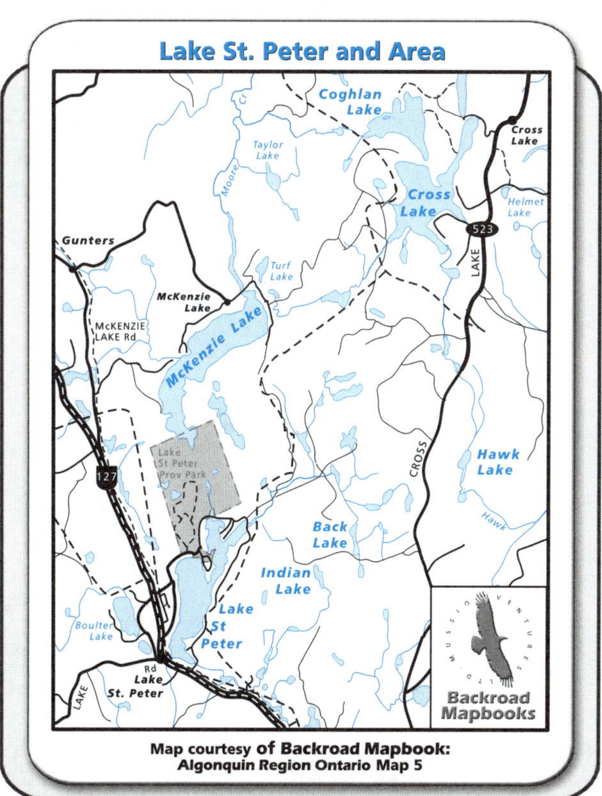

Map courtesy of Backroad Mapbook: Algonquin Region Ontario Map 5

Kennisis Lake

Fishing

The lake is a popular summer destination and a number of camps and cottages line the shoreline. With a maximum depth of 68 m (223 ft), the deep lake provides consistent fishing throughout the year with lake trout being the main attraction during the winter.

These naturally reproducing fish provide slow to fair at times for lakers that can reach up to 75 cm (30 in). Ice fishing is quite popular and is perhaps the most successful lake trout angling method on this lake. Be sure to practice catch and release for the preservation of the future sport fishery.

Access

Kennisis Lake is one of the larger lakes in the region and sits in a corner between the Leslie M. Frost Centre and the Haliburton Forest Reserve. From Haliburton, follow Highway 118 west to the Kennisis Lake Road (County Road 7). Kennisis Lake Road leads to the southern shore of the lake where one of the three access areas can be found.

Facilities

Along with the three access areas, there are a number of rental cottages and other privately run accommodations available on the lake. For the adventurous, the Leslie M. Frost Centre to the west of Kennisis Lake is home to numerous backcountry lakes and campsites. To the east, the Haliburton Forest Reserve, a privately organized recreation area, has plenty to offer visitors. At the reserve visitors can camp, rent cabins, stay in a fabulous lodge and explore the many backcountry lakes and trails in the area.

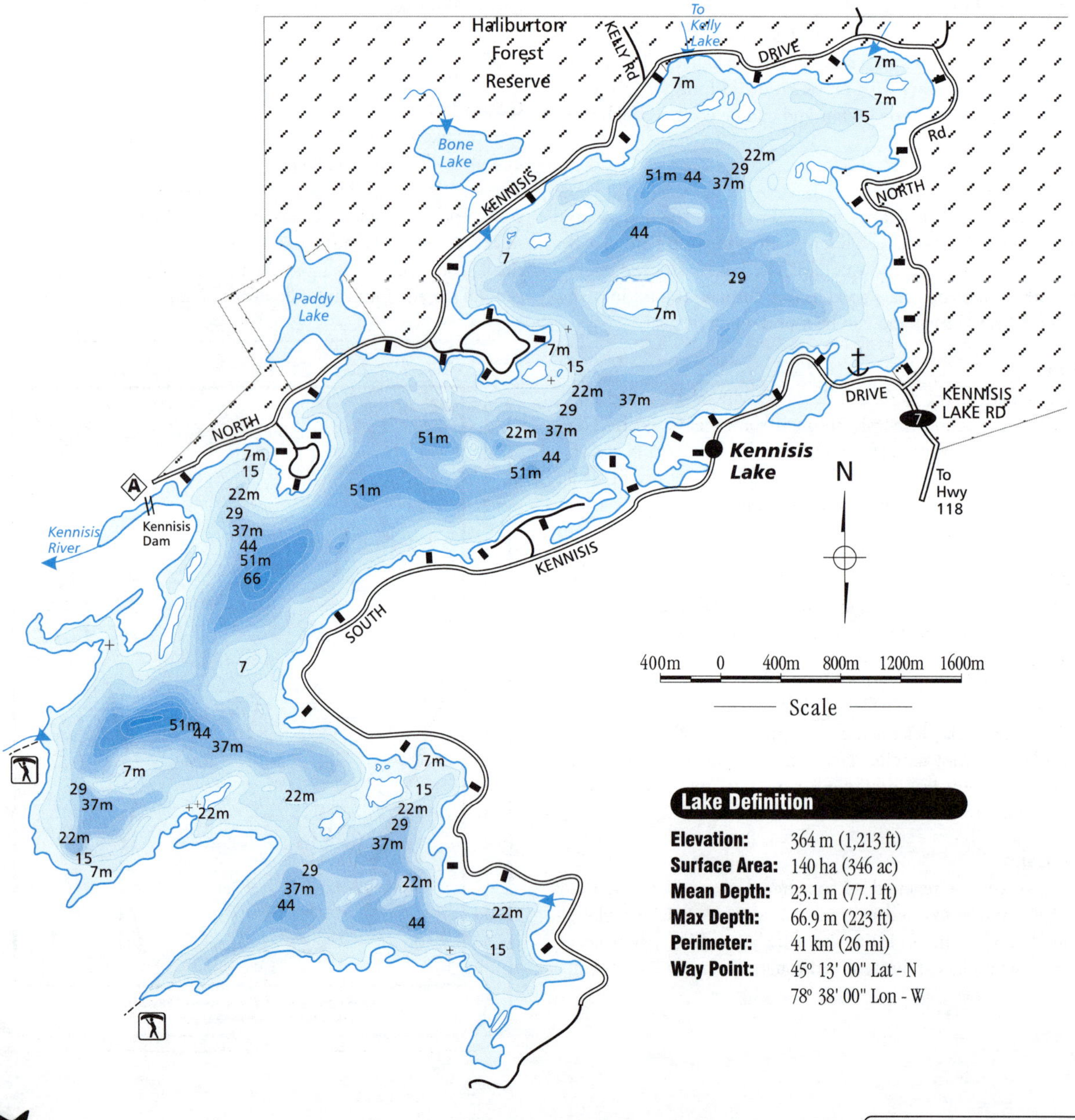

Lake Definition

Elevation:	364 m (1,213 ft)
Surface Area:	140 ha (346 ac)
Mean Depth:	23.1 m (77.1 ft)
Max Depth:	66.9 m (223 ft)
Perimeter:	41 km (26 mi)
Way Point:	45° 13' 00" Lat - N 78° 38' 00" Lon - W

Gostling Lake

Gostling Lake is a small lake found off the east side of Highway 35 north of Dorset. The lake offers slow fishing most of the time for small brook trout. Ice anglers should try jigging small spoons through the ice.

Guilford Lake

Guilford Lake is accessible via a road east of Redstone Lake, which can be easily traveled by snowmobile. The lake is stocked every few years with splake and fishing for nice sized fish is fair throughout the winter. Try jigging a small silver spoon while ice fishing.

Gun Lake

Found to the northwest of Halfway Lake, Gun Lake is stocked every few years with splake. Anglers can expect fair fishing for the hybrid species, which can reach sizes in the 45+ cm (18+ in) range. Surrounded by Crown Land, this lake is a good choice if you are looking for a peaceful ice fishing destination.

Halfway Lake

Found north of the village of Combermere, Halfway Lake has a number of cottages along its shoreline. The lake is divided into two sections that provide fair fishing for stocked splake. Anglers can expect fair fishing for the hybrid species, which can reach sizes in the 45+ cm (18+ in) range.

Hardwood Lake

Hardwood Lake is found not far from Highway 28 and is stocked every few years with splake that can grow to some decent sizes. The fast growing hybrid is very aggressive in winter and can provide some surprising results through the ice. Try jigging a small spoon or even a light coloured jig through the ice.

Harp Lake

Harp Lake is located east of Huntsville to the north of Highway 60. Harp Lake Road skirts the south end of the lake, which is stocked every few years with lake trout. Fishing for lakers can be good at times through the ice. The lake is also rumoured to have a small population of brook trout available.

Harvey and Wylie Lake

To find these lakes take the Ashport Road south of Rolphton. Harvey Lake is accessible off the east side of the road and Wylie Lake is a mere 0.5 km east of Harvey Lake. Both lakes are stocked every few years with brook trout and are popular ice fishing destinations. Fishing is regarded as fair for brookies that can reach 30+ (12+ in) in size.

Harvey Lake

Harvey Lake is a decent sized lake found northeast of Dorset not far off the Kawagama Lake Road. The majority of the shore of this lake is Crown Land. The lake has been stocked in the past with splake and there once was a natural population of brook trout. Ice fishing is rumoured to be fair for splake, but success for brook trout is unknown.

Haskins Lake

This small, hidden trout lake is found southeast of Aylen Lake among a series of well-developed snowmobile trails. Haskins Lake has been stocked with lake trout and fishing for small lakers is often good through the ice. Try jigging spoons in this lake.

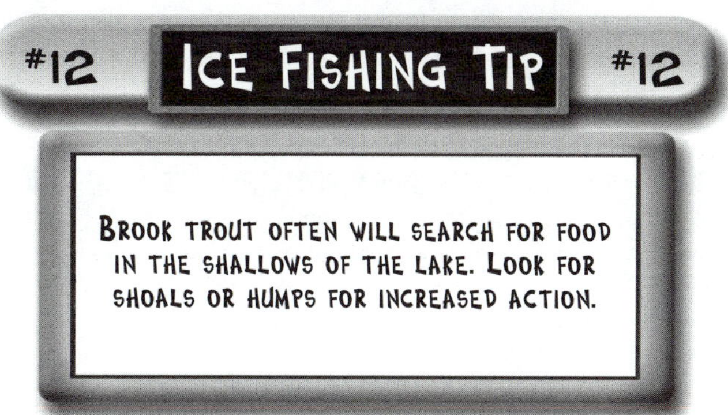

Havelock Lake

Accessible by trail within the Haliburton Forest Reserve, Havelock Lake is one of the better lake trout lakes in the area. The deep lake reaches depths of 30 m (100 ft) and has been stocked in the past with lake trout. Fishing can be good through the ice.

Hawk Lake

Hawk Lake is a secluded brook trout lake that can be accessed by snowmobile through dense bush from Cross Lake Road (County Road 523). Fishing for average sized brookies is fair throughout the year with ice fishing being one of the most productive periods.

Headstone Lakes

The Headstone Lakes are two lakes surrounded by Crown Land that are located close to Algonquin Park's east gate border north of the village of Whitney. Both lakes are only accessible via snowmobile during the winter. West Headstone Lake is stocked every few years with splake and offers good fishing at times. Splake can reach 55 cm (22 in) in size.

Heifer and Steer Lake

These are two small lakes that are stocked with brook trout every few years. Fishing for brookies is often good for trout in the 25+ cm (10+ in) range, especially during winter. The lakes can be accessed via snowmobile and are surrounded by Crown Land. The lakes lie north of the southwestern arm of Black Donald Lake.

James Lake

James Lake is a small lake that is located just north of Purdy Lake. Most visitors come via snowmobile in the winter. The lake is stocked every few years with brook trout and fishing can be good in winter for brookies in the 30 cm (12 in) range.

Johnsons Lake

Northwest of Golden Lake, this small lake can be accessed by a snowmobile trail. Brook trout are stocked in the lake every few years and provide fair fishing for brookies to 30 cm (12 in). Ice fishing can be productive for brook trout.

Kennisis Lake

See Page 80

Kamaniskeg Lake

Kamaniskeg Lake can be found off Highway 62 west of the village of Combermere. There are several cottages along the shoreline of this scenic lake. Lake trout are a much sought after species on Kamaniskeg Lake, but fishing is generally slow even during the more productive ice fishing season. Lakers can be found to 80 cm (31 in) in the lake. Watch for slot size restrictions for lake trout as well as special winter regulations. Northern pike and walleye are also found in the lake in fair numbers.

Lake St. Peter

This popular lake can be found off Highway 127, north of the village of Maynooth. There are a number of cottages along the southern shore, however the northern portion of the lake is a part of Lake St. Peter Provincial Park. The lake used to be stocked with lake trout in the past. Today, Lake St. Peter relies on natural reproduction; therefore, it is imperative to practice catch and release whenever possible. Fishing for lakers is fair during winter and can be found up to 80 cm (31 in) in size. Watch for slot size restrictions and special winter regulations.

Lake Vernon

See Page 85

Lasseter Lake

This small lake can be easily accessed off the north side if Millar Hill Road east of Huntsville. The lake offers fair fishing for small brookies.

Lee Lake

Lee Lake is found on the unplowed Lost Road, which can be picked up off the Millar Hill Road east of Huntsville. Accessed by snowmobile, the lake provides good ice fishing at times for brook trout to 35 cm (14 in) in size.

Little Clear, Long and Turtle Lake

These three small trout lakes are all easily accessed by snowmobile via Boundary Road east of Lake Nosbonsing. The lakes are stocked regularly and offer good fishing at times with ice fishing being one of the most productive periods. Brookies are small, but have been caught to 35+ cm (14 in).

Long Lake

Long Lake is a small lake found within Samuel De Champlain Provincial Park. The lake is stocked annually with brook trout since the lake receives significant angling pressure throughout the year. Fishing is fair at times through the ice.

Long Lake

Located north of Black Donald Lake, Long Lake is best accessed by snowmobile from the east side of Highway 41 north of Griffith. Fishing through the ice can be good at times for stocked brook trout that vary in size from very small to the 30 cm (12 in) range.

Longline Lake

Longline Lake can be easily accessed off the north side of Highway 117 west of Dorset. The lake is stocked with splake every few years that provide for fair fishing through the ice. There also once was a natural population of brook trout in the lake, although current fishing success for brookies is unknown.

Louie Lakes

Northeast of Dorset, these two small lakes can be accessed off County Road 12. Both lakes offer slow fishing for brook trout. Louie Lake is also stocked every few years with splake, which offer good fishing at times through the ice.

Loxton Lake

Accessible by snowmobile northeast of Kawawaymog Lake, Loxton Lake supports a natural brook trout population. Fishing is generally fair through the ice for brookies to 35 cm (14 in). The easiest access is found by following the Forestry Road east from Trout Creek on Highway 11. Look for the Smyth Lake Dam turnoff and follow this road south to Loxton Lake.

McDonald Lake

McDonald Lake is a secluded trout lake that can only be accessed by snowmobile in the winter. The lake lies right along the southern border of Algonquin Park just west of the Bonnechere River. For access details, inquire locally or consult a copy of the Backroad Mapbook for the Algonquin Region. The lake is stocked with brook trout every few years and offers good fishing for brookies to 30 cm (12 in). Jig a Little Cleo through the ice in winter for added success.

McHale Lake

This small lake can be found just off a rough road, west of the village of Griffith. The lake is stocked almost annually with brook trout that usually provide good fishing for trout in the 20-30 cm (8-12 in) range. Ice fishing with small spoons or white jigs is quite popular. Inquire at the general store in Griffith for access details.

McKenzie Lake

McKenzie Lake is a productive fishing lake with a number of cottages along its northern shoreline. A good gravel road leads to the public access point on the northern point, while the southern tip of the lake lies within the northern boundary of Lake St. Peter Provincial Park. Lake trout are caught up to 60 cm (24 in) in length. Watch for slot size restrictions and special winter regulations.

Martin (Boundary) Lake

Martin Lake is accessible via snowmobile north of East Lake. The smaller lake is stocked every two years with brook trout. Fishing can be good fishing through the ice for brook trout that average 25-35 cm (10-14 in) in size.

Meach Lakes

The Meach Lakes are two average sized brook trout lakes that can be accessed via snowmobile west of the village of Lake St. Peter. Fishing can be good through the ice for brook trout to 40+ cm (16+ lb) in size.

Menet Lake

Access to Menet Lake is via the Menet Lake Road southwest off Highway 17 near Driftwood Provincial Park. The lake is stocked annually with splake, which provide for fair fishing for splake to 40+ cm (16 in). White jigs through the ice can be effective.

Middle Shanty Lake

This lake is stocked with brook trout every few years that provide good fishing for fish in the 20-35 cm (8-14 in) range. Try a small white jig through the ice in winter. Access to the lake is by snowmobile south off the Forestry Tower Road east of Sand Lake. Across the road from Middle Shanty Lake lies a small, unnamed lake that also has a good population of brookies in it. There is also another, larger lake just south of there that holds nice sized brook trout.

Mink Lake

Mink Lake is a secluded lake that is most often visited by snowmobile. The lake offers fair fishing for small brook trout through the ice or in spring, just after ice off. To reach the lake take Highway 117 west of Dorset and look for the Paint Lake Road. The Paint Lake Road heads southwest past Paint Lake. Mink Lake is about a 1.5 km (1 mi) snowmobile ride north off Paint Lake Road.

Monkshood Lake

Monkshood Lake can be found by snowmobile trail from Aylen Lake Road east of Madawaska. The secluded lake is stocked every few years with splake and provides good fishing through the ice for nice sized fish.

Moonbeam Lakes

To find these lakes from Madawaska, follow the McCauley Lake Road north to Major Lake Road. Continue north to the power line and follow the power line road south. North Moonbeam Lake is found on the west side of the power line road. Moonbeam Lake is further southwest and will require a bit of bushwhacking to find it. The lakes are stocked every few years with brook trout. Brookies can reach 35 cm (14 in) in size and fishing can be good through the ice.

Morrow Lake

Morrow Lake is stocked annually with lake trout. Fishing is usually good through the ice for lakers that average 35-40 cm (14-16 in) in size, although they do grow bigger. The access to the lake is by snowmobile southeast of the village of Griffith. Look for the Morrow Lake Road.

Mousseau Lake

Southwest of the village of Bissett Creek, this lake can be accessed by snowmobile. We have provided an inset map showing you the road systems in the area. Mousseau Lake is stocked every few years with splake, which can be found in the 40+ cm (16+ in) range. Fishing is fair during winter.

Murphy Lake

Murphy Lake is found south of Highway 132 and the Mount St. Patrick Road. A snowmobile is needed to negotiate the series of logging roads in the area. Fishing through the ice can be good at times for stocked brook trout that vary in size from very small to the 30 cm (12 in) range.

Nehemiah Lake

This small, secluded lake is found in the Leslie M. Frost Centre, on the north side of the Sherborne Access Road. The lake is stocked ever few years with brook trout and the fishing for brookies that average 20-25 cm (8-10 in) is often good through the ice.

Nelson Lakes

To reach these lakes, follow the Limberlost Road (County Road 8) northeast from Huntsville to the Tasso Lake Road. The Tasso Lake Road provides easy snowmobile access to both lakes. Nelson Lake offers fair fishing for brook trout that can be slow at times. Little Nelson Lake lies west of the much larger Tasso Lake and is stocked every few years with brook trout. These brookies can grow to 35 cm (14 in) in size and offer fair fishing in spring and through the ice.

Niger Lake

Niger Lake can be located by snowmobile south of Highway 60 near the entrance to Algonquin Park. The lake is stocked periodically with brook trout and fishing for brookies to 30 cm (12 in) is fair. Fishing is often better in the winter at this secluded lake.

Oxbend Lake

This secluded lake can only be accessed by snowmobile. Most visitors follow the TOPS Feeder Trail south from Highway 127 between Maynooth and Lake St. Peter. The lake is stocked periodically with splake and fishing is fair through the ice. This species is a cross between brook trout and lake trout that can grow to good sizes in this lake. In fact, fish in the 60+ cm (24 in) range have been caught here using a silver spoons.

Papineau Lake

Papineau Lake is a scenic lake that has several cottages along its shoreline. Fishing for average sized northern pike is slow to fair at times in the winter. Best results occur during overcast periods and in the evening. Lake trout anglers will find some nice sized fish (to 70 cm/28 in) with fishing being fair on occasion through the ice. There are two public access points, one on the north side and one on the south side of the lake. County Road 62 passes near the southern portion of the lake. Check regulations for slot size and special winter restrictions.

Pat Lake

This small brook trout lake is found a few kilometres west of Lake St. Peter via snowmobile. The lake is stocked every few years with brook trout that average 20-25 cm (8-10 in) in size. However, by winter some of these trout have grown to be over 30 cm (12 in) in size.

Pell Lake

Pell Lake is a small brook trout lake that is stocked every few years

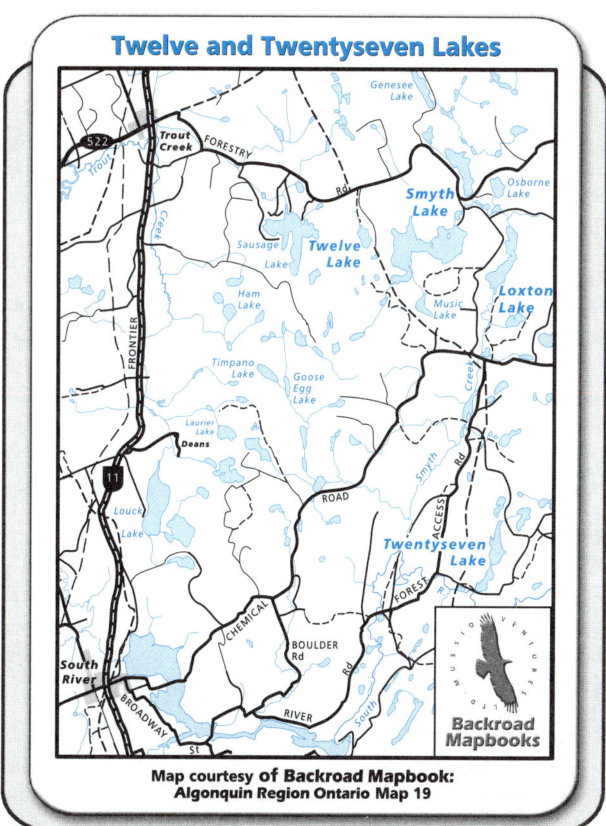

Map courtesy of Backroad Mapbook: Algonquin Region Ontario Map 19

with brook trout. The only access to the lake is by snowmobile in winter from Coghlan Lake northeast of the village of Lake St. Peter. Brookies can be found to 40+ cm (15.5 lb), although are generally much smaller. Ice fishing can be good at times.

Percy Lake

Percy Lake has cottages along its shoreline and can be found via the Percy Lake Road east of Lake Haliburton. The lake is stocked every few years with lake trout and fishing for lakers to 75 cm (30 in) is fair and can be good at times. Action usually increases at dusk and during overcast periods.

Peyton Lakes

The Peyton Lakes are two remote, picturesque lakes found amid the Almaguin Highlands. The only access to the lakes is by trail, which has helped immensely in maintaining the quality of the lakes. Almost all of the fishing on these lakes is done through the ice in winter. Both lakes are inhabited by natural brook trout and offer quite good fishing at times. Brookies in the lakes are not very big (they average 20-35 cm/8-14 inches in size), but they do hit hard at times. Practicing catch and release can go a long way in helping maintain the quality of this fishery. Inquire locally or consult the Backroad Mapbook for the Algonquin Region for detailed directions.

Pine Lake

A remote lake that is accessed by a logging road in summer, Pine Lake is best accessed by snowmobile in winter. The logging road system branches from the Forestry Tower Road east of Sand Lake. The Backroad Mapbook for Algonquin Region provides a good map of the area. The lake is stocked with brook trout every few years that provide good fishing for fish in the 20-35 cm (8-14 in) range. Try a small white jig through the ice in winter.

Purdy Lake

Purdy Lake lies off County Road 62 east of Maynooth. The lake is a popular cottage destination lake that is stocked with lake trout. Lakers can be found up to 65 cm (26 in) and are best caught through the ice. Be sure to check special lake trout regulations for Purdy Lake.

Raglan (White) Lake

Raglan Lake is another lake trout lake that has become solely dependant on stocking for its angling opportunities. The lake is stocked every few years with lake trout and provides fair fishing during ice fishing season. Lakers can grow to sizes exceeding 70+ cm (28 lb). To reach the lake, take Highway 515 southeast from Combermere to County Road 514 south. County Road 514 passes by a few short unplowed access roads that lead to the lake.

Rattail Lake

A 4wd road, which doubles as a snowmobile trail in winter, passes near Rattail Lake. The lakes lie northwest of the Bissett Creek Algonquin Park access point. We have provided an inset map showing you how to find the lake. Brook trout are found to 40 cm (16 in) in size and fishing can be fair through the ice.

Ronald Lake

If you are looking for seclusion then Ronald Lake will certainly meet that need. The lake is found via a 455 m (1,493 ft) portage/snowmobile trail from the north end of Nehemiah Lake. Nehemiah on the other hand is found off the north side of the Sherborne Access Road in the Leslie M. Frost Centre. Ronald Lake is stocked every few years with brook trout that provide fair to good fishing in the winter. Fish over 30 cm (12 in) in size are reported annually.

Ross Lake

Ross Lake is stocked every few years with splake and provides fair to good fishing at times for average sized splake. Access to the lake is by the Ross Lake Road off the Haliburton Lake Road north of the town of Haliburton.

Sand Lake

This is one of the larger lakes in the Kearney area and is a popular summer destination lake. Many cottages line the scenic shoreline. The lake is stocked every few years with lake trout, which provide fair fishing for trout to 70 cm (28 in). Ice fishing for lakers is the most productive method to catch the elusive fish.

Sandox Lake

This secluded lake can only be accessed by snowmobile. Most visitors follow the TOPS Feeder Trail south from Highway 127 between Maynooth and Lake St. Peter. The lake is stocked periodically with splake and fishing is fair through the ice. Silver spoons are known as one of the more productive winter lures for these fish that are rumoured to reach 60 cm (24 in) in size in this lake.

Sears Lake

Found north of the Brain Lake access point of Algonquin Park, Sears Lake is a remote lake that will require a good map and navigational skills to find. The lake can be found by snowmobile along a rustic trail east from the Brain Lake access road. Natural brook trout are found in the lake in fair numbers.

Shaw Lake

Found on a branch road north of Chemical Road near Kawawaymog Lake, Shaw Lake has been stocked with rainbow trout. Fishing can be good at times for rainbows to 35 cm (14 in).

Silversheen Lake

This small brook trout lake is found a few kilometres west of Lake St. Peter via snowmobile. Look for a major road branching north about 4 km along the Mink Lake Road. This road leads by the west side of Silversheen Lake. The lake is stocked every few years with brook trout that average 20-25 cm (8-10 in) in size. Fishing can be good through the ice at times.

Smyth Lake

The easiest access into Smyth Lake is found by following the Forestry Road east from Trout Creek on Highway 11. Look for the Smyth Lake Dam turnoff and follow this road south to the northern end of the lake. Smyth Lake is stocked every few years with rainbow trout.

Soaking Lake

Soaking Lake is a small, secluded lake that can be found via a rough road northwest of the village of Lake St. Peter. Ice fishing is generally fair for small brook trout. The road to the lake may be difficult to find due to the maze of logging offshoot roads in the area. However, there should be a snowmobile track leading to the lake.

Sunken Lake

You can find this lake off the Kawagama Road (County Road 8)

Lake Vernon

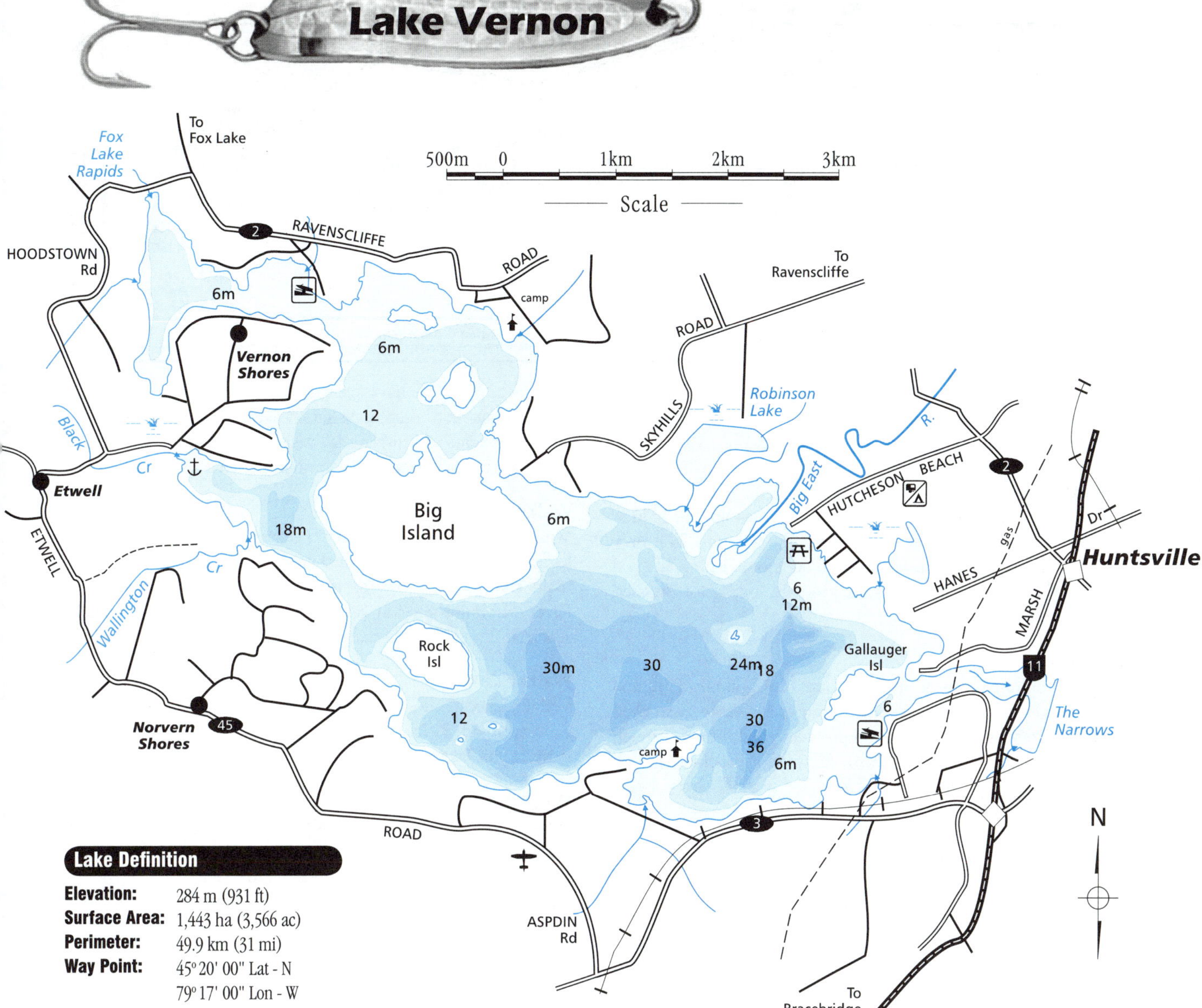

Lake Definition

Elevation:	284 m (931 ft)
Surface Area:	1,443 ha (3,566 ac)
Perimeter:	49.9 km (31 mi)
Way Point:	45° 20' 00" Lat - N 79° 17' 00" Lon - W

Fishing

Over the last several decades, Lake Vernon has become a very popular cottage destination lake. It was named as far back as 1861 and has seen over 140 years of changes since then. Originally, the main species in the lake were lake trout and brook trout. Over the years, new species have been introduced into the lake including, smallmouth bass, largemouth bass, rainbow trout and there has even been a confirmed report of a brown trout caught in the lake in 1966. Today, trout are only a memory but both bass species, lake trout and northern pike, provide a fairly decent fishery.

During winter anglers scout the lake in pursuit of both lake trout and northern pike. Lakers are stocked every two to three years but fishing still remains fairly slow, even through the ice. Lake trout prefer the deeper water in the east part of the lake during the summer; however, during winter there have been reports of catches each year in the west side of the lake. Northern pike fishing is fairly steady in winter and this aggressive fish can provide quite the surprise at times. Look for pike off shoal areas around Big Island and Rock Islands.

Access

Lake Vernon is located to the east of the town of Huntsville. To access the southeastern shore of the lake, take Highway 11 to County Road 3 (Yearly Road) and head west along that secondary highway. Almost immediately after you turn onto County Road 3, look for boat launch signs to direct yourself to the access point. Another access point is found off County Road 2 (Ravenscliffe Road). This road eventually brings you to the northwest end of the lake and a boat launch access point there. Snowmobilers use these launches in the winter.

Facilities

Lake Vernon lies in the heart of the cottage country and just to the west of the bustling town of Huntsville. Huntsville has developed into a popular all season getaway town, hence there are a number of resorts and lodges found in the area and even on Lake Vernon.

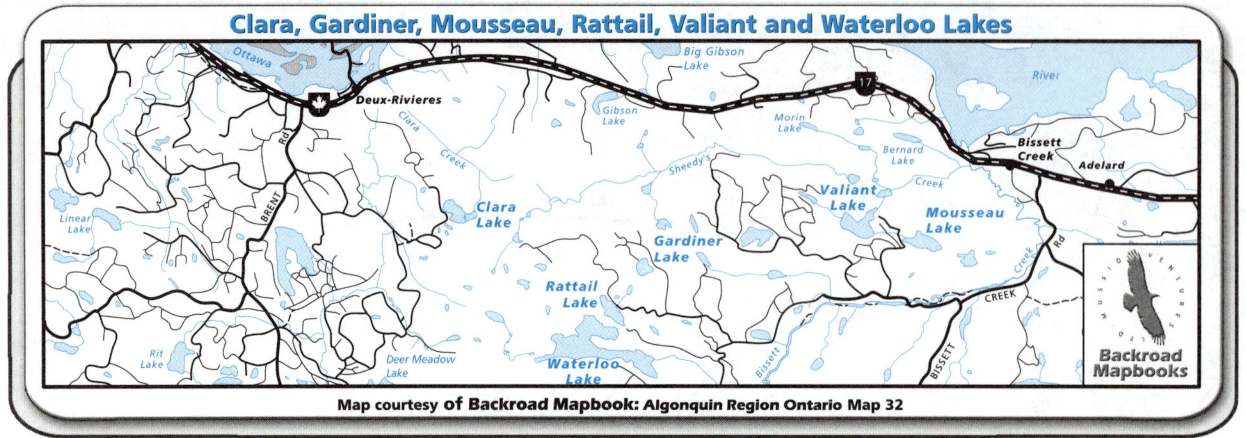

Map courtesy of Backroad Mapbook: Algonquin Region Ontario Map 32

east of Dorset. The lake has been stocked with rainbow trout and fishing for rainbows can be fair through the ice. Brook trout are also thought to inhabit the lake, although fishing reports are sketchy.

Trout Lake

A few kilometres northeast of the village of Madawaska this hidden trout lake is stocked every few years with brook trout. The only access to the lake is by snowmobile or on foot. Fishing is good through the ice for small brook trout. Inquire locally for detailed directions to the lake.

Troutspawn Lakes

These lakes lie just south of the West Gate of Algonquin Park and can be found via snowmobile. Little Troutspawn Lake is stocked every few years with brook trout and provides good fishing through the ice for brookies to 30 cm (12 in). Fishing for brookies to 35+ cm (14 in) is fair in Troutspawn Lake. Try a small silver spoon through the ice in either lake.

Tub Lake

A few kilometres northeast of the village of Madawaska this hidden trout lake is stocked every few years with brook trout. The best access to the lake is by snowmobile or on foot from an old road leading west from Opeongo River Provincial Park. Fishing is good through the ice for small brook trout.

Turtle Lake

Turtle Lake can be accessed via trail from a dirt road or from the bank of the Madawaska River east of Hardwood Lake. The secluded lake is quite beautiful and is stocked almost annually with brook trout. Ice fishing is often good through the ice.

Twelve Lake

This small hidden lake is set amid the Almaguin Highlands. The lake can only be accessed by trail, which helps reduce the fishing pressure on the lake. It has been stocked with brook trout and fishing can be good throughout the winter.

Twentyseven Lake

Twentyseven Lake can be accessed by snowmobile trail east of South River, not too far off the main Forest Access Road. The lake supports a natural brook trout fishery, which provides good fishing at times for some nice sized trout. Ice fishing with a small spoon or white jig can be effective.

Valiant Lake

Southwest of the village of Bissett Creek, this lake can be accessed by snowmobile. We have provided an inset map showing you the road systems in the area. Valiant Lake is stocked with lake trout every few years and fishing for lakers in the 40-50 cm (16-20 in) range can be good, especially through the ice.

Walker Lake

Walker Lake can be accessed by snowmobile only. The lake is located northwest of Bonnechere Provincial Park, look for the main trail leading towards the lake that follows along the Pine River. Fishing is good at times for stocked brook trout, which can reach 35 cm (14 in) in size.

Walker Lake

Walker Lakes is located east of Huntsville off the west side of County Road 8. Ice anglers will find a small population of lake trout in this lake.

Waterloo Lake

Waterloo Lake is one of the largest lakes in the area and is accessible via snowmobile west of the village of Bissett Creek on Highway 17. While a rough 4wd road leads to the lake, most of the fishing on this lake occurs during winter. Lake trout and brook trout are found in fair numbers. Lakers can reach 45+ cm (18+ in) and brook trout average 25-35 cm (10-14 in). The natural lake trout population has shown signs of stress and it is imperative to practice catch and release to maintain a quality fishery. Watch for special slot size restrictions and winter regulations.

West Aumond Lake

This secluded walleye lake can be accessed via snowmobile south of Mattawa. The lake receives most of its pressure in winter by ice fishing anglers. Fishing in the lake is fair, but can be slow at times. Walleye average 0.5-1kg (1-2 lbs).

Wish Lake

This lake is stocked with brook trout every few years and can be accessed by snowmobile in the winter. To find the lake from Madawaska, follow the McCauley Lake Road north to Major Lake Road. Continue north to the power line and follow the power line road north to the first branch off the north side. Brook trout average 20-30 cm (8-12 in) in size.

Wolf Lake

Wolf Lake lies in the Haliburton Forest and is home to a wide variety of sport fish species, including stocked splake. The lake lies just to the east of the much larger Little Kennesis Lake and can provide good fishing through the ice for small splake. Inquire at the Haliburton Forest Reserve front gate for detailed directions to the lake.

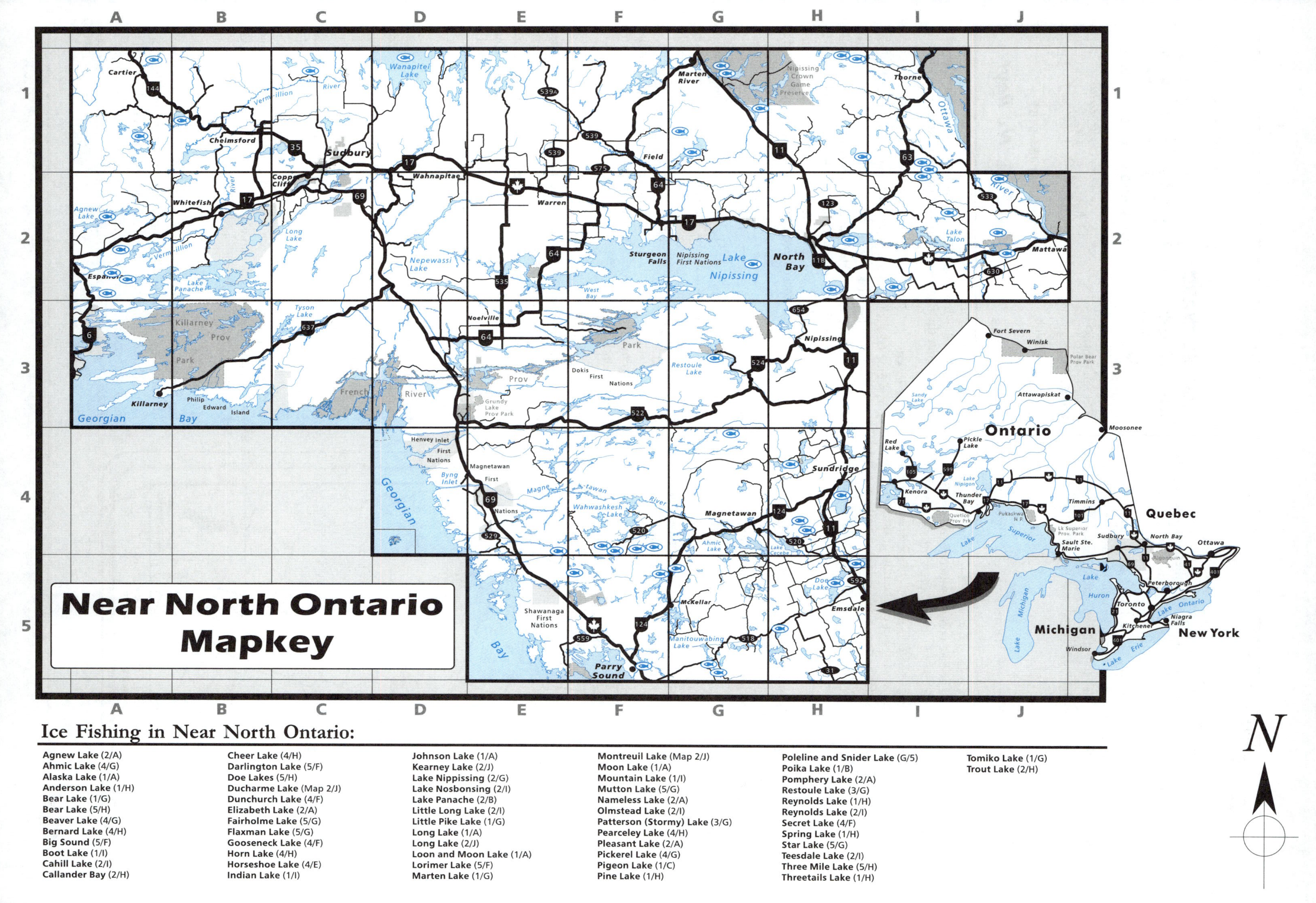
Near North Ontario
Mapkey
Cartier
Chelmsford
Sudbury
Whitefish
Copper Cliff
Wahnapitae
Warren
Field
Marten River
Thorne
Mattawa
North Bay
Sturgeon Falls
Nipissing First Nations
Lake Nipissing
Nepewassi Lake
Noelville
Killarney Prov Park
Killarney
Philip Edward Island
Georgian Bay
French River
Grundy Lake Prov Park
Dokis First Nations
Restoule Lake
Nipissing
Sundridge
Magnetawan
Magnetawan First Nations
Henvey Inlet First Nations
Byng Inlet
Shawanaga First Nations
Parry Sound
McKellar
Manitouwabing Lake
Emsdale
Doe Lake
Ahmic Lake
Wahwashkesh Lake
Lake Talon
Nipissing Crown Game Preserve
Ontario
Quebec
Michigan
New York
Fort Severn
Winisk
Attawapiskat
Moosonee
Pickle Lake
Red Lake
Kenora
Thunder Bay
Timmins
Sault Ste. Marie
Ottawa
Toronto
Peterborough
Kitchener
Niagra Falls
Windsor
Lake Superior
Lake Huron
Lake Michigan
Lake Ontario
Lake Erie
N
Ice Fishing in Near North Ontario:
Agnew Lake (2/A)
Ahmic Lake (4/G)
Alaska Lake (1/A)
Anderson Lake (1/H)
Bear Lake (1/G)
Bear Lake (5/H)
Beaver Lake (4/G)
Bernard Lake (4/H)
Big Sound (5/F)
Boot Lake (1/I)
Cahill Lake (2/I)
Callander Bay (2/H)
Cheer Lake (4/H)
Darlington Lake (5/F)
Doe Lakes (5/H)
Ducharme Lake (Map 2/J)
Dunchurch Lake (4/F)
Elizabeth Lake (2/A)
Fairholme Lake (5/G)
Flaxman Lake (5/G)
Gooseneck Lake (4/F)
Horn Lake (4/H)
Horseshoe Lake (4/E)
Indian Lake (1/I)
Johnson Lake (1/A)
Kearney Lake (2/J)
Lake Nipissing (2/G)
Lake Nosbonsing (2/I)
Lake Panache (2/B)
Little Long Lake (2/I)
Little Pike Lake (1/G)
Long Lake (1/A)
Long Lake (2/J)
Loon and Moon Lake (1/A)
Lorimer Lake (5/F)
Marten Lake (1/G)
Montreuil Lake (Map 2/J)
Moon Lake (1/A)
Mountain Lake (1/I)
Mutton Lake (5/G)
Nameless Lake (2/A)
Olmstead Lake (2/I)
Patterson (Stormy) Lake (3/G)
Pearceley Lake (4/H)
Pleasant Lake (2/A)
Pickerel Lake (4/G)
Pigeon Lake (1/C)
Pine Lake (1/H)
Poleline and Snider Lake (G/5)
Poika Lake (1/B)
Pomphery Lake (2/A)
Restoule Lake (3/G)
Reynolds Lake (1/H)
Reynolds Lake (2/I)
Secret Lake (4/F)
Spring Lake (1/H)
Star Lake (5/G)
Teesdale Lake (2/I)
Three Mile Lake (5/H)
Threetails Lake (1/H)
Tomiko Lake (1/G)
Trout Lake (2/H)

Agnew Lake (Map 18/B3)

Agnew Lake is one of the larger lakes in the area and can be accessed from a number of different dirt roads north off Highway 17 near Espanola. The lake is host to several camps and cottages, and remains a very scenic Near North lake. Fishing in the big lake is fair to good at times for northern pike that average 3+ kg (6.5+ lbs) in size. Walleye are also found in the lake in fair numbers and are best fished with minnows, although jigs can work quite well through the ice.

Ahmic Lake

Found close to the village of Magnetawan and Highway 124, Ahmic Lake is one of the larger lakes in the area. There are many access points as well as a popular snowmobile route that anglers can use to get out on the ice. The lake continues to offer decent fishing opportunities, despite increasing fishing pressure. Walleye and northern pike are the main sportfish anglers are looking for in the winter and fishing is generally fair but can be slow at times. Despite sometimes slower success for walleye, anglers do find walleye in the 4+ kg (9+ lb) range annually. Panfish also provide for some consistent action through the ice.

Alaska Lake

Found on the west side of Highway 144 north of Cartier, Alaska Lake is stocked almost annually with brook trout. Although not very big, these fish do provide fairly steady fishing through the ice.

Anderson Lake

The remote nature of this picturesque lake often rewards anglers with a peaceful setting and good fishing for natural brook trout. These feisty trout can be very aggressive in the winter. Try jigging a small silver spoon through the ice. For a detailed map of the area, please consult the Backroad Mapbook for Near North Ontario.

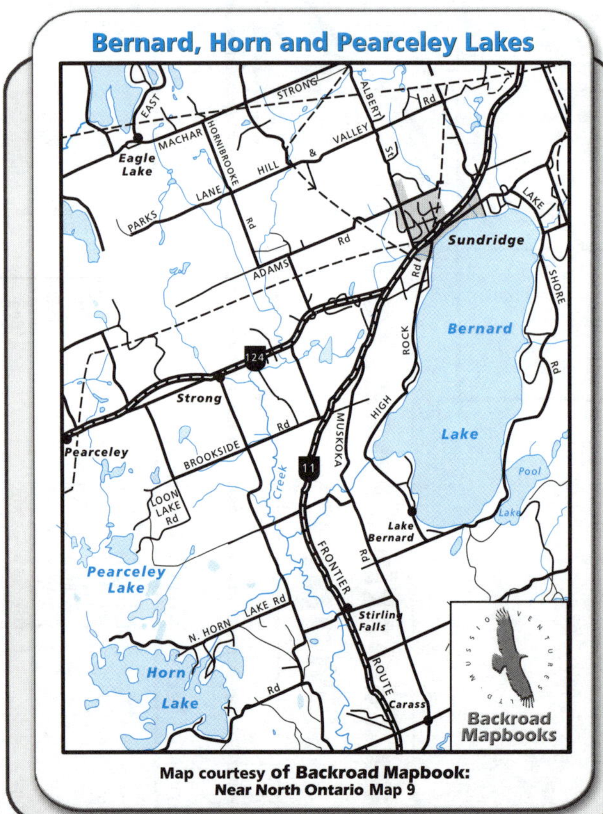

Map courtesy of Backroad Mapbook: Near North Ontario Map 9

Bear Lake

This scenic lake is found north of North Bay, not far from Highway 11. Smallmouth bass, lake trout and northern pike inhabit the lake. Bass are inactive during the winter months, while northern pike success is generally fair through the ice. Pike are found to 4+ kg (9+ lbs) in this lake. Lake trout are the most sought after sportfish in the lake and are stocked every few years. Lakers can be found to 3 kg (6.5 lbs) in size, with the most success coming through the ice.

Bear Lake

Bear Lake is located just off Highway 518 east of Orrville and has a number of cottages along its shoreline. Most of the ice fishing pressure is directed towards the northern pike and walleye in the lake. Pike are a little more common and can be found up to 3.5 kg (8 lbs) in size. The population of walleye is marginal, with fishing success generally slow. Ice fishing for perch is also popular during winter months.

Beaver Lake

Connected to the much larger Ahmic Lake, Beaver Lake offers similar fishing opportunities as the bigger lake. Walleye and northern pike are the main sportfish anglers are looking for in the winter and fishing is generally fair but can be slow at times. Despite sometimes-slower success for walleye, anglers do find walleye in the 4+ kg (9+ lb) range annually. Panfish also provide for some consistent action through the ice.

Bernard Lake

Accessible from the town of Sundridge, there are a number of cottages along its shoreline, although fishing continues to be productive year round. The main ice fishing attraction to the lake is lake trout, which can be caught to 70+ cm (28+ in). Another popular ice fishing attraction on Bernard Lake is the productive whitefish fishery. Whitefish grow to decent sizes in the lake and can provide great fun to anglers throughout the year. A small population of brook trout also remains in the lake, although the species is quite rare to find. Alternatively, panfish can provide for plenty of action in winter on this magnificent lake.

Big Sound

Big Sound is the large bay accessible from the town of Parry Sound. In winter, the bay is an outdoor playground with ice fishing and snowmobiling being the main activities enjoyed on the ice. The main attraction for ice anglers is the trout that can be caught in the bay. Lake trout, splake and rainbow trout can all be caught here in the winter months, with lake trout being the main draw. Other species that are present in the area include northern pike and walleye. The bay is quite productive for ice fishing and certainly rivals some of the more popular ice fishing destinations in this part of the province.

Boot Lake

Located between Highways 533 and 63 north of Mattawa, Boot Lake is a peaceful lake to visit in winter. The natural brook trout that inhabit the lake can provide some good fishing at times through the ice. Overcast periods seem to be more productive on these lakes in the winter.

Cahill Lake

Only accessible via snowmobile in the winter, Cahill Lake is found south of the power line that can be picked up off Olrig Road west of Mattawa. The medium sized lake is stocked annually with splake that provide fair fishing during the winter. Trout in this lake are usually not very big, although some 30+ cm (12+ in) trout are taken annually.

Callander Bay

Callander Bay is a part of the world-renowned Lake Nipissing. The bay has quickly grown to be perhaps the number one ice fishing destination in the province. In winter, several different sportfish species can be found in the bay, including northern pike, walleye, muskellunge, jumbo perch and whitefish. Northern pike can be found to 5+ kg (11+ lbs) in size and fishing can be fair to good in a few areas. Walleye fishing in the bay is also quite productive. The prized sportfish can reach sizes of up to 3+ kg (6.5+ lbs). Jigging can be an effective method for finding walleye during winter although most anglers use live minnow presentations. In addition to a few muskellunge, there are also are plenty of panfish available to keep the lines active throughout the day in Callander Bay.

Please note: the walleye of Lake Nipissing are often over targeted due to the easy access of the lake. Be sure to help maintain the fishery and be sure to practice catch and release when possible.

#13 **ICE FISHING TIP** #13

DRILLING CAN GENERATE A LOT OF NOISE. TRY DRILLING ALL OF YOUR HOLES AT ONE TIME AS OPPOSED TO FISHING ONE HOLE THEN DRILLING THE NEXT. THIS WILL HELP KEEP THE NOISE DOWN THROUGHOUT THE DAY.

Cheer Lake

Cheer Lake lies just south of Eagle Lake west of Sundridge, although permission must be obtained to cross private property to access the lake. A fair population of brook trout remains in the lake, although fishing success is usually limited.

Darlington Lake

Found just north of Parry Sound near Highway 69, Darlington Lake offers slow to fair fishing for lake trout. Lake trout are stocked annually and average 30 cm (12 in) in size. Lakers are best caught with minnows or by jigging small spoons.

Doe Lakes

The Doe Lakes can be easily accessed just west of Highway 11, north of the town of Emsdale. The lakes are some of the larger water bodies in the area and have a number of cottages along their shorelines. Walleye and northern pike can be found in fair numbers, with walleye to 3 kg (6.5 lbs) and northern pike 3.5 kg (8 lbs) still caught annually. Lake trout can also be found in the lakes, although success is usually quite slow.

Ducharme Lake

This lake is stocked annually with brook trout, which provide for good fishing through the ice in winter. Spoons or small white jigs can be productive. The lake is accessible by snowmobile north of Mattawa off of Highway 533.

Dunchurch Lake

Dunchurch Lake is a secluded lake that is mainly fished in the winter through the ice. Access to the lake in winter months is limited to snowmobile trails west of the village of Dunchurch. A good map and a GPS unit can definitely help access the lake. A fair population of small brook trout inhabits the lake.

Elizabeth Lake

East of the town of Espanola, Elizabeth Lake can be found off Panache Lake Road. The lake is stocked almost annually with lake trout, which provide for good fishing through the ice. Northern pike are also present in the lake in fair to good numbers and can be found in the 4+ kg (9+ lb) range.

Fairholme Lake

Stocked every few years with lake trout, the trout of Fairholme Lake provide for slow to fair fishing in the winter months. The lake lies just off Highway 124 north of the settlement of McKellar.

Flaxman Lake

This lake lies to the south of the Seguin Trail between Orrville and Parry Sound. While there is a road into Flaxman Lake, it is rarely plowed; therefore, access is via snowmobile. The medium sized lake is stocked every few years with lake trout, which provides for fair fishing at times for lakers in the 35 cm (14 in) range. Slot size limits and special restrictions are in effect on Flaxman Lake for lake trout. Be sure to check the regulations before heading out.

Gooseneck Lake

Gooseneck Lake can be accessed just off the north side of Highway 520 west of the settlement of Whitestone. A number of cottages are located along the shoreline of this beautiful lake and fishing is generally fair in winter for panfish and northern pike. Walleye also inhabit the lake, although they are harder to find comparative to other species.

Horn Lake

Horn Lake is accessible via the North or South Horn Lake Roads near Burk's Falls. A natural population of lake trout inhabits the lake and fishing is generally fair through the ice. Please check for special lake trout restrictions on Horn Lake before heading out.

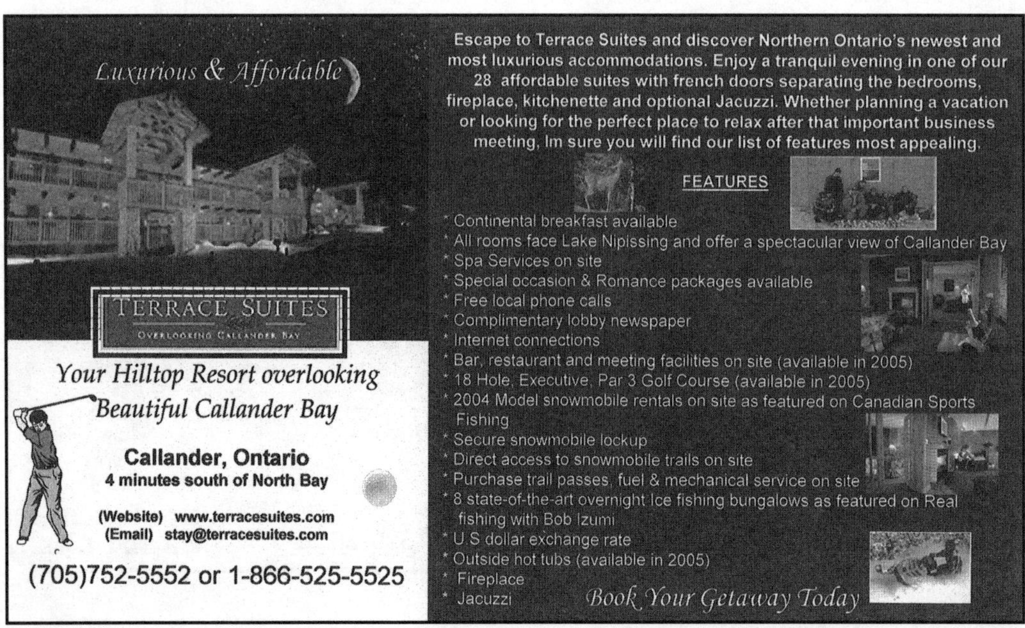

Horseshoe Lake

This small, hidden lake can be accessed by snowmobile from the much larger Six Mile Lake. Horseshoe Lake offers good fishing at times in the winter for decent sized northern pike. A fair walleye population is also present in the lake and this prized sportfish receives significant pressure during ice fishing season.

Indian Lake

Accessible by snowmobile, this lake is found just east of Highway 63 northeast of North Bay. The lake is home to natural brook trout, which provide fair fishing for above average sized brookies.

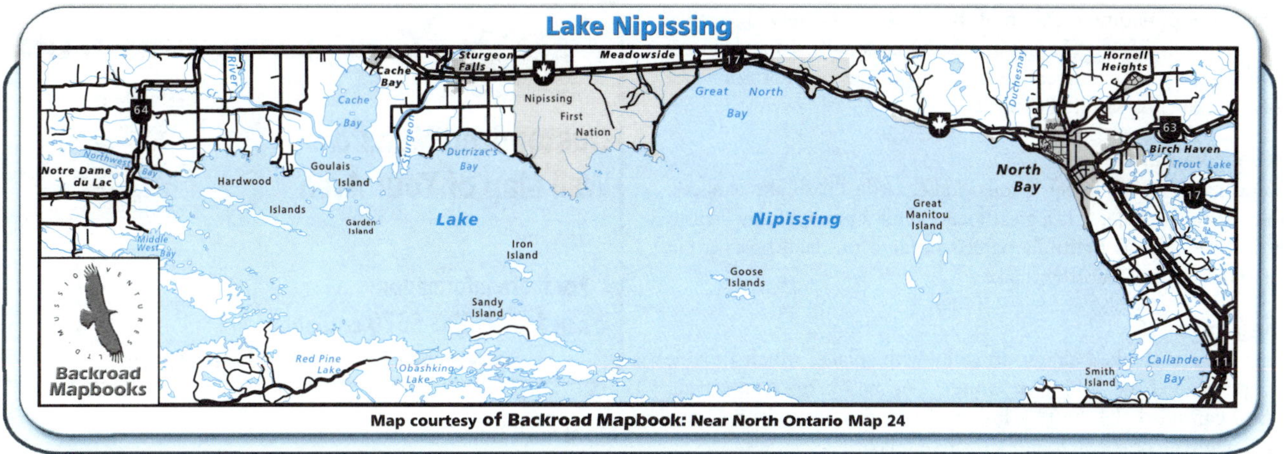

Map courtesy of Backroad Mapbook: Near North Ontario Map 24

Johnson Lake

Johnson Lake once had a seemingly endless natural brook trout population. Unfortunately over fishing has significantly slowed angling success although ice fishing can still be fairly productive. Look for the small lake on the east side of Highway 144 north of Cartier.

Kearney Lake

Located just north of Samuel De Champlain Provincial Park, Kearney Lake is accessible by snowmobile only. The scenic lake is inhabited by lake trout, which usually provide slow fishing. The best time to try for the lakers in this lake is in winter through the ice.

Lake Nipissing

Over the past decade, Lake Nipissing has become one of the most popular ice fishing destinations in Ontario. In winter, anglers can enjoy fishing for a number of different sportfish species. These species include northern pike, walleye, muskellunge, jumbo perch and whitefish. Walleye fishing in the lake is the main attractant for anglers to Nipissing and the prized sportfish can reach sizes of up to 3+ kg (6.5+ lbs). Jigging is an effective method for finding walleye at times, although most anglers use live minnows for the best success. The walleye of Nipissing are often over targeted due to the popularity of the lake. Be sure to release walleye when possible to aid the natural walleye population in this fabulous lake. Northern pike can also be found to 5+ kg (11+ lbs) in size and fishing can be fair to good in a few areas. When these sportfish are not hitting, there are plenty of panfish to keep the lines active throughout the day.

Lake Nosbonsing

This popular, large lake offers anglers a wide range of fish species to fish for. Most of the ice fishing is for walleye to 3 kg (6.5 lbs) and northern pike in the 2-3 kg (4.5-6.5 lb) range. A good holding area for walleye and pike is near the mouth of the Kaibushkong River. Other species include the odd muskellunge, Atlantic salmon (Ouananiche) and even sturgeon. Ouananiche, along with various trout species have been stocked in the past and there are still reports each year of an odd fish like a brown trout caught. Whether these species still exist or they are a case of mistaken identity is always unclear. Be sure to check the special regulations for this lake, as there are numerous special regulations in effect.

Lake Panache

Lake Panache is the largest lake in the immediate area and is found east of the town of Espanola. Although there are many cottages and camps on this lake, the size of the lake makes it relatively easy to find seclusion. Lake trout, walleye and northern pike are the main winter attraction in the lake and fishing success is usually fair for the three species. Lake trout and walleye can be found to about 60 cm (14 in) in size, although bigger catches are not uncommon. This lake has sustained its fish population even though the effects of acidification have definitely hampered fish stocks. With the latest improvements on Sudbury smelters, local lakes like Panache are slowly improving.

Little Long

This remote, snowmobile access lake is inhabited by fair to good populations of natural brook trout. Brookies are not very big as they average about 25 cm (10 in) in size. Occasionally a much larger trout will surprise unsuspecting ice anglers. The lake lies northeast of North Bay not far off Highway 63.

Little Pike Lake

Found north of the larger Tomiko Lake, Little Pike Lake is accessible by snowmobile. It is a great location for a peaceful day fishing. Little Pike Lake is rightfully named because the lake hosts a fair population of small northern pike.

Long Lake

Long Lake is stocked almost annually with splake, which provide for quite good ice fishing in winter. The brook trout/lake trout hybrid can reach 1+ kg (2+ lbs) in size in this lake. Try jigging a small white jig or spoon to attract active splake.

Long Lake

Long Lake is a small lake found within Samuel De Champlain Provincial Park. The lake is stocked annually with brook trout that provide fair fishing opportunities through the ice. The lake receives significant angling pressure throughout the year and brookies are usually small.

Loon and Moon Lakes

These small lakes lie to the west of Highway 144 north of Cartier. They are stocked almost annually with brook trout that provide for good fishing through the ice. Loon Lake can be accessed from the highway, while a snowmobile is recommended to get into Moon Lake during the winter.

Lorimer Lake

This beautiful Near North Ontario lake has a number of cottages and camps along its shoreline. The lake is stocked every few years with lake trout and fishing is good at times through the ice for lakers in the 35 cm (14 in) range. Northern pike are also found in the lake in fair numbers and can be found up to 3.5 kg (8 lbs). You can find the lake by taking Highway 124 north from Parry Sound to Lorimer Road.

Marten Lake

Marten Lake is one of the larger lakes in the area and is accessible just off the east side of Highway 11, near Marten River. There are a few camps on the lake, although most of the lake is surrounded by Crown Land. Walleye and lake trout inhabit the lake, but fishing can be slow for both species. The best time of year to find lakers and walleye is in the winter. Northern pike can also be found in the lake.

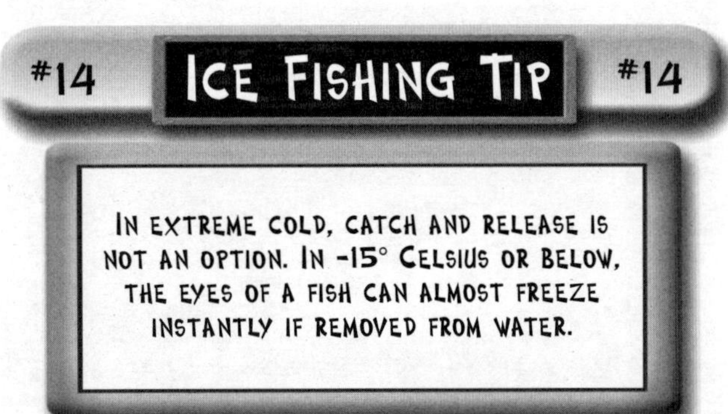

Montreuil Lake

This lake is stocked annually with brook trout, which provide for good fishing through the ice in winter. Spoons or small white jigs can be productive. The lake is accessible by snowmobile north of Mattawa off of Highway 533.

Mountain Lake

Located between Highways 533 and 63 north of Mattawa, Mountain Lake sees few visitors throughout the year. As a result, anglers who are willing to bushwhack in should find some good fishing for natural brook trout. Overcast periods seem to be more productive on these lakes in the winter.

Mutton Lake

Accessed south of Orrville off maintained roads, Mutton Lake is home to a fair number of northern pike. These predatory fish are most readily caught as evening approaches in the winter.

Nameless Lake

Nameless Lake is stocked almost annually with brook trout, which provide for good fishing through the ice. Try a minnow or small spoon through the ice. The lake is accessible by snowmobile and is located just north of Elizabeth Lake east of Espanola.

Olmstead Lake

Accessible via snowmobile in the winter, Olmstead Lake is found north of the power line that can be picked up off Olrig Road west of Mattawa. Stocked regularly with brook trout, the fishing in this lake can be fair to good at times during the winter. Trout in this lake are usually not very big, although some 30+ cm (12+ in) trout are taken annually.

Patterson (Stormy) Lake

Best accessed through Restoule Provincial Park, Patterson or Stormy Lake offers good fishing at times for northern pike in the 2+ kg (4.5+ lb) range. However, lake trout, walleye and even muskellunge fishing ranges from fair to slow during winter. The big lake is stocked almost annually with lake trout to aid that fishery. There are special restrictions on Stormy Lake.

Pearceley Lake

This small lake lies just south of Highway 124, southwest of Sundridge. The lake is stocked every few years with splake and fishing for the brook trout/lake trout hybrid can be quite good through the ice. Try a small silver spoon for good results.

Pine Lake

This small lake lies west of Thorne and is accessible from a rough road that is rarely plowed during the winter. Pine Lake is stocked annually with brook trout and provides for good fishing through the ice. Watch for special bait restrictions on the lake.

Pleasant Lake

Pleasant Lake is stocked annually with splake and provides for good fishing at times in winter through the ice. Try jigging a small spoon to find cruising splake.

Pickerel Lake

This lake is accessible via snowmobile trail or by following the summer road off of Spring Lake Road. Anglers will find good fishing at times for northern pike. Walleye are also found in the lake in fair numbers and are best fished through the ice.

Pigeon Lake

Pigeon Lake is a small lake found north of Val Caron off the North Rang Mine Road. The lake is stocked every few years with brook trout and fishing is good at times for trout in the 30 cm (12 in) range. Winter and early spring are the most productive fishing periods. Try a small spoon through the ice.

Poleline and Snider Lake

Both of these lakes are stocked almost annually with brook trout. Fishing for brookies can be good at times for trout in the 30 cm (12 in) range. Trout can be found bigger and the big ones are usually caught during ice fishing season.

Poika Lake

Poika Lake is a small lake that is located just south of the much larger Windy Lake south of Onaping. The small lake is stocked every few years with brook trout and provides for good fishing, especially through the ice. Although brookies averaging only about 30 cm (12 in) in size, larger trout are not uncommon.

Pomphery Lake

Located just south of Highway 17 west of the village of Nairn, Pomphery Lake is stocked with splake every year. Visiting anglers can expect good fishing through the ice. Try jigging a small spoon or white jig to find active brookies.

Restoule Lake

Restoule Lake is a large lake that is home to a number of cottages and camps as well as the popular Restoule Provincial Park. Fishing can be good at times for northern pike in the 2+ kg (4.5+ lb) range, while lake trout, walleye and even muskellunge fishing ranges from fair to slow during winter. Since Restoule Lake holds a natural population, watch for special restrictions on the lake.

Reynolds Lake

This remote, snowmobile access lake is inhabited by fair to good populations of natural brook trout. Brookies are not very big as they average about 25 cm (10 in) in size. Occasionally a much larger trout will surprise unsuspecting ice anglers. The lake lies northeast of North Bay at the end of a logging road leading east from Highway 63.

Secret Lake

Anglers can expect good fishing at times for brook trout in this secluded lake. The main angling period on this lake is during winter. The lake is only accessible by snowmobile northwest of the settlement of Ardberg off Highway 520.

Map courtesy of Backroad Mapbook: Near North Ontario Map 26

Spring Lake

Spring Lake offers fair fishing for a natural lake trout population. These lakers are small, but are quite enjoyable to catch. Watch for special bait restrictions on the lake.

Star Lake

Accessed south of Orrville off maintained roads, Star Lake is stocked every few years with lake trout. Lakers provide fair fishing through the ice. Northern pike are also found in this lake and are best caught as evening approaches in the winter.

Teesdale Lake

Found south of the bigger Cahill Lake, Teesdale Lake sees fewer visitors than most lakes in the area. The lack of pressure and the regular stocking program for brook trout can result in some good ice fishing. Trout over 30 cm (12 in) are not uncommon.

Three Mile Lake

Three Mile Lake offers fair fishing for both lake trout and walleye to about 3 kg (6.5 lbs) in size. The most successful period for these fish is usually in winter. Minnow presentations are usually the bait of choice when angling through the ice. Three Mile Lake can be easily accessed just east of Highway 11, north of the town of Emsdale.

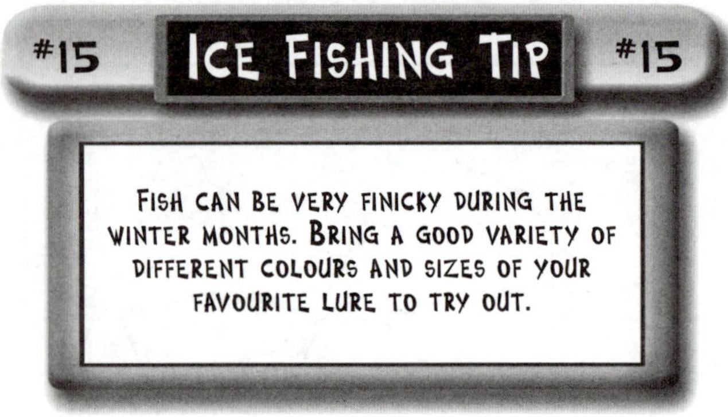

Threetails Lake

This small lake lies west of Thorne and is accessible from a rough 2wd road that is rarely plowed during the winter. Threetails Lake is stocked annually with lake trout and offers quite good fishing for the popular species in winter. Watch for special bait restrictions on the lake.

Tomiko Lake

Tomiko Lake can be reached by a series of roads that are found north of Sturgeon Falls not far off Highway 64. Fishing in the lake is slow to fair for smaller northern pike and walleye. Ice anglers will find panfish provide most of the action through the ice.

Twenty Minute Lake

Found just east of Highway 63 northeast of North Bay, a snowmobile is still recommended to find the lake. Fishing is generally fair for both brook trout and lake trout.

Trout Lake

Trout Lake is almost as popular for ice fishing as Lake Nipissing. The big lake is found east of the City of North Bay and is home to many homes and cottages. Anglers will find a wide variety of sportfish present including lake trout, muskellunge, northern pike, ouananiche and walleye. There are also some panfish to provide action through the ice. The most sought after species are the lake trout and walleye. Lakers average 40+ cm (16+ in), while walleye average 0.5-1 kg (1-2 lbs). Despite their popularity, patience is needed to lure one of these elusive fish. Northern pike fishing in the lake is generally fair, and seems to pick up as evening approaches during winter. Some good sized pike are taken out of Trout Lake annually. Be sure to check the regulations as there are very specific regulations concerning this important lake.

Valin Lake

Adventurous snowmobilers will find a series of logging roads lead to this remote lake. Those anglers that make it in should find a peaceful setting with good fishing for natural brook trout. These feisty trout can be very aggressive in the winter. Try jigging a small silver spoon through the ice. For a detailed map of the area, please consult the Backroad Mapbook for Near North Ontario.

Wanapitei Lake

Wanapitei Lake is one of the largest, most scenic lakes in the region. Snowmobile trails crisscross the big lake, while Wanapitei Provincial Park and the Wanapitei First Nation territory is located on the northwest side of the lake. Fishing in the lake can be challenging, due to its size. However, there is plenty of fishing opportunities. Panfish and northern pike seem to provide the bulk of the action in winter despite the attention given to the more elusive lake trout and walleye. Lake trout are harder to find and some people say the stocks are approaching dangerously low levels. Walleye on the other hand are caught with some regularity and average about 2 kg (4.5 lbs) in size. The West Bay of the lake has been stocked periodically with brook trout and there have been reports of decent catches of this species in various parts of the lake.

Weeden Lake

This lake lies south of the Seguin Trail between Orrville and Parry Sound and is accessible via snowmobile. Weeden Lake is also stocked every few years with brook trout, which provides for good fishing through the ice for brookies to 30+ cm (12+ in).

Wolf Lake

Found north of the larger Tomiko Lake, Wolf Lake is accessible by snowmobile via logging roads east of Highway 64. The remote lake is stocked annually with splake, which often provide for good fishing, especially through the ice.

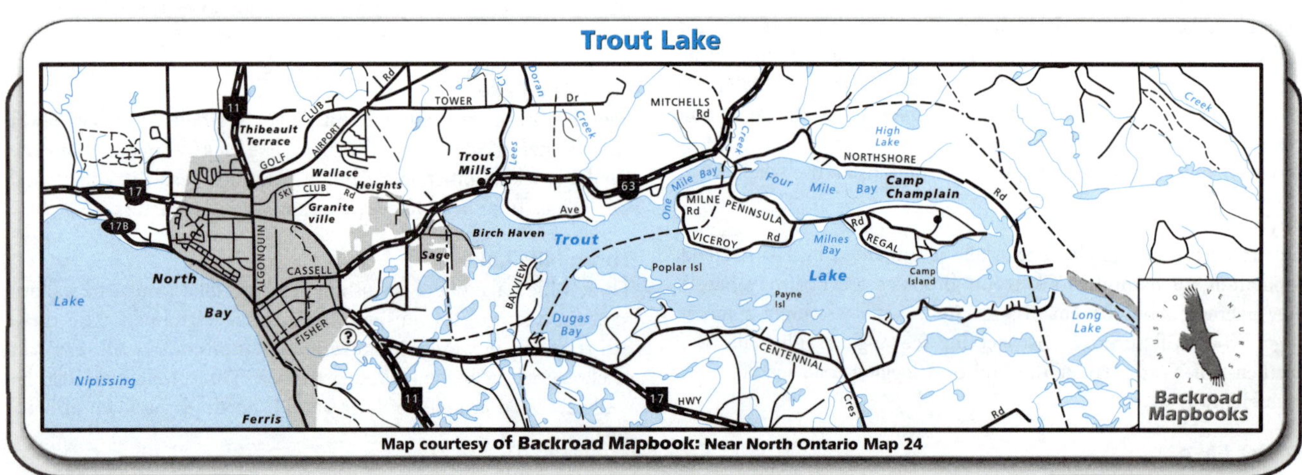

Map courtesy of Backroad Mapbook: Near North Ontario Map 24

Index

A
Adams Lake 18, 58
Agnew Lake 88
Ahmic Lake 88
Alaska Lake 88
Albion Lake 58
Anderson Lake 88
Anson (Montgomery) Lake 18
Arran Lake 12
Arrowhead lake 18, 77
Ashby White Lake 58
Avery Lake 18
B
Back Lake 58, 77
Bacon Lake 77
Bailey Lake 58
Baldcoot Lake 77
Ban (Band) Lake 18,77
Barns Lake 77
Bay (Bucktooth) Lake 77
Bear Lake 18, 88
Bear Mountain Lake 58
Beaudrie (Stringers) Lake 58
Beaver Lake 88
Beeches Lake 58
Bella Lake 18
Bells Lake 12
Belwood Lake 12
Bennett Lake 58
Bernard Lake 88
Big Gibson Lake 77
Big Gull Lake 58
Big Sound 88
Big Wind Lake 18
Birchy Lake 18, 77
Bitter Lake 18
Black Cat Lake 18
Black Lake 18
Blackstone Lake 18
Blue Lake 20, 58
Boat Lake 12
Bob's Lake 58
Boot Lake 89
Boshkung Lake 20
Boundary (Martin) Lake 20
Bow Lakes 58
Boy Lake 20
Brandy Lake 20, 23
Bright Lake 77
Buck Lake 77
Buckskin Lake 20
Buckskin Lake 77
Burdock Lake 20
Butternut Lake 58
C
Cahill Lake 89
Calabogie Lake 77
Callander Bay 89
Cameron Lake 12
Camp Lake 58
Cat Lake 20
Cat Lakes 18
Centre (Pivet) Lake 20
Charcoal Lake 20, 78
Charleston Lake 62
Cheer Lake 89
Cherry Lake 20
Chesley Lake 12
Chub Lake 20
Clara Lake 78
Claradeer Lake 78
Clear Lake 24, 62, 78
Cod Lake 24
Cod Lake 78
Coe (Island) Lake 62
Colpoy's Bay 12
Concession Lake 24
Constant Lake 78
Contestogo Lake 12
Cornick Lake 78
Coughlan Lake 78
Crane Lakes 24
Crevice Lake 78
Crosby Lake 62
Cross Lake 78
Crotch Lake 62
Crowe Lake 62
Crown Lake 24, 78
Cyprus Lake 12
D
Dalhousie Lake 62
Dan Lake 24
Darlington Lake 24, 89
Deermeadow Lake 78
Diamond Lake 62, 78
Dick Lake 79
Dixie Lake 24, 62
Dodds Lake 62
Doe Lakes 24, 90
Dog Lake 24, 64
Drag Lake 24
Draper Lake 64
Ducharme Lake 90
Duck Lake 24
Dunchurch Lake 90
Dutton Lake 27, 79
Dyson Lake 27
E
Eagle Lake 27
East Jeannie Lakes 27, 79
East Lake 27, 79
East Paint Lake 27, 79
Eastell Lake 79
Effingham Lake 64
Eiler Lake 27
Elephant Lake 64
Elizabeth Lake 90
Elzevir Lake 64
Esson (Otter) Lake 27
Eugenia Lake 13
Evelyn Lake 64
F
Fairholme Lake 90
Fairy Lake 30, 79
Farren Lake 64
Finger Lake 79
Flat Iron Lake 79
Flaxman Lake 90
Fletcher Lake 30, 79
Forget Lake 30
Fork Lake 79
G
Gardiner Lake 79
Genesee Lake 79
Glennies Pond 30
Go Home Lake 30
Godin Lake 64, 79
Gooseneck Lake 90
Gostling Lake 81
Gould Lake 13
Grace Lake 64
Green Lake 64
Grimsthorpe Lake 64
Grindstone Lake 30, 64
Guelph Lake 13
Guilford Lake 81
Gun Lake 81
H
Haines Lake 30
Halfway Lake 81
Halls Lake 30, 64
Hardwood Lake 81
Harp Lake 30
Harp Lake 81
Harvey Lake 30, 81
Haskins Lake 81
Havelock Lake 30, 81
Hawk Lake 81
Headstone Lakes 81
Heifer Lake 64, 81
Horn Lake 90
Horse Lake 30
Horseshoe Lake 30, 90
Hurst Lake 33
Hypothermia 9
I
Ice Thickness 9
Imp Lake 66
Indian Lake 64, 90
Indian Lake 77
Irish Lake 13
Isaak Lake 13
Isabella Lake 33
J
Jack Lake 33
James Lake 81
Johnson Lake 91
Johnsons Lake 81
K
Kabakwa Lake 33
Kahshe Lake 33
Kamaniskeg Lake 81
Kashagawigamog Lake 33
Kasshabog Lake 66
Kawagama Lake 33
Kearney Lake 91
Kennebec Lake 66
Kennisis Lake 81
Ketch Lake 33
Klaxton Lake 33
Koshlong Lake 33
L
Lake Erie 13
Lake Joseph 33
Lake Nipissing 91
Lake Nosbonsing 91
Lake Panache 91
Lake St. Clair 13
Lake St. Peter 82
Lake Vernon 82
Langford Lake 33
Lasseter Lake 33, 82
Lee Lake 33, 82
Liebeck Lake 33
Limburner Lake 33
Lipsy Lakes 37
Little Anstruther Lake 66
Little Arrowhead Lakes 18, 77
Little Birchy Lake 37
Little Bob Lake 37
Little Clear Lake 37, 82
Little Echo Lake 66
Little Green Lake 66
Little Long 91
Little Mayo Lake 66
Little Otter Lake 37
Little Pike Lake 92
Little Round Lake 66
Littlecoot Lake 77
Livingstone Lake 37
Lonewolf Lake 66
Long Lake 37, 66, 82, 92
Long Mallory Lake 66
Longbay Lake 66
Longline Lake 37, 82
Loon Call Lake 37
Loon Lake 92
Lorimer Lake 92
Louie Lakes 37, 82
Lowry (Bluerock) Lake 68
Loxton Lake 82
M
Mackie Lake 68
Marten Lake 92
Martin (Boundary) Lake 82
Mary Lake 37
Mazinaw Lake 68
McCoy Lake 37
McCreary Lake 68
McCullough Lake 16
McDonald Lake 82
McDowall Lake 68
McEwen Lake 45
McGee Lake 45, 68
McHale Lake 68, 82
McKenzie Lake 82
Meach Lakes 45, 82
Menet Lake 45, 82
Merrill Lakes 68
Middle Shanty Lake 82
Mink Lake 45, 82
Mississagagon Lake 68
Mississippi Lake 68
Mitchell Lake 68
Mohan Lakes 45
Moira Lake 68
Monck Lake 45
Monkshood Lake 83
Monmouth Lake 45
Montreuil Lake 92
Moon Lakes 92
Moonbeam Lakes 83
Moore Lakes 45
Moose Lake 45
Morrow Lake 45, 68, 83
Mountain Lake 16, 45, 92
Mousseau Lake 68
Mousseau Lake 83
Murphy Lake 83
Mutton Lake 92
N
Nameless Lake 92
Nehemiah Lake 49, 83
Nelson Lakes 83
Niger Lake 83
North Lake 68
North Muldrew Lake 49
Nowlan Lake 68
O
Olmstead Lake 92
Orley Lake 49
Other Options 23
Owen Sound 16
Oxbend Lake 68, 83
Oxtongue Lake 49
P
Paint (Deer) Lakes 49
Papineau Lake 83
Parkhurst Lake 68
Partridge Lake 49
Pat Lake 83
Patterson (Stormy) Lake 92
Patterson Lake 70
Pearceley Lake 92
Pell Lake 83
Pencil Lake 49
Perch Lake 70
Percy Lake 49, 84
Peyton Lakes 84
Pickerel Lake 93
Pigeon Lake 93
Pike Lake 70
Pine Lake 84, 93
Pleasant Lake 93
Poika Lake 93
Poleline and Snider Lake 93
Pomphery Lake 93
Poplar Lake 70
Portable Huts 7
Purdy Lake 84
Q
Quinn Lakes 70
R
Rabbit Lake 49
Raglan (White) Lake 70, 84
Rainy Lake 70
Rattail Lake 84
Raven Lakes 77
Rebecca Lakes 49
Reid Lake 70
Restoule Lake 93
Reynolds Lake 93
Robson Lakes 16
Ronald Lake 49, 84
Ross Lake 49, 84
Ruby Lake 70
Rustyshoe Lake 49
S
Sand Lake 84
Sandox Lake 84
Sandox Lake 68
Scraggle Lakes 49
Sears Lake 84
Secret Lake 93
Shabomeka Lake 70
Sharbot Lake 70
Shaw Lake 84
Shoe Lake 49
Shoelace Lake 52
Silver Buck Lake 52
Silver Doe Lakes 52
Silver Lake 70
Silversheen Lake 84
Simpson Lake 70
Skeleton Lake 52
Skootamatta Lake 73
Sky Lake 16
Smyth Lake 84
Snowshoe Lakes 73
Soaking Lake 52, 86
South Muldrew Lake 52
Spring Lake 73, 93
Spry Lake 16
St. Nora Lake 52
Star Lake 52, 93
Steer Lake 64, 81
Straddlebug Lake 73
Sucker Lake 52
Sullivan Lake 73
Sunken Lake) 86
Surprise Lake 52
Sward Lake 52
T
Tedious Lakes 52
Teesdale Lake 93
Three Mile Lake 93
Threetails Lake 94
Tim Lake 73
Tip Ups 7
Tomiko Lake 94
Tory Lake 73
Triangle Lake 52
Trout Lake 86, 94
Troutspawn Lakes 86
Tub Lake 86
Turtle Lake 73, 86
Turtle Lake 82
Twelve Lake 86
Twelve Mile Lake 52
Twenty Minute Lake 94
Twenty Seven Lake 86
U
Upper Rock Lake 73
Urbach Lake 73
V
Valiant Lake 86
Valin Lake 94
Verner Lake 52
W
Walker Lakes 56, 86
Wanapitei Lake 94
Waterloo Lake 86
Weeden Lake 56, 94
West Aumond Lake 86
West Twinpine Lake 73
White Lake 73
Whitefish Lake 56
Whyte Lake 73
Wilbur Lake 56
Wilbur Lakes 78
Wilcox Lake 16
Wilder Lake 16
Williams Lake 16
Wish Lake 86
Wolf Lake 56, 86, 94
Wolfe Lake 73
Wood Lake 56
Wren Lakes 56
Wylie Lake 81

The Author

Jason Marleau was born in Sudbury, Ontario. While growing up in Central Ontario, he had the opportunity to experience and enjoy Ontario's great outdoors. After graduating from the University of Ottawa, Jason spent a few years exploring British Columbia, where he met Russell and Wesley Mussio from Backroad Mapbooks.

This monumental meeting not only changed the career path of Jason but has also benefited many outdoor enthusiasts in Ontario and across the country. Jason has authored or co-authored over a dozen **Backroad Mapbooks** and **Fishing Mapbook** titles.

Despite his growing family commitments (we are proud to welcome River J to our family), Jason continues to be an avid outdoorsmen. Whenever he is not working on guidebooks, he is enjoying the great outdoors.

Backroad Mapbooks

...the start of every adventure!

Algonquin Region

Cottage Country

Eastern Ontario

Near North Ontario

Southwestern Ontario

Montreal/ Laurentides

FISHING ONTARIO

...and much more!

Eastern Ontario

Haliburton

Kawarthas

FISHING ONTARIO Muskoka

Muskoka

To obtain your book see your local outdoor retailer, bookstore or contact:

Backroad Mapbooks
5811 Beresford Street
Burnaby, B.C.
V5J 1K1, Canada
P. (604) 438-3474
F. (604) 438-3470

orders@backroadmapbooks.com

Published By:

Pembroke District Map

www.backroadmapbooks.com

For a complete list of titles visit our website or call us toll free **1-877-520-5670** or **(604) 438-FISH (3474)**